Lecture Notes in Computer Science 4165

Commenced Publication in 1973
Founding and Former Series Editors:
Gerhard Goos, Juris Hartmanis, and Jan van Leeuwen

T0223643

Willem Jonker   Milan Petković (Eds.)

Secure
Data Management

Third VLDB Workshop, SDM 2006
Seoul, Korea, September 10-11, 2006
Proceedings

 Springer

Volume Editors

Willem Jonker
Philips Research Europe
High Tech Campus 34
5656 AE Eindhoven
The Netherlands
E-mail: willem.jonker@philips.com

Milan Petković
Philips Research Laboratories
High Tech Campus 34
5656 AE Eindhoven
The Netherlands
E-mail: Milan.Petkovic@philips.com

Library of Congress Control Number: 2006931629

CR Subject Classification (1998): H.2.0, H.2, C.2.0, H.3, E.3, D.4.6, K.6.5

LNCS Sublibrary: SL 3 – Information Systems and Application, incl. Internet/Web and HCI

ISSN   0302-9743
ISBN-10   3-540-38984-9 Springer Berlin Heidelberg New York
ISBN-13   978-3-540-38984-2 Springer Berlin Heidelberg New York

Springer is a part of Springer Science+Business Media

springer.com

© Springer-Verlag Berlin Heidelberg 2006

Typesetting: Camera-ready by author, data conversion by Scientific Publishing Services, Chennai, India
SPIN: 11844662   06/3142   5 4 3 2 1 0

Preface

Recent developments in computer, communication, and information technologies, along with increasingly interconnected networks and mobility have established new emerging technologies, such as ubiquitous computing and ambient intelligence, as a very important and unavoidable part of everyday life. However, this development has greatly influenced people's security concerns. As data is accessible anytime from anywhere, according to these new concepts, it becomes much easier to get unauthorized data access. As another consequence, the use of new technologies has brought some privacy concerns. It becomes simpler to collect, store, and search personal information and endanger people's privacy. Therefore, research in the area of secure data management is of growing importance, attracting the attention of both the data management and security research communities. The interesting problems range from traditional ones such as access control (with all variations, like role-based and/or context-aware), database security, operations on encrypted data, and privacy preserving data mining to cryptographic protocols.

The call for papers attracted 33 papers both from universities and industry. The program committee selected 13 research papers for presentation at the workshop. These papers are also collected in this volume, which we hope will serve you as useful research and reference material.

The volume is divided roughly into four major sections. The first section focuses on privacy protection addressing the topics of indistinguishability, sovereign information sharing, data anonymization, and privacy protection in ubiquitous environments. The second section changes slightly the focal point to privacy preserving data management. The papers in this section deal with search on encrypted data and privacy preserving clustering. The third section focuses on access control which remains an important area of interest. The papers cover role-based access control, XML access control and conflict resolution. The last section addresses database security topics.

Finally, let us acknowledge the work of Richard Brinkman, who helped in the technical preparation of these proceedings.

July 2006   Willem Jonker and Milan Petković

Organization

Workshop Organizers

Willem Jonker (Philips Research/University of Twente, The Netherlands)
Milan Petković (Philips Research, The Netherlands)

Program Committee

Gerrit Bleumer, Francotyp-Postalia, Germany
Ljiljana Branković, University of Newcastle, Australia
Sabrina De Capitani di Vimercati, University of Milan, Italy
Ernesto Damiani, University of Milan, Italy
Eric Diehl, Thomson Research, France
Csilla Farkas, University of South Carolina, USA
Ling Feng, Twente University, Netherlands
Eduardo Fernández-Medina, University of Castilla-La Mancha, Spain
Elena Ferrari, Università degli Studi dell'Insubria, Italy
Simone Fischer-Hübner, Karlstad University, Sweden
Tyrone Grandison, IBM Almaden Research Center, USA
Ehud Gudes, Ben-Gurion University, Israel
Hacan Hacigümüş, IBM Almaden Research Center, USA
Marit Hansen, Independent Centre for Privacy Protection, Germany
Pieter Hartel, Twente University, The Netherlands
Dong Hoon Lee, Korea University, Korea
Mizuho Iwaihara, Kyoto University, Japan
Sushil Jajodia George Mason University, USA
Ton Kalker, HP Research, USA
Marc Langheinrich, Institute for Pervasive Computing ETH Zurich, Switzerland
Nick Mankovich, Philips Medical Systems, USA
Sharad Mehrotra, University of California at Irvine, USA
Stig Frode Mjølsnes, Norwegian University of Science and Technology, Norway
Eiji Okamoto, University of Tsukuba, Japan
Sylvia Osborn, University of Western Ontario, Canada
Günther Pernul, University of Regensburg, Germany
Birgit Pfitzmann, IBM Zurich Research Lab, Switzerland
Bart Preneel, KU Leuven, Belgium
Kai Rannenberg, Goethe University Frankfurt, Germany
Andreas Schaad, SAP Labs, France
Morton Swimmer, IBM Zurich Research Lab, Switzerland
Sheng Zhong, Stevens Institute of Technology, USA

Additional Referees

Srikanth Akkiraju, University of Twente, The Netherlands
Richard Brinkman, University of Twente, The Netherlands
Ileana Buhan, University of Twente, The Netherlands
Lothar Fritsch, Johann Wolfgang Goethe University, Germany
Ludwig Fuchs, University of Regensburg, Germany
Bijit Hore, University of California at Irvine, USA
Ravi Chandra Jammalamadaka, University of California at Irvine, USA
Heiko Rossnagel, Johann Wolfgang Goethe University, Germany
Falk Wagner, Johann Wolfgang Goethe University, Germany
Lingyu Wang, George Mason University, USA
Chao Yao, George Mason University, USA
Xingbo Yu, University of California at Irvine, USA

Table of Contents

Database Security

Indistinguishability: The Other Aspect of Privacy*

Chao Yao[1,**], Lingyu Wang[2], Sean X. Wang[3], and Sushil Jajodia[1]

[1] Center for Secure Information Systems
George Mason University
{cyao, jajodia}@gmu.edu
[2] CIISE, Concordia University
wang@encs.concordia.ca
[3] Department of Computer Science
The University of Vermont
xywang@cs.uvm.edu

Abstract. Uncertainty and indistinguishability are two independent aspects of privacy. Uncertainty refers to the property that the attacker cannot tell which private value, among a group of values, an individual actually has, and indistinguishability refers to the property that the attacker cannot see the difference among a group of individuals. While uncertainty has been well studied and applied to many scenarios, to date, the only effort in providing indistinguishability has been the well-known notion of k-anonymity. However, k-anonymity only applies to anonymized tables. This paper defines indistinguishability for general situations based on the symmetry among the possible private values associated with individuals. The paper then discusses computational complexities of and provides practical algorithms for checking whether a set of database views provides enough indistinguishability.

1 Introduction

In many data applications, it's necessary to measure privacy disclosure in released data to protect individual privacy while satisfying application requirements. The measurement metrics used in prior work have mainly been based on uncertainty of private property values, i.e., the uncertainty what private value an individual has. These metrics can be classified into two categories: non-probabilistic and probabilistic. The non-probabilistic metrics are based on whether the private value of an individual can be uniquely inferred from the released data [1,20,7,17,5,16] or whether the cardinality of the set of possible private values inferred for an individual is large enough [26,27]. The probabilistic metrics are based on some characteristics of the probability distribution of the possible private values inferred from the released data [3,2,10,9,15,4] (see Section 4 for more details).

* The work was partially supported by the NSF grants IIS-0430402, IIS-0430165, and IIS-0242237.
** Part of work of this author was done while visiting the University of Vermont.

W. Jonker and M. Petkovic (Eds.): SDM 2006, LNCS 4165, pp. 1–17, 2006.

However, uncertainty is only one aspect of privacy and it alone does not provide adequate protection. For example, we may reveal employee John's salary to be in a large interval (say, $100K$ to $300K$ annually). There may be enough uncertainty. However, if we also reveal that the salaries of all other employees are in ranges that are totally different from John's range (say, all are subranges of $50K$ to $100K$), then John's privacy may still be violated. As another example, suppose from the released data we can infer that all patients in a hospital may only have *Cold* or *SARS* except that *John* may have *Cold* or *AIDS*. Even though the uncertainty of *John*'s sickness has the same "magnitude" as that of the other patients, *John* may still feel his privacy is violated, since he is the only one who possibly has *AIDS*.

To adequately protect privacy, we need to consider the other aspect, namely, *indistinguishability*. Indeed, the privacy breach in the above examples can be viewed as due to the fact that from the released data, an individual is different from all other individuals in terms of their possible private values. In other words, the examples violate a privacy requirement, namely, the "protection from being brought to the attention of others" [11]. What we need is to have each individual belong to a group of individuals who are indistinguishable from each other in terms of their possible private values derived from the released data. In this way, an individual is hidden in a crowd that consists of individuals who have similar/same possible private values. For instance, in the above salary example, to protect John's privacy, we may want to make sure that attackers can only derive from the released data that a large group of employees have the same range as John's for their possible salaries.

Uncertainty and indistinguishability are two independent aspects for providing privacy; one does not imply the other. From the above examples, we can see that uncertainty cannot ensure good indistinguishability. Likewise, good indistinguishability cannot ensure enough uncertainty. For instance, if in the released data many employees have the same single possible salary value, then these employees are indistinguishable from each other in terms of their salaries, but there is not enough uncertainty to protect their privacy (all their salaries are the same and revealed!).

Our idea of indistinguishability is inspired by the notion of k-anonymization [24,25,21,14,18] as it can be viewed as a generalization of anonymization. The idea of k-anonymization is to recode, mostly by generalization, publicly available quasi-IDs in a single released table, so that at least k individuals will have the same recoded quasi-IDs. (Quasi-IDs are values on a combination of attributes that can be used to identify individuals through external sources [24,25].) In our view, this is an effort to provide indistinguishability among k individuals, since the recoding makes the individuals indistinguishable from each other. (As noted above, indistinguishability does not guarantee uncertainty. This is also true for k-anonymization, which is illustrated by the improvement reported in [19]. The authors impose an additional requirement on anonymization, namely, by requiring diverse private values among the tuples with the same recoded quasi-ID, in order to achieve, in our view, both indistinguishability and uncertainty.)

While k-anonymity is an interesting notion, it only applies to anonymized tables. In this paper, we define two kinds of indistinguishability, and the corresponding privacy metrics, that can be applied to general situations, including anonymized tables and relational views. We show that k-anonymization is a special case of one kind of indistinguishability under a certain assumption (see Section 2.3).

Both notions of indistinguishability introduced in this paper are based on certain symmetry between individuals and their private values in the released data. More specifically, the first definition requires symmetry for all possible private values while the second definition bases on symmetry referring only to certain subsets of possible private values. With the two kinds of indistinguishability defined, we turn to study the problem of deciding whether a set of database views provides enough indistinguishability. We study the computational complexity as well as practical algorithms. We focus on checking for indistinguishability since checking for uncertainty has been extensively studied [1,7,17,5,26,16,27].

We summarize the contributions of this paper as follows. (1) We identify indistinguishability as a requirement for privacy in addition to uncertainty, provide formal definitions of different kinds of indistinguishability, and study their properties. (2) We analyze the computational complexity and introduce practical checking methods for deciding whether a set of database views provides enough indistinguishability.

The rest of paper is organized as follows. We give formal definitions of indistinguishability and privacy metrics in Section 2. We then focus on checking database views against these privacy metrics in Section 3. In Section 4 we review the related work. Finally, we conclude with a summary in Section 5.

2   Indistinguishability

2.1   Preliminaries

In this paper, we consider releasing data from a single private table Tbl with schema D. The attributes in D are partitioned into two sets, B and P. The set B consists of the public attributes; P consists of the private attributes. For simplicity and without loss of generality, we assume P only has one attribute.

We assume that the projection on B, $\Pi_B(Tbl)$, is publicly known. In the salary example, this means that the list of employees is publicly known. We believe this assumption is realistic in many situations. In other situations where this is not true, we may view our approach as providing a conservative privacy measure.

Given a relation r_B on B, we will use $\mathcal{I}^B$ to denote the set $\{I | \Pi_B(I) = r_B\}$, i.e., the set of the relations on D whose B-projection coincides with r_B. The domain of P is denoted by $Dom(P)$. A tuple of an instance in $\mathcal{I}^B$ is denoted by t or (b, p), where b is in $\Pi_B(Tbl)$ and p is in $Dom(P)$. The set $\mathcal{I}^B$ corresponds to all possible private table instances by only knowing $\Pi_B(Tbl)$.

Furthermore, we assume B is a key in D, which means that each composite value on B appears at most once in the private table. We also assume B is a quasi-ID, and hence, the tuples in Tbl describe associations of the private attribute values with individuals. (Recall that a quasi-ID is a combination of attribute values that can be used to identify an individual.) Such associations are the private information to be protected.

In Figure 1, our running example is shown. The public attributes in B are *Zip, Age, Race, Gender*, and *Charge*. We use $t_1, ..., t_{12}$ to denote the tuples in the table. By the assumption that B is a quasi-ID, $t_i[B]$ identifies a particular individual for each i. In the sequel, we use $t_i[B]$ and the individual identified by $t_i[B]$ interchangeably. The private attribute is *Problem*. Here, *Problem* is drawn from a finite discrete domain. (In general the private attribute also can be drawn from an infinite or a continuous domain; but it should not be difficult to extend our study to infinite discrete or continuous domains).

We assume that the data in *Tbl* are being released with a publicly-known function M. We also use v to denote the result of $M()$ on the private table, i.e., $v = M(Tbl)$. Examples of function $M()$ include an anonymization procedure, and a set of queries (views) on a single table on D.

	Zip	Age	Race	Gender	Charge	Problem
t_1	22030	39	White	Male	1K	Cold
t_2	22030	50	White	Male	12K	AIDS
t_3	22030	38	White	Male	5K	Obesity
t_4	22030	53	Black	Male	5K	AIDS
t_5	22031	28	Black	Female	8K	Chest Pain
t_6	22031	37	White	Female	10K	Hypertension
t_7	22031	49	Black	Female	1K	Obesity
t_8	22031	52	White	Male	8K	Cold
t_9	22032	30	Asian	Male	10K	Hypertension
t_{10}	22032	40	Asian	Male	9K	Chest Pain
t_{11}	22033	30	White	Male	10K	Hypertension
t_{12}	22033	40	White	Male	9K	Chest Pain

Fig. 1. A patient table (Tbl)

	Zip	Problem
t_9	22032	Hypertension
t_{10}	22032	Chest Pain
t_{11}	22033	Hypertension
t_{12}	22033	Chest Pain

Fig. 2. A released view $\Pi_{Zip, Problem}(Tbl)$ $\sigma_{Zip='22032' or '22033'}(Tbl)$ provides 2-SIND

2.2 Symmetric Indistinguishability

As $v = M(Tbl)$ is released, we denote by $\mathcal{I}^v$ the subset of possible instances in $\mathcal{I}^B$ that yield v. We introduce the definition of indistinguishability based on $\mathcal{I}^v$.

Definition 1. *(Symmetric Indistinguishability) Given a released data v and two tuples b_i and b_j in $\Pi_B(Tbl)$, we say b_i and b_j are symmetrically Indistinguishable w.r.t. v if the following condition is satisfied: for each instance I in $\mathcal{I}^v$ containing (b_i, p_i) and (b_j, p_j), there exists another instance I' in $\mathcal{I}^v$ such that $I' = (I - \{(b_i, p_i), (b_j, p_j)\}) \cup \{(b_i, p_j), (b_j, p_i)\}$.*

We abbreviate Symmetric Indistinguishability as *SIND*. This definition requires that for each possible instance in $\mathcal{I}^v$, if two symmetrically indistinguishable B tuples swap their private values while keeping other tuples unchanged, the resulting new instance can still yield v. In the sequel, we say *two B tuples $t_1[B]$ and $t_2[B]$ can swap their private values in an instance*, or simply *$t_1[B]$ swaps with $t_2[B]$*, if the resulting instance can still yield v.

Note that such a swap is required for all the instances yielding v, hence this definition is in terms of v, not the current table Tbl (although we used the projection $\Pi_B(Tbl)$ in the definition, this projection is not Tbl itself and is assumed publicly known). In other words, to be SIND is to be able to swap their private values in all the possible instances, including Tbl.

For example, consider the released view v in Figure 2 on the table in Figure 1. The two B tuples $t_9[B]$ and $t_{10}[B]$ are SIND, because they can swap their *Problem* values in any instance that yields v while still yielding the same v. Similarly, the two B tuples $t_{11}[B]$ and $t_{12}[B]$ are also SIND. However, $t_9[B]$ and $t_{11}[B]$ are not SIND, even though they have the same *Problem* value *Hypertension* in the current private table. To show this, consider an instance obtained by swapping the *Problem* values of t_9 and t_{10} in Tbl (while other tuples remain unchanged). So now t_9 has *ChestPain* while t_{10} has *Hypertension*. Denote the new instance Tbl'. Clearly, Tbl' also yields the view v. However, in Tbl', if we swap the *Problem* values of t_9 (i.e., *ChestPain*) with that of t_{11} (i.e., *Hypertension*), then both t_9 and t_{10} will have *Hypertension*. Therefore, the new instance obtained from Tbl' does not yield v, and hence t_9 and t_{11} are not SIND.

The definition of SIND requires a complete symmetry between two B tuples in terms of their private values. The sets of possible private values of the SIND tuples are the same, because in each possible instance two SIND B tuples can swap their private values without changing the views. Furthermore, the definition based on swapping makes SIND between two B tuples independent on other B tuples. That is, even if attackers can guess the private values of all other B tuples, they still cannot distinguish between these two B tuples because the two B tuples still can swap their private values without affecting the views.

We can also use a probability model to illustrate the indistinguishability by SIND. If we assume each B tuple has the same and independent *a priori* distribution over its private values, then we can easily prove that the two B tuples have the same *a posteriori* distribution over their private values after data released, due to complete symmetry in terms of their private values.

The binary relation SIND is *reflexive, symmetric* and *transitive*. That is, SIND is an *equivalence* relation. It is easy to see that it is reflexive and symmetric. We prove the transitivity as follows. If a B tuple b_1 can swap with another B tuple b_2 and b_2 can swap with b_3, then b_1 can swap with b_3 by the following steps: b_1 swaps with b_2; b_2 swaps with b_3; b_2 swaps with b_1; by the definition of SIND, the final instance still yields v.

Thus, all the B tuples that are indistinguishable from each other form a partition of the B tuples. Each set in the partition, which we call a *SIND set*, is the "crowd" that provides individual privacy. The sizes of these crowds reflect how much protection they give to the individuals in the crowd. So we have the following metric.

Definition 2. *(k-**SIND**) Given a released data v, if each SIND set has a cardinality of at least k, we then say v provides k-*SIND.

2.3   Relationship with k-Anonymity

In this subsection, we discuss the relationship between k-SIND and k-anonymity. In the k-anonymity literature (e.g., [24,25,21,14,18]), the released data is an anonymized table. Anonymization is a function from quasi-IDs to recoded quasi-IDs, and the anonymization process (the function M in Section 2.1) is to replace quasi-IDs with recoded quasi-IDs. We assume that the anonymization algorithm and the input quasi-IDs are known. In fact, we make a stronger assumption, called "mapping assumption", which says that (1) each quasi-ID maps to one recoded quasi-ID and (2) given a recoded quasi-ID, attackers know which set of quasi-IDs map to it.

As an example, there is a table and an anonymized table as the following, respectively. The tuples on $(Zip, Race)$ are quasi-IDs. Under the mapping assumption, attackers know which quasi-ID maps to which recoded quasi-ID. For instance, $(22031, White)$ maps to $(2203*, *)$ but not $(220**, White)$. (In contrast, without the mapping assumption, only from the anonymized table, $(22031, White)$ may map to either $(2203*, *)$ or $(220**, White)$.)

Zip	Race	Problem
22021	White	Cold
22031	White	Obesity
22032	White	AIDS
22033	Black	Headache

Zip	Race	Problem
220**	White	Cold
220**	White	Obesity
2203*	*	AIDS
2203*	*	Headache

Under the above assumption, we have the following conclusion about the relationship between k-SIND and k-anonymity. Here the attributes of quasi-IDs are assumed to be exactly the public attributes B.

Proposition 1. *Under the mapping assumption, if an anonymized table v provides k-anonymity, where $k \geq 2$, then v provides k-SIND.*

Intuitively, if v provides k-anonymity, then at least k quasi-IDs map to each recoded quasi-ID in v. In any instance yielding v, suppose two quasi-IDs b_1 and b_2 map to the same recoded quasi-ID. Then swapping the private values of b_1 and b_2 in the original table gives an instance yielding the same v. Therefore, v provides k-SIND.

By definition, k-anonymity is applicable only to a single anonymized table, but not to other kinds of released data such as multiple database views.

2.4   Restricted Symmetric Indistinguishability

Since SIND requires symmetry in terms of all possible private values, it is a rather strict metric. We define another metric based on the symmetry in terms of not all possible private values but only a subset that includes the actual private values in the current private table. If B tuples are symmetric in terms of this subset of private values, even though they are not symmetric in terms of other values, we may still take them as indistinguishable. The intuition here is that we intend to provide more protection on the actual private values.

We associate each B tuple with a set of private values including its current private value. These sets form a collection. More specifically, we call a collection $\mathcal{P}$ of $Dom(P)$ value sets P_1, ..., P_n a *private value collection*, where $n = |\Pi_B(Tbl)|$ and $\Pi_B(Tbl) = b_1$, ..., b_n, if for each s, where $s = 1, ..., n$, $\Pi_P \sigma_{B=b_s}(Tbl) \in P_s$.

If two B tuples are symmetric w.r.t. a private value collection, then we take them as indistinguishable. More formally, we have the following definition. We abbreviate restricted symmetric indistinguishability as RSIND.

Definition 3. *(**RSIND***) Given a released data v on the current table Tbl and a private value collection P_1, ..., P_n, we say two B tuples b_i and b_j are RSIND w.r.t. P_1, ..., P_n if the following conditions are satisfied: (1) $P_i = P_j$ and (2) for each p_i in P_i and each p_j in P_j, if (b_i, p_i) and (b_j, p_j) are in an instance I in $\mathcal{I}^v$, I' is in $\mathcal{I}^v$ where $I' = (I - \{(b_i, p_i), (b_j, p_j)\}) \cup \{(b_i, p_j), (b_j, p_i)\}$.*

In this definition, unlike SIND, which swaps all possible private values, RSIND only swaps private values in a subset including the current private values. RSIND becomes SIND if $P_i = Dom(P)$ for each i.

For example, consider the two views in Figure 3 (see caption) on the table in Figure 1. From the view, we can deduce that in the private table Tbl, $t_1[B]$ cannot take *Obesity* but can take *Cold* and *AIDS*, and $t_2[B]$ can take all the three problems. Clearly, $t_1[B]$ and $t_2[B]$ are not SIND. But there exists a private value collection P_1, ..., P_4 with $P_1 = P_2 = \{Cold, AIDS\}$ and $P_3 = P_4 = \{Cold, AIDS, Obesity\}$, we have $t_1[B]$ and $t_2[B]$ are RSIND w.r.t. this collection. Indeed, P_1 and P_2 are identical, and they both include the current private values of $t_1[B]$ and $t_2[B]$, *Cold* and *AIDS*. In any instance yielding the views, if $t_1[B]$ and $t_2[B]$ have *Cold* and *AIDS*, or *AIDS* and *Cold*, respectively, then swapping their private values results in an instance yielding the same views.

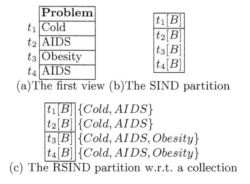

(a)The first view (b)The SIND partition

(c) The RSIND partition w.r.t. a collection

Fig. 3. Two released views $\Pi_{Problem}$ $\sigma_{Zip='22030'}(Tbl)$ and $\Pi_{Problem}$ $\sigma_{t_1\ and\ Problem='Obesity'}(Tbl) = \emptyset$

Given a private value collection P_1, ..., P_n, RSIND is also a binary equivalence relation, hence induces a partition over the B tuples; and each set in the partition is called an RSIND set w.r.t. P_1, ..., P_n.

Definition 4. (k-**RSIND**) *Given a released data v, if there exists a private value collection $\mathcal{P}$ such that each RSIND set in the induced partition has a cardinality of at least k, we then say v provides k-RSIND.*

Obviously, if v provides k-SIND, we can let $P_1, ..., P_n$ be the collection of all possible private values, i.e., $P_s = \{p | \exists I \in \mathcal{I}^v(b_s, p) \in I\}$, where $s = 1, ..., n$. Then each pair of SIND values are RSIND w.r.t. $P_1, ..., P_n$, hence the SIND partition is the RSIND partition w.r.t. $P_1, ..., P_n$. Clearly, the cardinality of each set in this RSIND partition is at least k since each set in the SIND partition is so. Thus, we have the following proposition. In Figure 3, the second view makes t_1 not have *Obesity* which others may have. The views do not provide 2-SIND, but do provide 2-RSIND.

Proposition 2. *k-SIND implies k-RSIND.*

From the definition of RSIND, we have the following conclusion. Given a set of tuples T in the current table Tbl, each private value collection w.r.t. which the B tuples in $\Pi_B(T)$ are RSIND from each other must include all of their current private values, $\Pi_P(T)$; $\Pi_B(T)$ are RSIND from each other w.r.t. $\Pi_P(T)$, if there exists a collection such that $\Pi_B(T)$ are RSIND from each other. More formally, we have the following proposition.

Proposition 3. *Given a private value collection $\mathcal{P} = P_0, P_1, ..., P_n$, released data v, and a set T of tuples in the current table, if the tuples in $\Pi_B(T)$ are RSIND from each other w.r.t. $\mathcal{P}$, then we have the following two facts. First, for each b_i in $\Pi_B(T)$, $\Pi_P(T) \subseteq P_i$. Second, for each b_i in $\Pi_B(T)$, if we replace P_i with $\Pi_P(T)$ to get a new private value collection $\mathcal{P}'$, then all the B tuples in $\Pi_B(T)$ are still RSIND w.r.t. $\mathcal{P}'$.*

Consider the example in Figure 3. $t_3[B]$ and $t_4[B]$ are RSIND w.r.t. the private value collection. Hence, in the collection, the corresponding sets of $t_3[B]$ and $t_4[B]$ are identical and have both their current private values, *Obesity* and *AIDS*. If we take their current private values as a collection, which means dropping *Cold* from their corresponding sets, $t_3[B]$ and $t_4[B]$ are still RSIND.

Proposition 3 implies the following property of RSIND. If the tuples in $\Pi_B(T)$ are RSIND from each other, then by Proposition 3, the tuples in $\Pi_B(T)$ are RSIND from each other w.r.t. $\Pi_P(T)$. By a repeated use of the definition of RSIND, for each set of tuple T' such that $\Pi_B(T') = \Pi_B(T)$ and the private values in T' is a permutation of the private values (with duplicates preserved) in T, we know there exists an instance I in $\mathcal{I}^v$ with $T \subseteq I$. This explains why we say these tuples are indistinguishable in terms of the current private values.

For example, consider the SIND partition of Figure 3(b) as an RSIND partition (note again that there are many RSIND partitions with difference private value collections and the SIND partition is one of them). We have that $t_2[B], t_3[B]$ and $t_4[B]$ are RSIND from each other w.r.t. $P_2 = P_3 = P_4 = \{Obesity, AIDS\}$. Then for each of the three different (repeated) permutations of $t_2[B], t_3[B]$, and $t_4[B]$ with *Obesity*, *AIDS* and *AIDS* values (i.e., $\langle (t_2[B], Obesity), (t_3[B], AIDS), (t_4[B], AIDS) \rangle$, $\langle (t_2[B], AIDS), (t_3[B], Obesity), (t_4[B], AIDS) \rangle$, and $\langle (t_2[B],$

$AIDS$), $(t_3[B], AIDS)$, $(t_4[B], Obesity)\rangle\rangle$, there exists at least one instance in $\mathcal{I}^v$ that contains that permutation.

The size of each set in a private value collection matters in measuring privacy disclosure, which is not reflected in k-RSIND. Generally, the more P values in the collection, the better indistinguishability we achieve since we ignore the fewer P values that may make B tuples distinguishable. Also, more private values may mean better uncertainty. However, in this paper, we are not pursuing this direction.

3   Checking Database Views

In this section, we focus on checking released data that are in the form of a view set for indistinguishability. A *view set* is a pair (V, v), where V is a list of selection-projection queries $(q_1, q_2, ..., q_n)$ on Tbl, and v is a list of relations $(r_1, r_2, ..., r_n)$ that are the results, with duplicates preserved, of the corresponding queries. We may abbreviate (V, v) to v if V is understood. In this paper, "view", "query" and "query result" are used interchangeably when no confusion arises. *Note all query results preserve duplicates, hence, are multisets and all relational operations in this paper are on multisets.*

3.1   Checking for k-SIND

In this subsection, we will show that checking for k-SIND is intractable. Then, we will present a subcase where checking is tractable, before which the basic checking mechanism is presented. Finally, we will also present a conservative checking methods that always catch k-SIND violation, but may make mistakes when a view set actually provides k-SIND.

Complexity. Checking for k-SIND is intractable. This is mainly because it is intractable to know whether a private value can associate with a particular B tuple by just looking at the view set.

Theorem 1. *Given a view set v containing only selection and projection, it is NP-hard to decide whether there exists an instance $I \in \mathcal{I}^v$ such that a tuple (b, p) is in I.*

The proof of the above theorem is by showing a reduction to our problem from the following NP-hard *Complement Boolean Auditing Problem* (whose complement, *Boolean auditing problem,* has been shown as coNP-hard [17]).

Theorem 2. *Given a view set v, whether v provides k-SIND is coNP-hard.*

We reduce the complement of the problem in Theorem 1 (that is, determining if a tuple (b, p) appears in at least one instance in $\mathcal{I}^v$) to the problem of checking k-SIND. Given any table Tbl and view set v, we construct another table Tbl' and view set v', such that v' violates 2-SIND iff (b, p) appears in at least one instance in $\mathcal{I}^v$. Because it is NP-hard to determine the latter by Theorem 1, it is coNP-hard to determine if v' satisfies 2-SIND.

Basic mechanism for checking. First, we introduce an important property of SIND in Proposition 4. This property will be used in the subsequent checking methods.

Proposition 4. *Given a view set v and two tuples b_1 and b_2 in $\Pi_B(Tbl)$, b_1 and b_2 are SIND w.r.t. v, iff for each pair of P values p_1 and p_2 associated with b_1 and b_2, respectively, in an instance in $\mathcal{I}^v$, and each query q in v, we have $q(\{(b_1, p_1), (b_2, p_2)\}) = q(\{(b_1, p_2), (b_2, p_1)\})$*

Assume b_1 and b_2 are SIND. Then for each view q in v, $q(\{(b_1, p_1), (b_2, p_2)\} \cup I_o) = q(\{(b_1, p_2), (b_2, p_1)\} \cup I_o)$ (all query results are multisets and relational operations are multiset operations), where I_o is an instance such that $\{(b_1, p_1), (b_2, p_2)\} \cup I_o \in \mathcal{I}^v$. Since q only contains selection and projection, $q(\{(b_1, p_1), (b_2, p_2)\} \cup I_o) = q(\{(b_1, p_1), (b_2, p_2)\} \cup q(I_o)$ and $q(\{(b_1, p_2), (b_2, p_1)\} \cup I_o) = q(\{(b_1, p_2), (b_2, p_1)\} \cup q(I_o)$. Thus, we have $q(\{(b_1, p_1), (b_2, p_2)\}) = q(\{(b_1, p_2), (b_2, p_1)\})$. The other direction holds for the same reason.

We call the equation in this proposition *swap equation*. This proposition suggests SIND for selection-projection views has the property of being "local". Indeed, to check SIND between given two B tuples, we do not need to see other B tuples.

More specifically, this proposition says that given v and two SIND B tuples b_1 and b_2, for each query q in v, if the tuples (b_1, p_1) and (b_2, p_2) are in an instance that yields v, and we swap the private values of (b_1, p_1) and (b_2, p_2) to get the two new tuples, i.e., (b_1, p_2) and (b_2, p_1), then we know that $\{(b_1, p_2), (b_2, p_1)\}$ yields the same result of q as $\{(b_1, p_2), (b_2, p_1)\}$ does. This is a necessary and sufficient condition.

As a simple example, given two B tuples b_1 and b_2, if in all the instances in $\mathcal{I}^v$, we know they associate either with p_1 and p_2, respectively, or p_2 and p_3, respectively. Then b_1 and b_2 are SIND iff

$$q\begin{pmatrix}(b_1, p_1)\\(b_2, p_2)\end{pmatrix} = q\begin{pmatrix}(b_1, p_2)\\(b_2, p_1)\end{pmatrix} \quad \& \quad q\begin{pmatrix}(b_1, p_2)\\(b_2, p_3)\end{pmatrix} = q\begin{pmatrix}(b_1, p_3)\\(b_2, p_2)\end{pmatrix}$$

To satisfy swap equation

$$q\begin{pmatrix}(b_1, p_1)\\(b_2, p_2)\end{pmatrix} = q\begin{pmatrix}(b_1, p_2)\\(b_2, p_1)\end{pmatrix}$$

there are only two possibilities: one is

$$q((b_1, p_1)) = q((b_1, p_2)) \quad \& \quad q((b_2, p_2)) = q((b_2, p_1))$$

and the other is

$$q((b_1, p_1)) = q((b_2, p_1)) \quad \& \quad q((b_1, p_2)) = q((b_2, p_2))$$

If a view has a projection on P and p_1 is distinct from p_2, we can easily prove that we only need to check the latter condition. Moreover, *if the projection of q contains P, and b_1 and b_2 have at least two possible private values, then it is* *a necessary and sufficient condition for b_1 and b_2 being SIND that $q((b_1, p)) = q((b_2, p))$ holds for each possible value p.*

For example, consider the view q in Figure 2 with the projection on P. Clearly, $q((t_9[B], H)) = q((t_{10}[B], H))$ and $q((t_9[B], C)) = q((t_{10}[B], C))$, where $H = Hypertension$ and $C = ChestPain$. Since H and C are the only possible values by looking at the view, we know $t_9[B]$ and $t_{10}[B]$ are SIND.

In the rest of this subsection, we use Proposition 4 to decide whether a view set v provides k-SIND.

Selection only on B attributes. This subcase is common, especially in statistical databases, and hence is extensively studied with uncertainty measures [1,17,16]. In this subcase, each query in the view set has a selection condition only on the attributes in B. If so, checking for k-SIND can be done in polynomial time in the size of the private table and the number of views.

We assume the projection of each view contains P; otherwise, no private information is involved since the selection condition also does not have P and the view may be removed from our consideration. By Proposition 4, we have following conclusion for checking.

Proposition 5. *Given a view set v with selection conditions only on the attributes in B, two B tuples b_1 and b_2 are SIND if for each query $q = \Pi_X \sigma_C(Tbl)$ in v, we have $\Pi_{X-\{P\}} \sigma_C(b_1) = \Pi_{X-\{P\}} \sigma_C(b_2)$. The inverse ("only if") holds if b_1 and b_2 have at least two distinct possible private values.*

For each query q in v, if we have $\Pi_{X-\{P\}} \sigma_C(b_1) = \Pi_{X-\{P\}} \sigma_C(b_2)$, then $q(b_1, p) = q(b_2, p)$ holds for each p in the domain. Because C does not contain p, we can apply the conclusion from Proposition 4. Thus, each pair of possible tuples (b_1, p_1) and (b_2, p_2) satisfies swap equation. Otherwise, $q(b_1, p) = q(b_2, p)$ can not hold, hence, swap equation can not be satisfied if b_1 and b_2 have at least two distinct possible private values (if there is only one possible private value, the swap results in the same instance, hence swap equation must be satisfied).

We assume that the set of k indistinguishable B tuples must have at least two distinct possible private values; otherwise, it must not be safe. Thus, the condition of Proposition 5 is a necessary and sufficient condition. By this proposition, we can present an efficient checking method through partitioning. The basic idea is that for each view, we can partition tuples such that each set in the partition are SIND w.r.t. this view, and we then intersect these partitions.

As an example of this procedure, consider the two views

$$\Pi_{Race, Problem} \; \sigma_{Zip='22030'} \; (Tbl) \text{ and}$$
$$\Pi_{Gender, Problem} \; \sigma_{Race='White'} \; (Tbl).$$

We partition the B tuples as Figure 4 (a) by the first view and by the second view as Figure 4 (b); the final result in Figure 4 (c) is the intersection of the two partitions shown in (a) and (b). For each view, the selected tuples that have the same values on the projection are grouped in the same set of the partition, $(Zip, Race)$ for the first and $(Race, Gender)$ for the second; the tuples that are not selected

(22030, White)	$t_1[B], t_2[B], t_3[B]$
(22030, Black)	$t_4[B]$
Others not selected	$t_5[B], t_6[B], ..., t_{12}[B]$

(a) By the first view

(White, Male)	$t_1[B], t_2[B], t_3[B], t_6[B],$ $t_8[B], t_{11}[B], t_{12}[B]$
(White, Female)	$t_6[B]$
Others not selected	$t_4[B], t_5[B], t_7[B],$ $t_9[B], t_{10[B]}$

(b) By the second view

| $t_1[B], t_2[B], t_3[B]$ |
| $t_4[B]$ |
| $t_5[B], t_7[B], t_9[B], t_{10}[B]$ |
| $t_6[B]$ |
| $t_8[B], t_{11}[B], t_{12}[B]$ |

(c) The final partition

Fig. 4. The partition of B tuples by views

are grouped into another set in the partition. If two B tuples are in the same block of the final partition, they are SIND. In this case, we only have 1-SIND.

Now we analyze the computational complexity of this checking procedure. The partitioning for each view q in this procedure needs to search for the set of B tuples yielding the same result of q. Such searching can be done using a hash data structure, hence is constant time. And each partition needs to scan all the B tuples in Tbl once. Thus the computing time is $O(nS)$, where S is the size of Tbl and n is the number of views in the view set.

Conservative checking. Because checking a view set for k-SIND is generally intractable, we may want to perform a conservative-style checking that is polynomial time and suitable for all cases. With a conservative algorithm, we always catch k-SIND violation, but we may make mistakes when a view set actually provides k-SIND.

First, we can use a conservative checking method for each single view q. The basic idea is that if two B tuples have the same characteristics in the selection condition and have the same value on the B attributes in the projection of q, then they are SIND for q.

More specifically, if two B tuples b_1 and b_2 have the same values on the B attributes in the projection of q, and after substitute B with b_1 and b_2, respectively, in the selection condition, the two substituted conditions have the same set of P values making the conditions true, then they are SIND. We can see that this method does not look for the possible private values. Thus, it has the similar procedure as the checking method for the case where v selects only B

attributes in Subsection 3.1. That is, generate a partition for each view by the corresponding attribute values of B tuples and intersect these partitions.

For example, consider the view $\Pi_{Zip}\sigma_{Charge>Salary}(Tbl)$ on the table Tbl. Each distinct $Charge$ value c has the different set of $Salary$ values making the selection condition true when you substitute $Charge$ with c in the condition. Thus, if two B tuples have the same $(Zip, Charge)$ value, then we take them as SIND; otherwise, we do not.

Clearly, this method for checking each single view is polynomial time. Then we can use the following conclusion to check a set of views. We have that if two b tuples are SIND w.r.t. each view in v, then then b_1 and b_2 are SIND w.r.t. v. Therefore, we can generate a SIND partition for each view in v, and then intersection these partitions to get a SIND partition for v. All the B tuples in the same set of the partition for v must be SIND. Then if the cardinality of each set of the final partition is at least k, the view set provides k-SIND. Otherwise, it may not do.

Checking in this way can be done in polynomial time, and is a conservative method to check the sufficient condition of SIND. We believe this conservative checking is practical, since we do not check what possible private values each individual has. In fact, it has the similar idea as k-anonymization methods [24,25,21,14,18]. Indeed, this checking does not look for the possible private values but looks at the public values while k-anonymization recodes only the public values of tuples to achieve k-anonymity.

3.2   Checking for k-RSIND

In this section, we turn to checking whether there exists an RSIND partition such that the cardinality of each set in the partition is at least k. By Proposition 3, we can check whether there exists this kind of partition by looking for the B tuples in each set that are RSIND from each other w.r.t. their current private values.

To do this, given a set T of tuples in Tbl, we need to check whether for each pair of B tuples b_1 and b_2 in $\Pi_B(T)$, each pair of P values p_1 and p_2 in $\Pi_P(T)$, and each instance I in $\mathcal{I}^v$ that contains (b_1, p_1) and (b_2, p_2), there exists an instance I' in $\mathcal{I}^v$ such that $I' = (I - \{(b_1, p_1), (b_2, p_2)\}) \cup \{(b_1, p_2), (b_2, p_1)\}$. Through the similar deduction as in Proposition 4, this swap is equivalent to that for each query q in v, we must have $q(\{(b_1, p_1), (b_2, p_2)\}) = q(\{(b_1, p_2), (b_2, p_1)\})$.

For each pair of B tuples in $\Pi_B(T)$ and each pair of private values in $\Pi_P(T)$, this swap equation needs to be checked. Then, for n tuples, it needs to be checked $O(n^4)$ times (there are $O(n^2)$ pairs of B tuples and $O(n^2)$ pairs of private values), where n is the cardinality of T. Obviously, this is costly.

However, in most cases, if each two B tuples in $\Pi_B(T)$ can swap their current values, then the two B tuples can swap each two private values in $\Pi_P(T)$. For instance, given $T = \{(b_1, p_1), \{(b_2, p_2), \{(b_3, p_3)\}$, if b_1 and b_2 can swap for p_1 and p_2, b_2 and b_3 for p_2 and p_3, and b_3 and b_1 for p_3 and p_1, then any two B tuples, for example, b_1 and b_2, can swap for all pairs of the current private values, p_1 and p_2, p_2 and p_3, and p_3 and p_1.

For convenience, we introduce another concept. Given two B tuples b_1 and b_2, and (b_1, p_1) and (b_2, p_2) in the current table, we say b_1 and b_2 are *CSIND* (currently SIND) if for each query q in v, we have either (1) q contains the projection on P, and $q((b_1, p_1)) = q((b_2, p_1))$ and $q((b_1, p_2)) = q((b_2, p_2))$, or (2) q does not contain the projection on P, but $q((b_1, p_1)) = q((b_1, p_2))$ and $q((b_2, p_1))) = q((b_2, p_2))$. Intuitively, if b_1 and b_2 are CSIND, we can swap their private values in the current table without affecting the view set.

Clearly, if each two tuples in $\Pi_B(T)$ are CSIND, then each two B tuples in $\Pi_B(T)$ satisfies swap equation for all the private values in $\Pi_P(T)$, hence, $\Pi_B(T)$ are RSIND from each other. Indeed, if each q contains the projection on P, this is a necessary and sufficient condition; otherwise, it is a sufficient condition.

Therefore, we apply the following checking method. If we can find a maximal partition over the B tuples $\Pi_B(Tbl)$ such that each pair of B tuples in each set in the partition are CSIND, then this partition is an RSIND partition. Here, "maximal" means that the union of any two sets in the partition cannot result in a set in which each pair of B tuples are still CSIND. In this way, we can find an RSIND partition by checking whether each pair of tuples in the current table is able to swap their private values. This provides a conservative checking algorithm for k-RSIND as follows.

Construct a graph G. Each tuple maps to a node. If two tuples are CSIND, which can be easily checked based on the current private table, add an edge between the corresponding nodes. Then a complete subgraph of G is a subset of an RSIND set. Therefore, finding an RSIND partition can be transformed to finding a maximal clique partition. If each query of v contains the projection on P, the above checking algorithm is a precise (not conservative) algorithm.

It is known, however, that finding a clique partition with each block's size of at least k is NP-hard [13]. It is not difficult to prove that it is NP-hard to decide whether v provides k-RSIND in the special case where each query of v contains the projection on P. Therefore, given a released view set v, it is NP-hard to decide whether v provides k-RSIND.

Nevertheless, we can use the heuristic algorithms in [13] to find a clique partition with each block size at least k. This will result in a conservative algorithm even for the special case where each query in v contains the projection on P.

For example, consider the views in Figure 3. We construct a graph as Figure 5. Each edge represents that the B tuples corresponding to the two adjacent nodes are CSIND. An RSIND partition maps to a maximal clique partition in the graph.

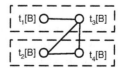

Fig. 5. An RSIND partition for the views in Figure 3 maps to a maximal clique partition

4   Related Work

The most relevant work to indistinguishability is k-anonymization, which focuses on how to gain k-anonymity by recoding the quasi-IDs in a single view, e.g., [24,25,21,14,18]. Recently, there is another work [19] aiming to achieve good uncertainty while gaining k-anonymity by imposing additional requirements on anonymization. But k-anonymity applies only to the case where released data is an anonymized table. In our work, we introduced different definitions of indistinguishability that apply to more general situations, and focused on checking data base views against these indistinguishability metrics. We also discussed the relationship between k-anonymity and indistinguishability.

Some work studies the privacy or secrecy disclosure by general database views. The conditions of perfect secrecy are studied in [22,8] using probability model, and in [28] using query conditional containment. In this paper, we addressed the case where we intend to release data if some partial disclosure by database views is tolerated, and hence the disclosure needs to be measured.

Except for the study of k-anonymity, the privacy metrics used in prior work have mainly been based on uncertainty of private property values, i.e., the uncertainty what private value an individual has. These metrics can be classified into two categories: non-probabilistic and probabilistic.

The non-probabilistic metrics are mainly used in the fields of inference problem of statistical databases [1,17,16,26], multilevel databases [20,5] and general purpose databases [7,5,27]. The most often used one is that if the private value of an individual cannot be uniquely inferred, released data about the individual are considered safe [1,20,7,17,5,16]. The other one is the cardinality of the set of possible private values for each individual, among which attackers cannot determine which one is the actual one [26,27] (The metric used in [27] is an uncertainty metric in spite of the notion of k-anonymity introduced).

In the above fields, some uncertainty metrics are based on probability. Authors use the probability value associated with the actual value [12,16] or the variance of the probability distribution of private values [1,23]. Most work in privacy-preserving data mining uses probability-based metrics. Their metrics are based on only the characteristics of the *a posteriori* probability distribution of private values [3,2,10], or on both *a priori* and the *a posteriori* distribution [2,9,15,4]. The work in [6] uses indistinguishability based on probability "distance" as privacy metric.

In this work, we used symmetry-based indistinguishability metrics. And we illustrated that uncertainty needs to be supplemented with indistinguishability.

5   Conclusions

In this paper, we identified a requirement of privacy in data release, namely indistinguishability, in addition to uncertainty. We first gave two definitions of indistinguishability, namely, SIND and RSIND. Then we focused on checking database views against these indistinguishability metrics. Generally, checking for k-SIND is intractable. We presented a case where polynomial algorithms are possible. Furthermore, we presented a conservative checking method. Checking for RSIND is easy, but checking for k-RSIND is intractable and can be done in a conservative way with heuristic polynomial algorithms.

References

1. N. R. Adam and J. C. Wortmann. Security-control methods for statistical databases: a comparative study. *ACM Computing Surveys*, 21(4):515–556, December 1989.
2. D. Agrawal and C. C. Aggarwal. On the design and quantification of privacy preserving data mining algorithms. In *Proceedings of the Twenty-third ACM SIGACT-SIGMOD-SIGART Symposium on Principles of Database Systems (PODS)*, 2001.
3. R. Agrawal and R. Srikant. Privacy-preserving data mining. In *Proceedings of the ACM SIGMOD International Conference on Management of Data (SIGMOD Conference)*, pages 439–450, 2000.
4. S. Agrawal and J. R. Haritsa. A framework for high-accuracy privacy-preserving mining. In *Proceedings of the 21st International Conference on Data Engineering (ICDE)*, pages 193–204, 2005.
5. A. Brodsky, C. Farkas, and S. Jajodia. Secure databases: Constraints, inference channels, and monitoring disclosures. *IEEE Transactions on Knowledge and Data Engineering*, 12(6):900–919, 2000.
6. S. Chawla, C. Dwork, F. McSherry, A. Smith, and H. Wee. Toward privacy in public databases. In *Theory of Cryptography, Second Theory of Cryptography Conference (TCC)*, pages 363–385, 2005.
7. H. S. Delugach and T. H. Hinke. Wizard: A database inference analysis and detection system. *IEEE Transactions on Knowledge and Data Engineering*, 8(1):56–66, 1996.
8. A. Deutsch and Y. Papakonstantinou. Privacy in database publishing. In *Database Theory - ICDT 2005, 10th International Conference*, pages 230–245, 2005.
9. A. V. Evfimievski, J. Gehrke, and R. Srikant. Limiting privacy breaches in privacy preserving data mining. In *Proceedings of the Twenty-third ACM SIGACT-SIGMOD-SIGART Symposium on Principles of Database Systems (PODS)*, pages 211–222, 2003.
10. A. V. Evfimievski, R. Srikant, R. Agrawal, and J. Gehrke. Privacy preserving mining of association rules. In *Proceedings of the Eighth ACM SIGKDD International Conference on Knowledge Discovery and Data Mining (KDD)*, pages 217–228, 2002.
11. R. Gavison. Privacy and the limits of the law. In D. G. Johnson and H. Nissenbaum, editors, *Computers, Ethics, and Social Values*. 1995.
12. J. Hale and S. Shenoi. Catalytic inference analysis: Detecting inference threats due to knowledge discovery. In *Proceedings of the 1997 IEEE Symposium on Security and Privacy*, pages 188–199, 1997.
13. X. Ji and J. E. Mitchell. Branch-and-price-and-cut on clique partition problem with minimum clique size requirement. In *IMA Special Workshop: Mixed-Integer Programming*, 2005.
14. R. J. B. Jr. and R. Agrawal. Data privacy through optimal k-anonymization. In *Proceedings of the 21st International Conference on Data Engineering (ICDE)*, pages 217–228, 2005.

15. M. Kantarcioglu, J. Jin, and C. Clifton. When do data mining results violate privacy? In *Proceedings of the Tenth ACM SIGKDD International Conference on Knowledge Discovery and Data Mining (KDD)*, pages 599–604, 2004.

16. K. Kenthapadi, N. Mishra, and K. Nissim. Simulatable auditing. In *Proceedings of the Nineteenth ACM SIGMOD-SIGACT-SIGART Symposium on Principles of Database Systems (PODS)*, pages 118–127, 2005.

17. J. M. Kleinberg, C. H. Papadimitriou, and P. Raghavan. Auditing boolean attributes. In *Proceedings of the Nineteenth ACM SIGMOD-SIGACT-SIGART Symposium on Principles of Database Systems (PODS)*, pages 86–91, 2000.

18. K. LeFevre, D. J. DeWitt, and R. Ramakrishnan. Incognito: Efficient full-domain k-anonymity. In *Proceedings of the ACM SIGMOD International Conference on Management of Data (SIGMOD Conference)*, pages 49–60, 2005.

19. A. Machanavajjhala, J. Gehrke, D. Kifer, and M. Venkitasubramaniam. l-diversity: Privacy beyond k-anonymity. In *Proceedings of the 22nd International Conference on Data Engineering (ICDE)*, pages 24–35, 2006.

20. D. G. Marks. Inference in MLS database systems. *IEEE Transactions on Knowledge and Data Engineering*, 8(1):46–55, 1996.

21. A. Meyerson and R. Williams. On the complexity of optimal k-anonymity. In *Proceedings of the Twenty-third ACM SIGACT-SIGMOD-SIGART Symposium on Principles of Database Systems (PODS)*, pages 223–228, 2004.

22. G. Miklau and D. Suciu. A formal analysis of information disclosure in data exchange. In *Proceedings of the ACM SIGMOD International Conference on Management of Data (SIGMOD Conference)*, pages 575–586, 2004.

23. K. Muralidhar and R. Sarathy. Security of random data perturbation methods. *ACM Transactions on Database Systems (TODS)*, 24(4):487–493, 1999.

24. P. Samarati. Protecting respondents' identities in microdata release. *IEEE Transactions on Knowledge and Data Engineering*, 13(6):1010–1027, 2001.

25. L. Sweeney. Achieving k-anonymity privacy protection using generalization and suppression. *International Journal on Uncertainty, Fuzziness and Knowledge-based Systems*, 10(5):571–578, 2002.

26. L. Wang, D. Wijesekera, and S. Jajodia. Cardinality-based inference control in sum-only data cubes. In *Proceedings of 7th European Symposium on Research in Computer Security (ESORICS)*, pages 55–71, 2002.

27. C. Yao, X. S. Wang, and S. Jajodia. Checking for k-anonymity violation by views. In *Proceedings of the 31st International Conference on Very Large Data Bases (VLDB)*, pages 910–921, 2005.

28. Z. Zhang and A. O. Mendelzon. Authorization views and conditional query containment. In *Database Theory - ICDT 2005, 10th International Conference*, pages 259–273, 2005.

Sovereign Information Sharing
Among Malicious Partners

Stefan Böttcher and Sebastian Obermeier

University of Paderborn
Fürstenallee 11
33102 Paderborn, Germany
{stb, so}@upb.de

Abstract. A secure calculation of common data $R \cap S$ without disclosing R or S is useful for many applications and has been widely studied. However, proposed solutions assume all participants act "semi-honest", which means participants may neither stop the protocol execution nor fake database content. In this contribution, we focus on a malicious participant behavior and prove that an atomic exchange of common data is not possible under the assumption of malicious participants. However, we propose mechanisms that not only reduce the damage in case a participant alters the exchange protocol, but also give a means to impede database content faking.

1 Introduction

Enterprise information stored in databases is often confidential and should not be accessed by other companies. However, there are situations in which two companies want to know whether they have common data and which data this is, but the parties are not willing to disclose any other data than that what both have in common. We call this problem the *sovereign information sharing* problem. In this contribution, we focus on protocols for the atomic exchange of the common data without having a trusted third party. In particular, we address the problem that participants may get an advantage by changing the exchange protocol in such a way, that the party that receives and encrypts the common data first can suppress the sending of the corresponding information that is necessary for the other party.

In the context of enterprise information sharing, the interesting data is often stored within database tables, say within database tables R and S of two different companies. The partners demand a protocol that returns the intersection $R \cap S$ without disclosing any other information; it even should not disclose size information like $|R|$ or $|S|$.

For example, let us look at a company C_R and its competitor C_S doing business in the service sector. Both companies want to know whether they have common customers in order to check whether their customers play one company off against the other. A customer of both companies may, for instance, pretend

W. Jonker and M. Petkovic (Eds.): SDM 2006, LNCS 4165, pp. 18–29, 2006.
© Springer-Verlag Berlin Heidelberg 2006

that one company has delivered a certain service cheaper than the other company and demand a discount. Therefore, C_R and C_S want to examine their customer databases for common customers. However, both parties are not willing to disclose any information about customers that the other party does not have, and they do not want to disclose information about their number of customers, i.e. about the sizes $|S|$ and $|R|$.

Existing approaches and proposals that also address the sovereign information sharing problem [1,2] either disclose $f(R, S)$ to a *single* party only, or they assume that participants will follow the protocol strictly and send – as the protocol's last step – the information that the other party needs to calculate $f(R, S)$. In a world of mobile networks and growing evilness, there might be situations in which the participant that has just decoded valuable information suppresses the sending of information that is required by the other participant for decoding the information as well. In addition, [1,2] require that the database sizes $|R|$ and $|S|$ are disclosed, which may also be sensitive information. A sharing of these size information may be not acceptable for companies, e.g. if $|R|$ represents the number of a company's customers. Even if a third party is available and only used for message exchange, this third party can suppress messages and thereby prevent one company from getting to know the intersection information. For this reason, we focus on the problem that each participant may stop the protocol execution whenever there is an advantage for him.

First, we prove that when no trustworthy third party is available, an atomic exchange of the common data is not possible if participants may cheat in terms of altering the protocol. Second, we provide a mechanism that allows participants to exchange a bunch of information units like customer data or supplier information without having the risk of being cheated by more than one information unit.

Unfortunately, when "cheating" in terms of creating faked data is considered as a possibility, theoretical boundaries arise. For example, one participant could invent a lot of customer data in order to get the complete customer data set of the other party as intersection. The only possibility to achieve that stored data complies with reality, i.e., to prevent participants from faking data, is a third-party auditing device that punishes participants for cheating [3]. Contrary to this approach, we present a mechanism appropriate especially for practical applications that makes it hard to create faked data that will not be identified as such.

The remainder of the paper is organized as follows. We identify requirements and assumptions to our protocol in Section 2. In Section 3.1, we prove that the requirement of having an atomic data exchange cannot be fulfilled. However, in Section 3.4, we introduce an exchange algorithm that reduces the amount of data that is disclosed in case a party cheats to one independent information unit. The concept of adding tuple-specific information to prevent participants from getting advantage of data faking is explained in Section 3.2. Finally, Section 4 discusses related work and Section 5 concludes the paper.

2   Basic Assumptions and Requirements

As we cannot guarantee that each party provides all its data for the computation of an intersection $R \cap S$, we assume that each partner contributes only that data to the intersection computation, which it accepts to disclose if it is in the intersection.

Besides the requirement to disclose only the intersection $R \cap S$ of two tables R and S to their owners, namely C_R and C_S, we also need to guarantee that no party can cheat within the disclosing process by suppressing messages or manipulating them. We cannot tolerate that one company that receives the intersection $R \cap S$ can actively prevent the other party from also receiving this information. However, we do not demand a failure-free network, and distinguish between message loss and active message suppression. We assume that each participant acknowledges the received messages and a sender repeats the sending of non-acknowledged messages until the network will finally deliver the message.

An additional requirement is, that size information like $|S|$ or $|R|$ should not be disclosed to the opposite party.

There are business settings in which the partners do not want to rely on a trusted third party that performs a significant part of an intersection computation for a varyity of reasons, e.g. a trusted third party may be too difficult or too time-consuming to find, it may be too expensive or simply not wanted for political reasons. Therefore, in our scenario, we assume that both parties will not trust a third party. This especially means that protocols that disclose $R \cap S$ only to one party (e.g. [4]) are not suitable since we cannot guarantee that the other party will also receive the intersection if none of the companies trusts a third party. Therefore, we need a protocol that guarantees atomicity for the exchange of $R \cap S$. Unfortunately, we can prove in Section 3.1 that a complete atomic exchange of $R \cap S$ cannot be guaranteed. Therefore, we need a protocol that at least reduces the suffered damage in the case that a company cheats.

The problem of cheating does not only concern the data exchange, there is another way of cheating within the data exchange scenario: faked data. Although, it may be difficult or even impossible to detect faked data in general ("is this really a customer, or only a prospective buyer"), the detection of faked data is relevant in practice and can be achieved under certain assumptions. We assume that each data item contributed to the intersection problem is associated with a unique information, which is visible only to the owner of the data item. For example, in the introduced scenario, a company that wants to fake customer data must get in real contact with the customer.

3   Solution

We first prove that an atomic exchange of the common data is not possible if participants may cheat in terms of message suppression. However, for many database and application scenarios, the algorithm proposed in Section 3.4 does not require that the whole intersection must be disclosed at once and furthermore allows to determine whether the other party is cheating.

3.1 Impossibility of Atomic Data Exchange

Our proof that the atomic exchange of common data is not possible is based on a proof idea of the two generals' problem [5, 6], where two generals want agree on an attack time by using an uncertain medium.

In our case, there might be a guaranteed message exchange, but the participants may not behave correctly, i.e., they may suppress messages. Therefore, we can reduce cheating in terms of suppression of messages to the problem of having an uncertain medium that swallows some messages.

Definition 1. *Let C_R and C_S be the owners of the data R and S. A sovereign information sharing protocol IP is said to be* intersection safe, *if it fulfills the following two conditions:*

1. *P discloses $(R \cap S)$ to C_S exactly if it discloses $(R \cap S)$ to C_R.*
2. *P discloses no tuple of R - $(R \cap S)$ to C_S, and it discloses no tuple of $S - (R \cap S)$ to C_R.*

A participant C_R is called distrustful, *if it will not send $(R \cap S)$ or the information that is necessary to completely disclose $(R \cap S)$ to the other participant C_S without the guarantee that C_R will also learn $(R \cap S)$.*

Lemma 1. *Let C_R and C_S be the owners of the data sets R and S respectively. Without a trusted third party, there is no intersection safe protocol if both participants are distrustful.*

Proof. By contradiction. Assume, there is an intersection safe protocol IP that delivers $R \cap S$ to both distrustful participants C_R and C_S.

Then, there also exists a minimal protocol, i.e. a protocol that does not contain a superfluous message, to let both parties learn $R \cap S$, namely either the original protocol, or an equivalent protocol in which all superfluous messages are left out. To let the protocol compute and deliver the intersection, C_S must receive at least one message from C_R, and C_R must receive at least one message from C_S. Because each message that is received has been sent before, there must be also at least one last message M_{last} received by one partner after this partner has sent his last message. As the situation is symmetric, let us assume that M_{last} has been sent from C_R to C_S. Since C_R does not get something in return for sending M_{last} to C_S, C_R must have learned $S \cap R$ before M_{last} could be send. Since our protocol is minimal, C_s cannot have learned $S \cap R$ before M_{last} is sent (otherwise M_{last} would not be necessary and the protocol would not be minimal). However, in this case, C_S must have sent the information that is necessary for C_R to learn $S \cap R$ although C_S has not had the guarantee that it will also receive $S \cap R$, since the last message could be suppressed by C_R.

This behavior of C_s is a contradiction to the assumption that both participants act distrustful. □

The conclusion of this proof is that one party must take the risk of being cheated and be the first who sends the information which is necessary to disclose $R \cap S$.

Otherwise, there would be no exchange, since one party must be the first who completely discloses information of $R \cap S$.

However, although atomicity is not possible, we try to reduce the damage that the one-sided disclosure of the common data involves by an approach outlined in Section 3.4. Our idea is to send only a small part of the intersection $R \cap S$, and let the other party send the next part in return. In this case, if the other party cheats, only a small part of the intersection is disclosed, which might reduce the damage.

However, as we can see in the next section, we cannot make the disclosed information parts, which we call *information units*, arbitrary small.

3.2   Information Units

Let R be arbitrary information of company C_R and S be arbitrary information of C_S. If we partition R into several disjointed smaller parts $j_1 \ldots j_n$, we call each j_i an *information unit* of R. The information units are those parts of the common data of R and S that we want to disclose during one protocol exchange step. Note that information units are only considered for exchange purposes, and not for the calculation of the common data of $R \cap S$, which is based on tuples and not on the information units.

If we cannot conclude any unit j_i that belongs to $R \cap S$ with $|R|, |S| > |R \cap S|$, as long as we do not have all information units of $R \cap S$, we call the set $j_1 \ldots j_n$ *independent*.

Example 1. Let R and S be customer database relations with $|R|, |S| > |R \cap S|$, and $j_1 \ldots j_n$ information units of R, such that each information unit j_i represents a *customer*, and the customers occur in a randomized order. In this case, the set $\{j_1, ..., j_n\}$ is independent since we cannot clearly identify a customer $j_k \in R \cap S$ even if we know $\{j_l \mid j_l \in (R \cap S) \wedge j_l \neq j_k\}$, i.e. the complete intersection except the missing customer, because there are at least two remaining customers who might be j_k due to $|R| > |R \cap S|$.

Note that an independent information unit may contain more than one customer, but an independent information unit cannot be made arbitrarily small, as the next example shows.

Example 2. Let R and S be customer database relations and $j_1 \ldots j_n$ information units representing *characters* occurring in customers of R. This means, each customer is represented by several information units $j_i \ldots j_l$. However, the set $j_1 \ldots j_n$ is not independent for the following reason. If we can use R to identify the customer cu that is represented partially by the characters $j_i \ldots j_k$ with $cu \in R \cap S$, we can conclude the next character of the customer. For example, if $j_i...j_k$ discloses the substring "`Miller, Flori`" of a customer name and we have only one Miller from Florida in our customer database R, we know that this Miller belongs to $R \cap S$ and that further information units j_{k+1} and j_{k+2} will disclose "d" and "a". Therefore, the information units used during the exchange process are not independent.

For this reason, if non-independent information units are used, a party can some-times conclude more than one information unit while the other party may not necessarily know which data is meant. For example, if C_R knows which data is in the intersection and cheats by stopping the exchange of non-independent in-formation units, the other party C_S may have no chance to conclude any missing information unit.

When exchanging only independent information units, we can reduce the ad-vantage that a cheating party may get by altering the protocol to one indepen-dent information unit (c.f. Section 3.4).

3.3 Cryptographic Basis

Our solution is based on commutative encryption, which means that given two cryptographic encryption keys $ek(r)$ used by C_R and $ek(s)$ used by C_S, the encryption order of applying an encryption function E is commutative:

$$E_{ek(r)}\left(E_{ek(s)}(d)\right) = E_{ek(s)}\left(E_{ek(r)}(d)\right) = c_d$$

Since the order of applying the encryption functions $E_{ek(r)}$ and $E_{ek(r)}$ and the corresponding decryption functions does not matter, we call this *commutative encryption*.

Cryptographic functions and their implementation have already been dis-cussed in various cryptographic publications [7, 8, 9, 10]. Therefore, we assume that for the commutative encryption and decryption properly selected encryp-tion functions and and decryption functions and secure algorithms are used, such that keys cannot be broken even if plain and ciphered text are known.

3.4 Exchange Algorithm

Figure 1 summarizes our exchange algorithm that fulfills the requirement of reducing the damage in case a party cheats.

We will explain what happens in each step, which is shown at the left side of the sequence diagram.

1. The parties agree on the data field(s) that they want to check for common data, and both parties suggest a common database size sz_i, of which the following can be expected: $sz_i > \max(|R|, |S|)$. The parties can either send sz_i in plain text and agree on the greater value $sz = \max(sz_1, sz_2)$, or they can use Yao's Millionaire Protocol [11] to conceal the smaller value of the two sz_i values. Then, each party adds randomly created data to their databases R and S until $|R| \approx |S| \approx sz$.
2. Each party hashes every tuple with the same hash function $h(R)$, and en-crypts the hashed values of the tuples with its commutative encryption func-tion $E_{ek(r)}$ with encryption key $ek(r)$ and $E_{ek(s)}$ with key $ek(s)$ respectively.[1]

---

[1] $h(R)$ should not produce collisions and make the hashed values to "appear random", which means there should be no dependency between them to prevent attacks on the encryption key if encrypted and decrypted hash values are known.

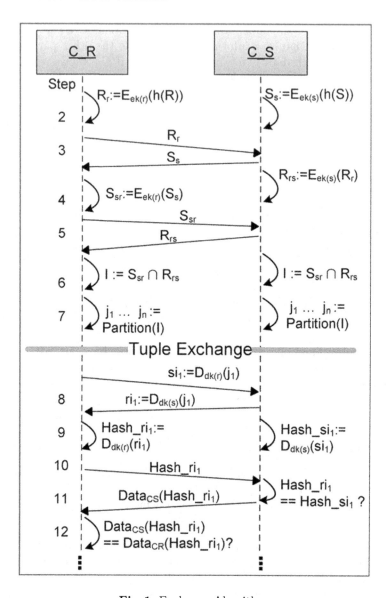

Fig. 1. Exchange Algorithm

3. The hashed and encrypted data is exchanged.
4. Every party encrypts the data it received in Step 3 with its own key. Thus, the resulting data sets R_{rs} and S_{sr} are hashed and thereafter encrypted by both partners, C_R and C_S.
5. The twice encrypted data is exchanged. Now every party owns two files that were hashed and encrypted by each party.

6. Due to commutative encryption, the intersection of the files R_{rs} and S_{sr} represents the intersection of the original data $R \cap S$. Both parties sort R_{rs} and S_{sr} lexicographically and determine the tuples of the intersection.
7. The intersection is partitioned into independent information units, e.g. into packages containing 5 tuples.
8. C_R computes si_1 by decrypting the first information unit j_1 with its decryption key $dk(r)$, and sends si_1 to C_S. C_S analogously does the same, and sends ri_1 to C_R.
9. C_R decrypts ri_1 with its key $dk(r)$, and gets the plain hash value(s) Hash_ri_1. (For simplicity of the following presentation, we assume that an information unit contains a single hash value). C_S does the same with si_1 and also gets the plain hash value Hash_si_1. Now both parties can identify the data associated with the hash value, which is a part of the information both have in common.
10. However, in order to check that no participant cheated, C_R sends Hash_ri_1 to C_S and demands the original data as proof that the data is in the database of C_S.
11. C_S checks, whether the received hash value Hash_ri_1 is equal to the value that it decrypted itself in Step 9, namely Hash_si_1. If this is the case, C_S sends the data belonging to the hash value to C_R.
12. C_R checks whether the received data from C_S corresponds to the data of Hash_ri_1, which C_R has in its own database.

This algorithm does not only hide the data of R and S, it also hides all size information except $|S \cap R|$, since each participant adds a bunch of random data to its database. Therefore, e.g. C_S cannot use $|R|$ to conclude the number of the real data inside the database of C_R.

Furthermore, message manipulation can be detected directly after uncovering a single information unit. If any message is manipulated before Step 6, e.g. some data of the other party is altered before or after the encryption, the intersection computation in Step 6 would not find two identical encrypted tuples of the altered data, and would therefore neither disclose the altered data nor any corresponding real data. If any data si_i or ri_i is manipulated after Step 6, the manipulating party cannot predict the hash value, to which the manipulated data is decrypted. If, for example, C_R sends manipulated data as si_1 in Step 8, it does not know the resulting Hash_si_1 to which C_S decrypts si_1. Therefore, this manipulation will be detected by C_S in step 11, since the two hash values differ. If, the other way round, C_S cheats by sending an $ri_1 \in R_r$, C_R will decrypt this to Hash_ri_1, which is in the database of C_R. However, in Step 11, C_R demands the data corresponding to Hash_ri_1, and if C_S does not have this data, it cannot send it. If C_S has this data and can send it, the manipulation of ri_1 was no manipulation at all since intersecting tuples are meant to be exchanged. This means, any cheating in Step 8 can be detected.

Cheating in Step 10 can be detected as well, since no party knows the hash value to which ri_1 and si_1 are decrypted.

Cheating in Step 11 is not possible as well if we assume the hash method to be secure. This means, given a hash value Hash_ri_1, we assume that it is not possible to calculate the data which C_R has in its database that leads to the hash value.

Therefore, altering the protocol by suppressing or manipulating messages may only prevent the other party from learning one information unit of the intersection, but does not disclose the complete set $R \cap S$.

3.5 Impeding Tuple Faking

Although cheating in terms of message suppression and manipulation can be detected by our algorithm and therefore the damage is reduced, one problem remains, which is faking database tuples. In our example, an evil participant can add a huge amount of telephone book entries to his customer database in order to abuse the intersection computation to check which customers the other side has. To prevent this kind of faking, the parties must agree to additionally supply *tuple-specific information* that both parties have due to the real existence of the tuple in their database.

data tuple	tuple specific information

This tuple-specific information should not be of such a kind that it can not be guessed or concluded from information that is available for public. An address field, for instance, is no tuple-specific information since it can be easily obtained from public resources.

Example 3. Consider the common customers example. Each party expands the set of tuples that it wants be checked for being in $R \cap S$ with tuple-specific information, i.e. the customers' credit card details, such that the extended data record may look like this:

name	surname	street	place	*credit card number*

Then this data fields is hashed, encrypted and sent to the other side. If faked credit card data is generated, the customer belonging to the generated card number will not match with the real customer, since both entries differ in their hash values.

While we used the credit card number as an example, other scenarios will rely on different tuple specific information, for example a social security number, income tax number, student number, etc.

3.6 Exchange Speed Versus Trust

The efficiency of our intersection computation algorithm depends on given parameters like the intersection size, the connection speed, and on a choseable parameter, i.e. the size of exchanged information units. As the exchange of small information units needs more communication steps than exchanging larger ones, we have a trade-off between trust and speed. When both parties do not expect a malicious behavior, an information unit may contain more data than it may contain when two competing parties act. Whenever an application does not require a fast intersection computation, the use of information units containing only a single data tuple can be preferred, which reduces the disadvantage in case of cheating to the risk of disclosing only one data tuple.

4   Related Work

Within the sovereign information sharing scenario, two aspects are important and have been studied: the secure computation of the intersection, and the fair exchange of the data. The *Secure Multiparty Computation* problem, for instance, focuses on a joint computation of $f(r, s)$ without disclosing r or s. Examples of functions f to be computed are cooperative scientific computations arising in linear programming [12], or Yao's Millionaire's protocol [11], in which f returns the information of whether or not $r > s$.

In an enterprise context where databases are used to store information, solutions exist [4, 13] that focus on the multi-party computation problem within a database context. The secure computation of the join-operator, for instance, can be found in [4]. However, these solutions disclose not only size information like $|R|$ and $|S|$, they also assume an "semi-honest" behavior [14,15], which means that although a party might analyze messages, it will not alter the protocol execution.

[16, 17] tackle the problem from a cryptographic point-of-view, and show solutions where only one participant learns of the intersection, but not the other one. In addition, the cryptographic approaches assume the data is drawn from a large domain, and therefore participants that fake data will hardly get a match. Although even in our example the domain from which the data is taken is large, we consider this to be not sufficient for the following reason. This assumption does not prevent the participants from faking data in order to get the knowledge of whether the other participant has exactly this data (this customer) in its database. In contrast, our solution focuses on a model where each participant may act malicious and does not only stop the program execution, but may also change messages or fake data. We introduce the term information unit and show that no secure exchange protocol exists that can guarantee an atomic exchange of a single information unit.

For the *fair exchange* of the data, some proposals rely on a *trusted third party* [18, 19], while other proposals do not necessarily need this third party. [20, 21], for example, describe an approach, which focuses on a fair exchange of items by using a third party only if participants are dishonest. If a third party is present but not trustable, [22] shows a solution in which this third party helps to make an exchange fair. [20] classifies the type of the exchanged items, and can guarantee an atomic exchange for items belonging to the categories revocable or generatable, which is suitable for problems like contract signature or access to webpages. However, enterprise information is in many cases neither revocable nor generatable, and the approach to use a third party for collecting affidavits and starting law suits in case of malicious participants is suitable for goods and items, but cannot be used to revoke the reveal of sensible enterprise data. In contrast, our approach does not rely on a certain item category; it is useful for non-revocable and non-generatable items as well.

5   Summary and Conclusion

In this contribution, we have presented an application scenario where two parties need a secure exchange of common information, although they do not trust each other and assume malicious behavior. We have shown that atomicity for the exchange of the common data is not possible if no third party is used for this purpose. Furthermore, we have proposed a solution, which reduces the damage that a party suffers in case the other party alters the exchange protocol to the disclosure of one additional independent information unit. While the sending of faked data within our proposed protocol can be effectively detected by means of cryptography, the use and creation of faked database content has can be impeded by extending the datasets that should be compared with tuple-specific information. In addition, our solution conceals the database's input sizes and therefore does not allow to conclude important database properties, e.g. the number of customers.

References

1. Naor, M., Pinkas, B.: Oblivious transfer and polynomial evaluation. In: STOC '99: Proceedings of the thirty-first annual ACM symposium on Theory of computing, New York, NY, USA, ACM Press (1999) 245–254
2. Huberman, B.A., Franklin, M., Hogg, T.: Enhancing privacy and trust in electronic communities. In: ACM Conference on Electronic Commerce. (1999) 78–86
3. Agrawal, R., Terzi, E.: On honesty in sovereign information sharing. In: 10th International Conference on Extending Database Technology, Munich, Germany (2006) 240–256
4. Agrawal, R., Evfimievski, A.V., Srikant, R.: Information sharing across private databases. In: Proceedings of the 2003 ACM SIGMOD International Conference on Management of Data, San Diego, California, USA. (2003) 86–97
5. Akkoyunlu, E.A., Ekanadham, K., Huber, R.V.: Some constraints and tradeoffs in the design of network communications. SIGOPS Oper. Syst. Rev. **9** (1975) 67–74
6. Gray, J.: Notes on data base operating systems. In: Operating Systems, An Advanced Course, London, UK, Springer-Verlag (1978) 393–481
7. Diffie, W., Hellman, M.E.: New directions in cryptography. IEEE Transactions on Information Theory **IT-22** (1976) 644–654
8. Gamal, T.E.: A public key cryptosystem and a signature scheme based on discrete logarithms. In: Proceedings of CRYPTO 84 on Advances in cryptology, New York, NY, USA, Springer-Verlag New York, Inc. (1985) 10–18
9. Goldwasser, S., Micali, S.: Probabilistic encryption & how to play mental poker keeping secret all partial information. In: STOC '82: Proceedings of the fourteenth annual ACM symposium on Theory of computing, New York, NY, USA, ACM Press (1982) 365–377

10. Shamir, A., Rivest, R., Adleman, L.: Mental poker. In: Technical Report LCS/TR-125. (1979)
11. Yao, A.C.: Protocols for secure computations. In: Proceedings of the 21st Annual IEEE Symposium on the Foundations of Computer Science, Chicago, IEEE (1982) 160–164
12. Du, W., Atallah, M.J.: Secure multi-party computation problems and their applications: A review and open problems. In: New Security Paradigms Workshop, Cloudcroft, New Mexico, USA (2001) 11–20
13. Clifton, C., Kantarcioglu, M., Lin, X., Vaidya, J., Zhu, M.: Tools for privacy preserving distributed data mining (2003)
14. Goldreich, O.: Secure multi-party computation. Working Draft (2000)
15. Goldreich, O., Micali, S., Wigderson, A.: How to play any mental game. In: STOC '87: Proceedings of the nineteenth annual ACM conference on Theory of computing, New York, NY, USA, ACM Press (1987) 218–229
16. Kissner, L., Song, D.X.: Privacy-preserving set operations. (In: Advances in Cryptology - CRYPTO 2005: 25th Annual International Cryptology Conference)
17. Freedman, M., Nissim, K., Pinkas, B.: Efficient private matching and set intersection. (In: Advances in Cryptology — EUROCRYPT 2004.)
18. Ajmani, S., Morris, R., Liskov, B.: A trusted third-party computation service. Technical Report MIT-LCS-TR-847, MIT (2001)
19. Jefferies, N., Mitchell, C.J., Walker, M.: A proposed architecture for trusted third party services. In: Cryptography: Policy and Algorithms. (1995) 98–104
20. Asokan, N., Schunter, M., Waidner, M.: Optimistic protocols for fair exchange. In: CCS '97: Proceedings of the 4th ACM conference on Computer and communications security, New York, NY, USA, ACM Press (1997) 7–17
21. Asokan, N., Shoup, V., Waidner, M.: Asynchronous protocols for optimistic fair exchange. In: Proceedings of the IEEE Symposium on Research in Security and Privacy. (1998) 86–99
22. Franklin, M.K., Reiter, M.K.: Fair exchange with a semi-trusted third party (extended abstract). In: ACM Conference on Computer and Communications Security. (1997) 1–5

Temporal Context Lie Detection and Generation

Xiangdong An[1,2], Dawn Jutla[2], and Nick Cercone[1]

[1] Faculty of Computer Science
Dalhousie University
Halifax, NS B3H 1W5, Canada
{xan, nick}@cs.dal.ca
[2] Finance and Management Science Department
Saint Mary's University
Halifax, NS B3H 3C3, Canada
{xan, dawn.jutla}@smu.ca

Abstract. In pervasive (ubiquitous) environments, context-aware agents are used to obtain, understand, and share local contexts with each other so that all resources in the environments could be integrated seamlessly. Context exchanging should be made privacy-conscious, which is generally controlled by users' privacy preferences. Besides who has rights to get what true information about him, a user's privacy preference could also designate who should be given obfuscated information. By obfuscation, people could present their private information in a coarser granularity, or simply in a falsified manner, depending on the specific situations. Nevertheless, obfuscation cannot be done randomly because by reasoning the receiver could know the information has been obfuscated. An obfuscated context can not only be inferred from its dependencies with other existing contexts, but could also be derived from its dependencies with the vanished ones. In this paper, we present a dynamic Bayesian network (DBN)-based method to reason about the obfuscated contexts in pervasive environments, where the impacts of the vanished historical contexts are properly evaluated. On the one hand, it can be used to detect obfuscations, and may further find the true information; on the other hand, it can help reasonably obfuscate information.

Keywords: Privacy management, context inference, inference control, obfuscation, pervasive computing, dynamic Bayesian networks, uncertain reasoning.

1 Introduction

A pervasive (ubiquitous) environment [1,2] is an intelligent space that senses, learns, reasons and acts, where varied devices such as cell phones, PDAs (personal digital assistants) and computers use a wide range of heterogeneous networks to provide diverse services. There is also a lot of information (e.g. data about users and their activities) in such an environment. To integrate these resources and information transparently so that they are available for different tasks at all times and in all locations, contexts of entities in the environment need to be exchanged properly [3,4,5]. Here, by context we mean any information that can be used to characterize an entity in the environment, which could be locations, time, capabilities, lighting, noise levels, services offered and sought, activities and tasks engaged, roles, beliefs and the preferences [6,7]. Context-aware agents have been developed to capture, interpret, reason about, and share such

W. Jonker and M. Petkovic (Eds.): SDM 2006, LNCS 4165, pp. 30–47, 2006.

information in pervasive (ubiquitous) environments [8,9]. An example of the pervasive environment is like this: When Bob drives into a business site, his agent perceives his location and reminds him that he needs to buy a pair of shoes of size 9.5. The store agents detect (or are informed of) Bob's presence and exchange information with Bob's agent. Then each store agent checks their repository's catalog and tells Bob's agent if they have the right shoes and for how much they sell them. For another example, Bob's cell phone gets a text message about breakfast from a nearby restaurant when he approaches the restaurant in the early morning. By this, merchants advertise or promote their products timely to potential customers and users could get relevant information at proper times and places. Therefore, by context-perceiving and exchanging, an actionable understanding of a space would be constructed.

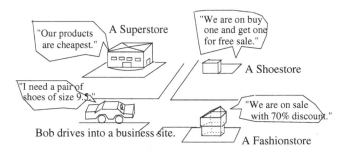

Fig. 1. A context-aware environment

However, a user's context may contain or imply his/her privacy. Privacy is the right of individuals to determine for themselves when, how, and to what extent information about them is communicated about [10], which can be divided into (1) bodily privacy, (2) territorial privacy, (3) communication privacy, and (4) information privacy. A user's context may contain or imply his/her information privacy, which a user may not like to unconditionally share with others [11]. For the example above, Bob's location, car driven, time arriving at the business site, goods bought, time spent at the site may all be private or privacy containing. To control the disclosure of our private information, we could specify privacy preferences [12]. In the privacy preferences, we may designate who has rights to have what information about us (e.g. only superstore X can have access to our location information when we enter a certain business site). In particular, we may also designate when to present abstracted or falsified answers to the queries regarding our contexts. The former is called *access control rules*, and the latter *obfuscation rules* [4].

We obfuscate our answers to queries about us because we may not want to completely block some enquirers from some information, or may not like to appear we are withholding some information. For example, Alice may have to tell her friend that she is currently on campus since her friend is going to pick her up soon. However, Alice may not necessarily tell her friend her current exact location (which room of which building) since exact location may imply some private activities. This is called *obfuscation by abstraction*. In some situations, Alice may not even want to tell her friend her location in a coarsest granularity. For instance, she is currently in the US instead of Canada where she is supposed to stay because she is studying there. She does not want anybody to know she is in the US for private issues. Nevertheless, to the query from her friend about her location, Alice may have difficulty to say nothing about it (*refusal*); Otherwise, her friend will know she is withholding some private things [13]. At such situations, Alice may have to give a false answer (e.g. telling her friend that she is eating in a restaurant far from her home). This is called *obfuscation by falsification*. In [14], context obfuscated by abstraction is also said to be made *imprecise* or *vague*, and context obfuscated by falsification is also said to be made *inaccurate*.

However, we cannot obfuscate our answers randomly. Our answers should be reasonable enough so that they are believable and will be treated seriously. For the examples above, Alice should not tell her friend that she is in downtown (suppose her university is in downtown) while asking her friend to pick her up from campus soon; Alice should not tell her friend that she is at home (actually in the US) in the case her friend is her roommate. This shows, on the one hand, we can reason about the possible obfuscations by others, and on the other hand, we should ensure that our obfuscations are inference-withstanding [15,16].

Since one's contexts in pervasive environments are generally ambiguous [17,18], especially from the points of view of others, we propose to reason about obfuscations probabilistically. We are bound to use probabilistic reasoning if we numerically represent uncertainty for a set of mutually exclusive and collectively exhaustive alternatives and want a coherent numerical model of human reasoning [19]. Bayesian networks (BNs) [20] have been widely accepted as an effective probabilistic inference formalism in uncertain domains [21], but BNs assume the problem domains are static. They do not have facilities to explicitly model temporal dependencies among domain events. That is, the effects of historical domain events on the current domain state may not be properly absorbed using BNs. Nevertheless, context information is highly history-dependent (e.g. Bob won't go to a barber's shop if he just got his hair cut). In this paper, we propose to use dynamic Bayesian networks (DBNs) [22] to detect obfuscation and to find true information (de-obfuscation) if possible, or to help generate convincing obfuscations. DBNs are extended from BNs for probabilistic inference in dynamic domains. Compared to BNs, DBNs can capture richer and more realistic domain dependencies [23], which have been applied in many areas such as domain state monitoring [24,25], activity or plan recognition [26], forecasting [27], speech recognition [28], medical diagnosis [29], and fault or defect detection [30]. To our best knowledge, this is the first work to apply dynamic Bayesian networks to context inference in context-aware systems.

The paper is organized as follows. We review related work in Section 2. In Section 3, we give an introduction to dynamic Bayesian networks. In Section 4, we present an example to show how dynamic Bayesian networks can be applied to obfuscation detection or obfuscation generation [1], and their effectiveness in the applications. Implementation details are discussed after the example. The two problems are then formally described and the corresponding algorithms are presented. Concluded remarks are made in Section 5.

---

[1] Which can also be called obfuscation recommendation or obfuscation suggestion.

2   Related Work

Inference has been applied in context-aware systems [5,9,6] to reason about new context information (e.g. a user's social relation), to check knowledge consistency, or to find matched rules to support decision-making. In these systems, however, inference is mostly done on rule-based knowledge-bases based on classical logic (e.g. first order predicate logic). Probability [6] and fuzzy logic [9] are used in some way in the inference. However, details are not reported. BNs have been used to represent and reason about uncertain contexts in pervasive environments [18]. Our paper introduces DBNs to context obfuscation detection and generation in uncertain domains.

To preserve certain secrets in information systems, two query answering approaches - refusal and lying - have been discussed [15,13,31]. Lying modifies the correct answer by returning its negation, and refusal just does not give any answer. It is assumed that, for an arbitrary sequence of queries, lyings or refusals are used only when they are necessary to protect secrets; otherwise the true answers have to be provided. Security policies for known potential secrets or known and unknown secrecies (secrets and their negations) are investigated respectively. A security policy for known or unknown secrecies aims at returning answers that are consistent with both alternatives of the specified secrecies (since both alternatives could reveal critical information), and a security policy based on known potential secrets aims at returning answers that are consistent with the falsity of all secrets [13]. The security policies can be specified using lyings or refusals uniformly [15,13] or their combination [31], depending on specific conditions and requirements. Nevertheless, the policies are proposed based on the assumption that the assumed initial belief of the enquirer is consistent by itself and does not imply any of secrecies, secrets or disjunction of secrets, and requiring that each answer the enquirer obtains, combined with his current belief, does not imply any of the secrecies, secrets or disjunction of secrets either. The assumption and requirement are sometimes too strong in the real world, especially in problem domains with uncertainties. In particular, the answer to a major problem - whether secrecies, secrets or disjunction of secrets are implied by a set of statements - are assumed to be known immediately, but it is a constraint satisfaction or propositional theorem proving problem which is generally intractable [32,33]. In this paper, we investigate this problem in uncertain domains. We show joint probability distribution (JPD) can be efficiently represented by exploring dependency structures among domain variables.

In multilevel statistical databases [34,35], inference control [16,36,37] has been used to protect information with a higher security level from being inferred. For exact inference control, many restriction based techniques have been studied which include restricting the size of query results [38,39], controlling the overlap of queries [40], generalizing or suppressing sensitive data values [41,42,43], and auditing queries to determine whether inference is possible [44,45]. For statistical inference control, some perturbation based techniques have been proposed such as adding noises to source data [46] or to the query results [47], swapping values among records [48], and sampling data to answer queries [49]. Our work can be considered to be about inference control when used for finding proper obfuscation for users' personal data. Compared to the statistical databases, users' personal data are usually much smaller in size and only correspond to a record in databases. Inference control techniques for databases are generally not applicable to personal data. Anyway, our work does not study how to add noises to obfuscate data but studies how to find the most believable obfuscation. Our work investigates how to audit queries to prevent the proposed obfuscations from being detected in dynamic uncertain domains.

Anonymity [50] and/or unlinkability [51] have been sought to protect users' identities, where information disclosed by users is processed in some way so that no private data (identity or location, etc.) can be derived conclusively. When used for obfuscation recommendation, our work seeks anonymity or unlinkability. Nevertheless, our work makes lie recommendations in uncertain domains.

Masquerader detection (user substitution detection) problem has been approached as an anomaly detection problem [52,53], which is close to our detection problem. However, dependencies among users' data are not explicitly modeled in the classifiers in [52,53]. We propose to use DBNs to explicitly model the uncertainties in personal data and their dependencies for lie detection.

3   Dynamic Bayesian Networks

Dynamic Bayesian networks (DBNs) are graphical models for probabilistic inference in dynamic domains, which are extended from Bayesian networks (BNs) for static domains. DBNs provide us with an easy and compact way to specify the conditional independencies in dynamic domains.

A DBN consists of a finite number of BNs, each of which (called a *slice* of the DBN) corresponds to a particular time instant (or interval). BNs corresponding to different instants are generally assumed to be the same in their structures and parameters. BNs corresponding to different instants are connected through arcs that represent how the state of the domain evolves over time. Like BNs, the structures of DBNs are directed acyclic graphs (DAGs), where each node represents a domain variable of interest at some time instant, and each directed arc represents the causal dependency between the two nodes it connects. The strength of dependencies is quantified by conditional probability distributions (CPDs) specifying the probabilities of children taking specific values given the values of their parents.

A DBN is generally assumed to be a first-order Markov process satisfying the *Markovian property*: the state of the domain at time $t + 1$ is independent of the states of the domain prior to time t, given the state of the domain at time t. That is, only successive BNs are connected with each other by evolving arcs. In particular, like in a BN, each node in a DBN is conditionally independent of its non-descendants given its parents. These properties allow us to solve complex problems by cheaper local computations.

As mentioned above, in a DBN, we generally assume the structures and parameters of slice i are identical to those of slice j, and in particular, the dependency and its strength between a pair of nodes across two successive instants won't change over time. This is called *time invariant* assumption for DBNs. Base on time invariant assumption, a DBN can be described by one and a half slices of the DBN (1.5TBN) and the entire DBN can be obtained by unrolling the 1.5TBN: one slice is used to represent the first slice of the DBN and a half slice is used to represent how the DBN evolves across consecutive slices. Below are the definitions of BNs and DBNs. We say a *graph* is a pair $G = (V, E)$, where V denotes a set of nodes (vertices), and E denotes a set of edges. In a directed graph $G = (V, E)$, we use $\pi(v)$ to denote the set of parents of $v(\in V)$ in G.

Definition 1. *A Bayesian network (BN) is a triplet $(V, G, \mathcal{P})$, where V is a set of variables, G is a connected DAG, and $\mathcal{P}$ is a set of probability distributions: $\mathcal{P} = \{P(v|\pi(v)) \mid v \in V\}$.*

It can be shown that the joint probability distribution (JPD) of all variables in V can be specified as:

$$P(V) = \prod_{v \in V} P(v|\pi(v)). \tag{1}$$

Definition 2. *A dynamic Bayesian network (DBN) is composed of a finite number of BNs $\{B_i=(V_i, G_i, \mathcal{P}_i) \mid 0 \le i < n, n > 1\}$ corresponding to n time instants (intervals). B_{i-1} and B_i $(0 < i < n)$ are connected by more than one edge directed from nodes in B_{i-1} to nodes in B_i. A DBN can be represented by a pair $(B_0, B_\rightarrow)$, where $B_0 = (V_0, G_0, \mathcal{P}_0)$ and $B_\rightarrow$ is a BN representing how DBN evolves across B_{i-1} and B_i $(0 < i < n)$. B_0 and $B_\rightarrow$ define*

$$P(V_i \mid V_{i-1}) = \prod_{v \in V_i} P(v|\pi(v)), 0 < i < n.$$

In Definition 2, for those $v \in V_i$ which has parents in V_{i-1}, $P(v|\pi(v))$ is defined by $B_\rightarrow$, and for those $v \in V_i$ which does not have parents in V_{i-1}, $P(v|\pi(v))$ is defined by B_0.

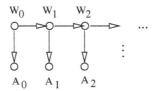

Fig. 2. A DBN about the weather and an old man's activities

Consider an example where an old man named John lives in a city far from the town his friend Peter lives. They talk with each other by phone every evening. John usually walks around if the weather of his city is *good*, and stays home otherwise. Peter does not know the weather condition of John's city, but can judge it from John's activities on that day. The example can be represented by a DBN as shown in Figure 2.

In the DBN, each node represents a random variable, and each arrowed arc represents the causal dependencies between the two nodes connected. The subscript of a variable indicates the corresponding time instant. Hence, in the DBN, each instant is represented by two random boolean variables, W_i and A_i $(i = 0, 1, 2, ...)$. The variable W_i represents the weather condition of John's city on day i, taking the value *good* when the weather is good and *bad* otherwise. The variable A_i represents John's activities on day i, taking the value *out* when John walks around, and *in* otherwise. Note that it is possible that John walks around while the weather is bad and vice versa. Nevertheless, John's activities are highly dependent on the weather conditions. The arrowed arc between two successive slices represents the evolution of the weather condition. The weather will very probably remain good next day if it is good today and bad if bad. The parameters are specified in Tables 1 and 2. Note the parameters specified in Table 2 will be repeated slice by slice. Hence, to describe a DBN, the first one and a half slices are actually enough (i.e. 1.5TBN).

Table 1. The prior belief about the weather condition

W_0	$P(W_0)$
good	0.75
bad	0.25

Table 2. The prior belief about the relationship between the weather condition and John's activities, and the evolution of the weather condition ($i \geq 0$)

W_i	A_i	$P(A_i\|W_i)$	W_i	W_{i+1}	$P(W_{i+1}\|W_i)$
good	in	0.10	good	good	0.75
good	out	0.90	good	bad	0.25
bad	in	0.80	bad	good	0.65
bad	out	0.20	bad	bad	0.35

Each slice of the DBN is a BN which includes two variables and an arc. Each separate BN can be used to reason about the weather condition based on John's activities at that day. However, historical dependencies on weather conditions are definitely lost if they are not connected into a DBN.

In Bayesian probability theory, probabilities are subjective corresponding to the degree of belief of reasoners in the truth of the statements. The degree of belief is different from the degree of truth. People with different prior knowledge could *correctly* obtain different results from Bayesian probability theory.

In the DBN as shown in Figure 2, variable A_i, representing the observation on day i, is often called *information, evidential* or *observable* variable. Variable W_i, representing the actual weather condition on day i, is called a *hypothesis* or *unobservable* variable. DBNs can, based on evidence collected from information variables, help efficiently evaluate the probabilistic state of hypothesis variables. In our case, with the help of the DBN model, Peter is able to determine the probabilities of the weather condition on some day given John's current and past activities. For instance, by talking over phone, Peter knows John's activities in the last 3 days are as follows: walked around on day 0, stayed at home on day 1, and walked around on day 2. By inference using the model, Peter knows it is 88.29% that the weather on day 0 was good, 65.35% on day 1 bad, and 78.52% on day 2 good. The model can also predict that the weather on day 3 will be good by 66.41%, and John will walk around on day 3 by 66.48%.

For the problem of context obfuscation detection and suggestion, information variables are associated with measurable contexts (e.g. one's own location), and the hypothesis variables are associated with unmeasurable (unobservable) contexts (e.g. somebody else's location).

4 Obfuscation Detection

People use context obfuscation to conceal and protect their privacy frequently. It could happen anywhere and anytime. In different environments, the specific obfuscation detection models could be different in variables used and dependencies among them. However, the principles of DBN obfuscation detection or suggestion would be the same: using DBNs to capture any anomalous events. In this section, we present a DBN model for obfuscation suggestion or detection in a pervasive environment.

4.1 The Problem and the Method

In a pervasive environment, a user may have many contexts such as his location, the food he likes, the local weather, the restaurants he often visits, how often he visits a barber's shop, etc. Some of these contexts could be disclosed to the others unconditionally (e.g. the makes of cars or painters he likes), some of them could be disclosed to the others conditionally (e.g. some of the diseases he has or had and how often he visits hospitals), and some of them may not be disclosed (e.g. the professors he hates, some of the diseases he has or had). The disclosed information could have been obfuscated.

We may be able or need to reason about obfuscation based on our prior knowledge and new evidence we observe about a user. Our prior knowledge about one could come from common senses (e.g. he is generally healthy), or from credible (verified) information he discloses to us (e.g. he attends a class 3:30pm-4:30pm on every Wednesday). New evidence can be observed (e.g. today's weather, somebody is attending a conference, etc.), which is believed to be true in general. An example could be like this: We know George attends some class 3:30pm-4:30pm every Wednesday in this term (prior knowledge). Today is Wednesday (new evidence). We wait for him outside the class room minutes before the class is over. However, we do not find him after the class is over (new evidence). We call and ask him where he is. He tells us he is on campus for attending the class. This is very probably a lie (it could be true if he had left before we arrived at the class room). We should be very confident that he obfuscates his location information for some reasons. With more evidence, say somebody saw his car parking outside a hospital, we could conclude that he went to see his doctor at that time.

If our prior knowledge on all contexts about a person and the relationships among them is accurate and certain, we would be able to reason about the state of the domain deterministically. For the instance above, George will attend the class 3:30pm-4:30pm today for sure if we assume our knowledge about this issue is accurate and certain. However, this is not always true in the real world. There generally always exist some exceptions to a rule or a statement. In this example, he may not attend the class today if he is too sick or today is a holiday. For another example, one could still be considered healthy if he is becoming thin due to his being on diet or his exercising. In particular, there may exist some contexts we have very little knowledge about (e.g. how much cash he has in his accounts, how much investment he has done, etc.). We need to figure out the credibility of any conclusions derived based on such uncertain knowledge.

On the other hand, contexts are generally time series data, which are developed over time. For example, one's social relationships will change each time his marriage status changes. For another example, one won't buy cars or houses too often. New contexts are developed from the old. Hence, knowing old contexts could help us reason about the new contexts and vice versa.

Dynamic Bayesian networks (DBNs), based on Bayesian probability theory, provide a coherent framework for knowledge representation and reasoning in dynamic uncertain domains. In next subsection, we, by an example, show how DBNs can be used to reason about context lies.

4.2 An Example

Suppose a person named John could appear in several different places in the evening after his getting off work: his home, a Gym, shopping malls, or restaurants. He almost can always be reached by his home phone if he is at home, and mostly plays badminton if he goes to the Gym. He usually visits the Gym or restaurants every other day (i.e. he will highly probably visit the Gym or restaurants this evening if he did not last evening). Most restaurants he visits are in downtown. He will very probably go shopping if the weather is good. Shopping malls are generally located out of downtown. The weather will more probably remain good next day if it is good today, and bad if bad.

The example can be modeled by a DBN whose first two slices are as shown in Figure 3, where each dotted box denotes one slice. As discussed in Section 3, we can unroll

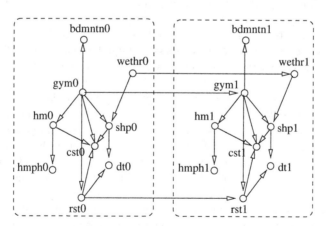

Fig. 3. A DBN for a location-sensitive environment

Table 3. Probability distributions of variables without any parents: $P(gym0)$, and $P(wethr0)$

gym0	$P(gym0)$	wethr0	$P(wethr0)$
true	0.5	good	0.75
false	0.5	bad	0.25

the two slices to get all slices of the DBN. In each slice, "bdmntn" represents "playing badminton" (true or false), "gym" "in Gym" (true or false), "hm" "at home" (true or false), "hmph" "reached by home phone" (true or false), "rst" "in a restaurant" (true or false), "dt" "in downtown" (true or false), "shp" "shopping" (true or false), "wethr" "weather condition" (good or bad), and "cst" "constraint parameter" (true or false). The digit ('0' or '1') following each label indicates the corresponding time instant. All variables are boolean. "cst" is a boolean constraint variable: it is *true* if and only if only one of the four variables connected to it (*gym, hm, shp*, and *rst*) is true. Before performing inference using the DBN, we set *cst* to be *true* so that John will not appear in more than one place at the same time. Hence, *cst* is a constant in inference over all slices of the DBN. Note "wethr", "gym", and "rst" are history dependent and evolve over time. The corresponding conditional probability distributions are specified in Tables 3, 4, 5, and 6 respectively. In Table 6, the dot '.' is the abbreviation of the corresponding conditions for saving space. For example, $P(rst_i|.)$ represents $P(rst_i|gym_i, rst_{i-1})$. These parameters reflect our knowledge about John stated in the beginning of this subsection.

Assume one evening John and his boss Bob go to a restaurant located in quiet uptown to have a dinner and discuss some issues within their company. Both John and Bob do not want their meeting to be known by their colleagues. However, while in the meeting,

Table 4. Conditional probability distributions of hm_i, $hmph_i$, and $bdmntn_i$ ($i \geq 0$)

gym_i	hm_i	$P(gym_i|hm_i)$	hm_i	$hmph_i$	$P(hmph_i|hm_i)$	gym_i	$bdmntn_i$	$P(bdmntn_i|gym_i)$
true	true	0.0	true	true	0.95	true	true	0.9
true	false	1.0	true	false	0.05	true	false	0.1
false	true	0.3	false	true	0.0	false	true	0.0
false	false	0.7	false	false	1.0	false	false	1.0

Table 5. Conditional probability distributions of rst_0, gym_i, and $wethr_i$ ($i \geq 1$)

gym_0	rst_0	$P(rst_0|gym_0)$	gym_{i-1}	gym_i	$P(gym_i|gym_{i-1})$	$wethr_{i-1}$	$wethr_i$	$P(wethr_i|wethr_{i-1})$
true	true	0.0	true	true	0.05	good	good	0.75
true	false	1.0	true	false	0.95	good	bad	0.25
false	true	0.3	false	true	0.9	bad	good	0.35
false	false	0.7	false	false	0.1	bad	bad	0.65

Table 6. Conditional probability distributions of rst_i ($i \geq 1$), shp_i, and dt_i ($i \geq 0$)

gym_i	rst_{i-1}	rst_i	$P(rst_i|.)$	gym_i	$wethr_i$	shp_i	$P(shp_i|.)$	shp_i	rst_i	dt_i	$P(dt_i|.)$
true	true	true	0.0	true	good	true	0.65	true	true	true	0.99
true	true	false	1.0	true	good	false	0.35	true	true	false	0.01
true	false	true	0.0	true	bad	true	0.3	true	false	true	0.25
true	false	false	1.0	true	bad	false	0.7	true	false	false	0.75
false	true	true	0.2	false	good	true	0.9	false	true	true	0.9
false	true	false	0.8	false	good	false	0.1	false	true	false	0.1
false	false	true	0.4	false	bad	true	0.1	false	false	true	0.1
false	false	false	0.6	false	bad	false	0.9	false	false	false	0.9

John gets a phone call from one of his colleagues named Alice. Alice is looking for John and wonders where he is. John cannot tell her where he is (and hence what he is doing) and has to provide an obfuscated answer.

Nevertheless, John cannot randomly pick an answer to respond Alice's query. John recalls that he has played badminton for two consecutive evenings, and he met Alice in both evenings. With the fact considered, the model shows that this evening John is 5.59% in the Gym, 25% at home, 30.58% shopping, 38.84% at a restaurant, and 45.66% in downtown.[2] Hence, being in the Gym is not a good answer. The model shows that this evening John is at home by 25%, which is close to the probability of John being shopping (30.58%) or at a restaurant (38.84%). Is being at home a good obfuscation? No, because Alice could have called his home. With the assumption entered, the model indicates that John is 7.33% in the Gym, 1.64% at home, 40.10% shopping, 50.93% at a restaurant, and 56.76% in downtown. Obviously being at home is also not a good answer. Then, which of the last two options (being shopping or being at a restaurant) is a better answer? The probability (40.10%) of John being shopping looks close to the probability (50.93%) of his being at a restaurant. Nevertheless, John knows being shopping is not a good answer because the weather of this evening is pretty bad. With the evidence entered, the model shows that he is 8.11% in the Gym, 2.47% at home, 12.81% shopping, 76.61% at a restaurant, and 73.21% in downtown.

So, eating in a restaurant is the only reasonable and specific answer. Does John have to tell Alice his real location and related activities? Not necessarily. The model shows that he is in downtown with a pretty high probability (73.21%), where at this time he could be shopping (though with a small probability), having a casual dinner (with a large probability), or performing some other activities (with a small probability). With the aid of the model, John believes being in downtown is a reasonable answer. John is glad to tell Alice that he is in downtown, and Alice is satisfied with the answer. The answer suggested by the model is an obfuscation by falsification (John is actually in uptown now). However, from Alice's perspective, the answer is pretty reasonable. Without the model, John could present a not properly obfuscated answer (e.g. telling Alice he is at home or in the Gym). With the model, these poorly obfuscated answers could be detected by Alice.

With the aid of the model, both John and Alice can also predict that the weather will be bad by 64.93% next day. Alice can predict that John will go to the Gym by 88.57% next day. In particular, if somebody just came back from abroad, he can from the model know that the weather on the yesterday was bad by 58.33%. Therefore, not only can the model help automate the obfuscation suggestion and detection, but also can help predict one's future contexts or find out past domain states, where the past and current events, and any uncertain factors in the domain are considered and modeled properly.

4.3   Discussion

In the example above, we assume a user processes answers or queries from the others. In pervasive environments, however, it is intelligent agents which collect information, perform inference, make decision and act on behalf of the respective users. To make proper decisions, an agent needs to have a good understanding about the world. To get

---

[2] Note downtown is not mutually exclusive with shopping malls or restaurants.

a good understanding about the world, an agent not only needs to capture and reason about the contexts of the represented user, but also needs to collect and reason about the contexts of the other interested users. Querying is one way for an agent to obtain more information about other users, but the interaction among agents may not be done frankly due to privacy concerns of the respective users. Agents generally need to interact with each other based on the respective users' privacy preferences. To protect its user's privacy, an agent may need to obfuscate its answer to a query about the user. In this paper, we present a DBN-based method to help an agent detect obfuscations or generate reasonable obfuscations.

At an agent, the obfuscation detection model against another agent is generally different from the obfuscation suggestion model against the same agent. This is because the two models are built and maintained based on different knowledge of different agents on different users. Let agent A_k represent user U_k ($0 \leq k < n, n > 1$). The obfuscation suggestion model at agent A_a against agent A_b is constructed and maintained based on the assumed knowledge of agent A_b on user U_a, whereas the obfuscation detection model at agent A_a against agent A_b is built and maintained based on agent A_a's knowledge about user U_b. Also, the obfuscation suggestion models against an agent A_c should be different at different agents $\{A_i \mid i \neq c, 0 \leq i < n\}$ since such models represent the assumed knowledge of the agent A_c on different users $\{U_i \mid i \neq c, 0 \leq i < n\}$. Since different agents may have different perspectives and knowledge about a same user U_c, the corresponding DBN obfuscation detection models against the agent A_c at different agents could be different. Some agents may have the same knowledge about a same user in the beginning, but their belief about the user could change over time due to the different evidence they may observe about the user [3]. Hence, the DBN obfuscation detection models against a same agent at different agents could eventually become different. On the other hand, at an agent A_a, the obfuscation detection models against other agents should be different since these models are made based on A_a's knowledge about different users. The obfuscation suggestion models against other agents at agent A_a could be different since other agents may have different knowledge about U_a. However, if agent A_a does not have too many levels of information to disclose, the obfuscation suggestion models at agent A_a against the agents which are believed to have the same information about U_a should be the same. For the similar reason, some of the obfuscation detection models at different agents against the same agent could be the same.

An agent could combine some of its obfuscation detection or obfuscation suggestion models based on dependencies among the corresponding users. Model combination would reduce the number of models to maintain. Especially, a combined model would be able to sense the world with more channels, which helps obfuscation detection or suggestion. For an example on obfuscation detection, I call Bob in a weekend and ask where he is. He tells me he is in a meeting with his boss. I may have difficulty to judge if this is a lie or not if I do not know his boss. Even I know his boss, it won't help if I do not examine his words against the activities of his boss. Nevertheless, I could verify his words in some degree if I could inspect these words based on his boss's activities. I would be able to find that Bob lies if I know his boss is in a trip. For

---

[3] Different agents may get different levels of information from the same agent.

another example on obfuscation suggestion, I may tell my wife that I am in a meeting with my boss. However, if my wife knows my boss, I should be careful in presenting a lie involving my boss to her, since she could have chances to verify it. In particular, the obfuscated answers presented to my wife may have to be consistent with those to my boss. A combined model could produce better results than individual models in obfuscation detection or generation, but this is achieved at the cost of the increase in the computational complexity. The more the users modeled together are, the higher the computational complexity of the model would generally be. We should try to take advantage of as much conditional independencies among users' contexts as possible in modeling. Conditional independencies allow cheaper local computations. In particular, we should focus on modeling stronger dependencies since weak dependencies may not affect inference results much but increase computational complexity without mercy.

A DBN obfuscation detection or suggestion model against a user can be constructed manually by experts in the corresponding problem domains or learned automatically from the live data captured about the user. There is a lot of work about DBN learning in literatures [54,55,56,57,58]. By DBN learning and inference, a DBN model can be obtained and improved over time. DBN learning explores as much independencies as possible among series data to make inference efficient. Note that Markovian assumption in this paper regarding DBN representation of historical dependencies can be relaxed so that higher order historical dependencies can be represented [54]. For obfuscation detection, the more an agent knows about a user, the preciser the corresponding model is, the more probably the lies from the user will be detected by the agent. However, for obfuscation recommendation, an agent A_a needs a DBN model which represents and reasons about the uncertain knowledge of the adversarial agent A_b about the user U_a. The more A_a assumes A_b knows about U_a, the more conservative the obfuscation recommendation made by A_a would be. However, the assumed upper bound knowledge A_b has about U_a is what A_a has about U_a, and the assumed lower bound knowledge A_b has about U_a can be limited to some publicly known information about U_a. Hence, a DBN model for obfuscation generation can be adjusted based on the assumed lower and upper bound knowledge. An obfuscation recommendation can be made from most conservatively to most imprudently depending on the degree of the concern on the protected context.

A probability threshold should be set for a DBN for obfuscation recommendation or detection. If a statement could be true by a probability above the threshold, the statement could be confidently considered true (e.g. a statement is considered a lie if the model indicates that its negation could occur by 90%, which is above the threshold, say, 80%).

4.4   Formal Description

Problem statement 3 is a formal description of the obfuscation detection problem we address in the paper.

Problem Statement 3. *In a pervasive environment E, each context-aware agent A_i $(0 < i \leq n, n \geq 2)$ corresponds to a user U_i in E. A_i has access to all available information[4] about U_i, but only has some prior knowledge K_{ij} about U_j ($j \neq i$, $0 <$*

---

[4] Which could be uncertain.

$j \leq n$). A_i could obtain more information O_{ij} about U_j ($j \neq i, 0 < j \leq n$) by its observation. O_{ij} is certain and is believed to be true by A_i. Then the obfuscation detection problem is if and how agent A_i, based on $K_{ij} \cup O_{ij}$, can judge whether an answer from A_j to its query is very probably, relative to a probability threshold, an obfuscated answer.

For the problem described in Problem statement 3, when agents' prior knowledge about the domain is ambiguous or uncertain, a DBN-based solution is proposed as Algorithm 1, where agent A_i's prior knowledge K_{ij} about U_j is represented by a DBN.

Algorithm 1 (DBNobfuscationDec). *An agent A_i receives an answer W from A_j to its query about the context C of U_j. By the following operations A_i figures out if W should be considered a lie about C using a DBN model M against user U_j based on observed evidence O_{ij}. Let T be the probability threshold for making confident judgment.*

1 enter evidence O_{ij} to M;
2 M indicates that W could occur by a probability p;
3 if $p \geq T$, W will not be considered as a lie and return;
4 otherwise, W will be considered as a lie;

Problem statement 4 is a formal description of the obfuscation recommendation problem we address in the paper.

Problem Statement 4. *In a pervasive environment E, each context-aware agent A_i ($0 < i \leq n, n \geq 2$) corresponds to a user U_i in E. A_i has access to all available information about U_i, but only has some prior knowledge K_{ij} about U_j ($j \neq i, 0 < j \leq n$). A_i could obtain more information O_{ij} ($j \neq i, 0 < j \leq n$) about U_j by its observation. O_{ij} is certain and is believed to be true by A_i. Then the obfuscation suggestion problem is if and how agent A_i, based on its guess G_{ij} about agent A_j's prior knowledge K_{ji} and guess H_{ij} about agent A_j's new evidence O_{ji}, can evaluate if a lie to a query from A_j will be considered reasonable by A_j.*

Algorithm 2 (DBNobfuscationRec). *Before agent A_i sends A_j a lie Y to the query about the context C of U_i, by the following operations, A_i evaluates if Y will be considered reasonable by A_j using a DBN model M constructed from G_{ij} based on guessed evidence H_{ij}. Let T be the probability threshold for making confident judgment.*

1 enter evidence H_{ij} to M;
2 M indicates that Y could occur by a probability p;
3 if $p \geq T$, Y will not be considered a lie and send it over;
4 otherwise, Y will be considered a lie and another lie needs to be tested;

For the obfuscation recommendation problem described in Problem statement 4, when agents' prior knowledge about the domain is ambiguous or uncertain, a DBN-based solution is proposed as Algorithm 2, where agent A_i's guess G_{ij} about prior knowledge K_{ji} of A_j is represented as a DBN.

5   Conclusion

In pervasive (ubiquitous) environments, agents should be made privacy conscious so that no private information will be disclosed improperly. Nevertheless, there exist some situations when users may like to disclose their private information partially or falsely through information obfuscation. The obfuscation should be made reasonable enough so that the enquirers won't be able to detect it. On the other hand, the enquirers should be able to detect any poorly obfuscated answers to their enquiries.

The paper presents an approach to automate the private context obfuscation suggestion and detection. Since one's contexts are usually uncertain, in particular from the points of view of the reasoners, and are highly history dependent, we propose to use dynamic Bayesian networks to model and reason about users' contexts. By an example, we show how DBNs can be applied to the problems and their effectiveness in the applications. Implementation details are discussed after the example. The obfuscation detection problem and the obfuscation suggestion problem are then formally described. Algorithms are proposed to solve these problems. To our best knowledge, this is the first paper proposing using dynamic Bayesian networks to deal with temporal dependencies and uncertainties in context inference. The method can also be used to predict future contexts, and to find out past domain states.

References

1. Abowd, G.D., Dey, A., Orr, R., Bortherton, J.: Context-awareness in wearable and ubiquitous computing. Virtual Reality **3**(3) (1998) 200–211
2. Davies, N., Gellersen, H.W.: Beyond prototypes: Challenges in deploying ubiquitous systems. IEEE Pervasive Computing **1**(1) (2002) 26–35
3. Khedr, M., Karmouch, A.: Exploiting agents and SIP for smart context level agreements. In: Proceedings of IEEE Pacific Rim Conference on Communications, Computers, and Signal Processing, Victoria, BC, Canada (2003) 1000–1003
4. Gandon, F.L., Sadeh, N.M.: Semantic web technologies to reconcile privacy and context awareness. Journal of Web Semantics **1**(3) (2005)
5. Khedr, M., Karmouch, A.: Negotiating context information in context-aware systems. IEEE Intelligent Systems **19**(6) (2004) 21–29
6. Chen, H., Finin, T., Joshi, A.: An ontology for context-aware pervasive computing environments. Knowledge Engineering Review, Special Issue on Ontologies for Distributed Systems **18**(3) (2004) 197–207
7. Dey, A.: Understanding and using context. Personal and Ubiquitous Computing **5**(1) (2001) 4–7
8. Chou, S.C., Hsieh, W.T., Gandon, F.L., Sadeh, N.M.: Semantic web technologies for context-aware museum tour guide applications. In: Proceedings of the 19th International Conference on Advanced Information Networking and Applications (AINA'05), Vol. 2. (2005) 709–714
9. Khedr, M., Karmouch, A.: ACAI: Agent-based context-aware infrastructure for spontaneous applications. Journal of Network and Computer Applications **28**(1) (2005) 19–44
10. Westin, A.F.: Privacy and Freedom. Atheneum, New York (1967)
11. Hull, R., Kumar, B., Lieuwen, D., Patel-Schneider, P.F.: Enabling context-aware and privacy-conscious user data sharing. In: Proceedings of the 2004 IEEE International Conference on Mobile Data Management (MDM'04). (2004) 103–109

12. Cranor, L., Langheinrich, M., Marchiori, M., Presler-Marshall, M., Reagle, J.: The platform for privacy preferences 1.0 (P3P 1.0) specification. Technical report, W3C Recommendation, http://www.w3.org/TR/P3P (2002)

13. Biskup, J., Bonatti, P.A.: Lying versus refusal for known potential secrets. Data & Knowledge Engineering **38** (2001) 199–222

14. Duckham, M., Kulik, L.: A formal model of obfuscation and negotiation for location privacy. In Gellersen, H.W., Want, R., Schmidt, A., eds.: Proceedings of the 3rd International Conference on Pervasive Computing (PERVASIVE 2005). Volume 3468 of LNCS., Munich, Germany, Springer-Verlag Berlin Heidelberg (2005) 152–170

15. Biskup, J.: For unknown secrecies refusal is better than lying. Data & Knowledge Engineering **33** (2000) 1–24

16. Denning, D.E., Schlörer, J.: Inference control for statistical databases. IEEE Computer **16**(7) (1983) 69–82

17. Dey, A., Mankoff, J., Abowd, G., Carter, S.: Distributed mediation of ambiguous context in aware environments. In Beaudouin-Lafon, M., ed.: Proceedings of the 15th Annual ACM Symposium on User Interface Software and Technology (UIST'02), Paris, France, ACM Press (2002) 121–130

18. Gu, T., Peng, H.K., Zhang, D.Q.: A Bayesian approach for dealing with uncertain contexts. In: Proceedings of the Second International Conference on Pervasive Computing (Pervasive'04), Vienna, Austria, Austrian Computer Society (2004)

19. Neapolitan, R.E.: Probabilistic Reasoning in Expert Systems: Theory and Algorithms. John Wiley & Sons, Inc., New York, NY, USA (1990)

20. Pearl, J.: Probabilistic Reasoning in Intelligent Systems: Networks of Plausible Inference. Morgan Kaufmann Publishers, San Franciso, CA, USA (1988)

21. Haddawy, P.: An overview of some recent developments in Bayesian problem solving techniques. AI Magazine **20**(2) (1999) 11–19

22. Dean, T., Kanazawa, K.: Probabilistic temporal reasoning. In: Proceedings of the 7th National Conference on Artificial Intelligence (AAAI-1988), St. Paul, Minnesota, AAAI Press (1988) 524–528

23. Dagum, P., Galper, A., Horvitz, E., Seiver, A.: Uncertain reasoning and forescasting. International Journal of Forecasting **11**(1) (1995) 73–87

24. Nicholson, A.E., Brady, J.M.: Dynamic belief networks for discrete monitoring. IEEE Transactions on Systems, Man, and Cybernetics, special issue on Knowledge-Based Construction of Probabilistic and Decision Models **24**(11) (1994) 1593–1610

25. Li, X., Ji, Q.: Active affective state detection and user assistance with dynamic Bayesian networks. IEEE Transactions on Systems, Man, and Cybernetics-Part A: Systems and Humans **35**(1) (2005) 93–105

26. Ardissono, L., Brna, P., Mitrovic, A., eds.: A comparison of HMMs and dynamic Bayesian networks for recognizing office activities. In Ardissono, L., Brna, P., Mitrovic, A., eds.: Proceedings of the 10th International Conference on User Modeling (UM-2005). Volume 3538 of Lecture Notes in Computer Science (LNCS)., Edinburgh, Scotland, UK, Springer (2005)

27. Dagum, P., Galper, A., Horvitz, E.: Dynamic network models for forecasting. In Dubois, D., Wellman, M.P., D'Ambrosio, B., Smets, P., eds.: Proceedings of the 8th Conference on Uncertainty in Artificial Intelligence (UAI-1992), Stanford, CA, USA, Morgan Kaufmann Publishers (1992) 41–48

28. Nefian, A.V., Liang, L., Pi, X., Murphy, K.: Dynamic Bayesian networks for audio-visual speech recognition. EURASIP Journal on Applied Signal Processing **11** (2002) 1–15

29. Hanks, S., Madigan, D., Gavrin, J.: Probabilistic temporal reasoning with endogenous change. In Besnard, P., Hanks, S., eds.: Proceedings of the 11th Conference on Uncertainty in Artificial Intelligence (UAI-1995), Montréal, Québec, Canada, Morgan Kaufmann Publishers (1995)
30. Salem, A.B., Bouillaut, L., Aknin, P., Weber, P.: Dynamic Bayesian networks for classification of rail defects. In: Proceedings of the Fourth International Conference on Intelligent Systems Design and Applications (ISDA'04), Budapest, Hungary (2004)
31. Biskup, J., Bonatti, P.: Controlled query evaluation for known policies by combing lying and refusal. Annals of Mathematics and Artificial Intelligence **40**(1-2) (2004) 37–62
32. Dorndorf, U., Pesch, E., Phan-Huy, T.: Constraint propagation techniques for disjunctive scheduling problems. Artificial Intelligence **122** (2000) 189–240
33. Cook, S.A.: The complexity of theorem-proving procedure. In Harrison, M.A., Banerji, R.B., Ullman, J.D., eds.: Proceedings of the 3rd Annual ACM Symposium on Theorey of Computing (STOC'71), Shaker Heights, OH, ACM Press (1971) 151–158
34. Jajodia, S., Sandhu, R.: Polyinstantiation integrity in multilevel relations. In: Proceedings of the 1990 IEEE Computer Symposium on Research in Security and Privacy, Oakland, CA, IEEE Computer Society (1990) 104–115
35. Cuppens, F., Gabillon, A.: Logical foundations of multilevel databases. Data & Knowledge Engineering **29**(3) (1999) 199–222
36. Yip, R.W., Levitt, K.N.: Data level inference detection in database systems. In: Proceedings of the 11th IEEE Computer Security Foundations, Rockport, MA (1998) 179–189
37. Staddon, J.: Dynamic inference control. In Zaki, M.J., Aggarwal, C.C., eds.: Proceedings of the 8th ACM SIGMOD Workshop on Research Issues in Data Mining and Knowledge Discovery (DMKD'03), San Diego, CA, ACM Press (2003) 94–100
38. Fellegi, I.: On the question fo statistical confidentiality. Journal of American Statistical Association **67**(337) (1972) 7–18
39. Denning, D.E., Denning, P.J., Schwartz, M.D.: The tracker: a threat to statistical database security. ACM Transactions on Database Systems **4**(1) (1979) 76–96
40. Dobkin, D., Jones, A., Lipton, R.: Secure databases: Protection against user influence. ACM Transactions on Database Systems **4**(1) (1979) 97–106
41. Cox, L.H.: Suppression methodology and statistical disclosure control. Journal of the American Statistical Association **75**(370) (1980) 377–385
42. Bayardo, R.J., Agrawal, R.: Data privacy through optimal k-anonymization. In: Proceedings of the 21st International Conference on Data Engineering (ICDE'05), Tokyo, Japan, IEEE Computer Society (2005) 217–228
43. Narayanan, A., Shmatikov, V.: Obfuscated databases and group privacy. In Atluri, V., Meadows, C., Juels, A., eds.: Proceedings of the 12th ACM Conference on Computer and Communications Security (CCS'05), Alexandria, VA, USA, ACM Press (2005) 102–111
44. Chin, F.Y., Özsoyoglu, G.: Auditing and inference control in statistical databases. IEEE Transactions on Software Engineering **8**(6) (1982) 574–582
45. Kleinberg, J., Papadimitriou, C., Raghavan, P.: Auditing boolean attributes. In: Proceedings of the 19th ACM SIGMOD-SIGART Symposium on Principles of Database Systems (PODS'00), Dallas, TX, ACM Press (2000) 86–91
46. Traub, J.F., Yemini, Y., Woznaikowski, H.: The statistical security of a statistical database. ACM Transactions on Database Systems **9**(4) (1984) 672–679
47. Beck, L.L.: A security mechanism for statistical databases. ACM Transactions on Database Systems **5**(3) (1980) 316–338
48. Reiss, S.P.: Practical data-swapping: The first steps. ACM Transactions on Database Systems **9**(1) (1984) 20–37
49. Denning, D.: Secure statistical databases with random sample queries. ACM Transactions on Database Systems **5**(3) (1980) 291–315

50. Díaz, C., Seys, S., Claessens, J., Preneel, B.: Towards measuring anonymity. In Federath, H., ed.: Proceedings of the 2nd Workshop on Privacy Enhancing Technologies (PET'02). Volume 2482 of LNCS., San Francisco, CA, Springer-Verlag (2002) 54–68

51. Steinbrecher, S., Köpsell, S.: Modelling unlinkability. In Dingledine, R., ed.: Proceedings of the 3rd Workshop on Privacy Enhancing Technologies (PET'03). Volume 2760 of LNCS., Dresden, Germany, Springer-Verlag (2003) 32–47

52. Mazhelis, O., Puuronen, S., Veijalainen, J.: Modelling dependencies between classifiers in mobile masquerader detection. In López, J., Qing, S., Olamoto, E., eds.: Proceedings of the 6th International Conference on Information and Communications Security (ICICS'04). Volume 3269 of LNCS., Malaga, Spain, Springer-Verlag (2004) 318–330

53. Mazhelis, O., Puuronen, S.: Combining one-class classifiers for mobile-user substitution detection. In: Proceedings of the 6th International Conference on Enterprise Information Systems (ICEIS'04), Porto, Portugal (2004) 32–47

54. Ghahramani, Z.: Learning dynamic Bayesian networks. In: Adaptive Processing of Sequences and Data Structures. Volume 1387 of Lecture Notes in Artificial Intelligence., Springer-Verlag (1998) 168–197

55. Friedman, N., Murphy, K., Russell, S.: Learning the structure of dynamic probabilistic networks. In Cooper, G.F., Moral, S., eds.: Proceedings of the 14th Conference on Uncertainty in Artificial Intelligence (UAI-1998), Madison, WI, USA, Morgan Kaufmann Publishers (1998)

56. Boyen, X.: Inference and Learning in Complex Stochastic Processes. PhD thesis, Computer Science Department, Stanford University, Stanford, CA, USA (2002)

57. Peña, J.M., Björkegren, J., Tegnér, J.: Learning dynamic Bayesian network models via cross-validation. Pattern Recognition Letters **26**(14) (2005) 2295–2308

58. Dojer, N., Gambin, A., Mizera, A., Wilczynski, B., Tiuryn, J.: Applying dynamic Bayesian networks to perturbed gene expression data. BMC Bioinformatics **7** (2006)

Secure Anonymization for Incremental Datasets

Ji-Won Byun[1], Yonglak Sohn[2], Elisa Bertino[1], and Ninghui Li[1]

[1] CERIAS and Computer Science, Purdue University, USA
{byunj, bertino, ninghui}@cs.purdue.edu
[2] Computer Engineering, Seokyeong University, Korea
syl@skuniv.ac.kr

Abstract. Data anonymization techniques based on the k-anonymity model have been the focus of intense research in the last few years. Although the k-anonymity model and the related techniques provide valuable solutions to data privacy, current solutions are limited only to static data release (i.e., the entire dataset is assumed to be available at the time of release). While this may be acceptable in some applications, today we see databases continuously growing everyday and even every hour. In such dynamic environments, the current techniques may suffer from poor data quality and/or vulnerability to inference. In this paper, we analyze various inference channels that may exist in multiple anonymized datasets and discuss how to avoid such inferences. We then present an approach to securely anonymizing a continuously growing dataset in an efficient manner while assuring high data quality.

1 Introduction

A model on which recent privacy-protecting techniques often rely is the *k-anonymity* model [22]. In the k-anonymity model, privacy is guaranteed by ensuring that any record in a released dataset be indistinguishable (with respect to a set of attributes, called *quasi-identifier*) from at least $(k - 1)$ other records in the dataset. Thus, in the k-anonymity model the risk of re-identification is maintained under an acceptable probability (i.e., $1/k$). Another interesting protection model addressing data privacy is the ℓ-diversity model [16]. The ℓ-diversity model assumes that a private dataset contains some sensitive attribute(s) which cannot be modified. Such a sensitive attribute is then considered disclosed when the association between a sensitive attribute value and a particular individual can be inferred with a significant probability. In order to prevent such inferences, the ℓ-diversity model requires that every group of indistinguishable records contains at least ℓ distinct sensitive attribute values; thereby the risk of attribute disclosure is kept under $1/\ell$.

Although the k-anonymity and ℓ-diversity models have led to a number of valuable privacy-protecting techniques [3,10,11,13,14,21], the existing solutions are limited only to static data release. That is, in such solutions it is assumed that the entire dataset is available at the time of release. This assumption implies a significant shortcoming, as data today are continuously collected (thus continuously growing) and there is a strong demand for up-to-date data at all times. For instance, suppose that a hospital wants to publish its patient records for medical researchers. Surely, all the published records must be properly anonymized in order to protect patients' privacy. At first glance, the

W. Jonker and M. Petkovic (Eds.): SDM 2006, LNCS 4165, pp. 48–63, 2006.

AGE	Gender	Diagnosis
21	Male	Asthma
23	Male	Flu
52	Male	Alzheimer
57	Female	Diabetes

Fig. 1. Initial patient records

AGE	Gender	Diagnosis
[21 − 25]	Male	Asthma
[21 − 25]	Male	Flu
[50 − 60]	Person	Alzheimer
[50 − 60]	Person	Diabetes

Fig. 2. 2-diverse patient records

AGE	Gender	Diagnosis
21	Male	Asthma
23	Male	Flu
52	Male	Alzheimer
57	Female	Diabetes
27	Female	Cancer
53	Male	Heart Disease
59	Female	Flu

Fig. 3. New patient records

AGE	Gender	Diagnosis
[21 − 30]	Person	Asthma
[21 − 30]	Person	Flu
[21 − 30]	Person	Cancer
[51 − 55]	Male	Alzheimer
[51 − 55]	Male	Heart Disease
[56 − 60]	Female	Flu
[56 − 60]	Female	Diabetes

Fig. 4. New 2-diverse patient records

task seems reasonably straightforward, as any of the existing anonymization techniques can anonymize the records before they are published. The challenge is, however, that as new records are frequently created (e.g., whenever new patients are admitted), the hospital needs a way to provide up-to-date information to researchers in timely manner.

One possible approach is to anonymize and publish new records periodically. Then researchers can either study each released dataset independently or merge multiple datasets together for more comprehensive analysis. Although straightforward, this approach may suffer from severely low data quality. The key problem is that small sets of records are anonymized independently; thus, records may have to be modified much more than when they are anonymized all together. Thus, in terms of data quality, this approach is highly undesirable.

A better approach is to anonymize and publish the entire dataset whenever the dataset is augmented with new records. In this way, researchers are always provided with up-to-date information. Although this can be easily accomplished using existing techniques (i.e., by anonymizing the entire dataset every time), there are two significant drawbacks. First, it requires redundant computation, as the entire dataset has to be anonymized even if only a few records are newly inserted. Another, much more critical, drawback is that even though published datasets are securely anonymous independently (i.e., each dataset is k-anonymous or ℓ-diverse), they could be vulnerable to inferences when observed collectively. In the following section, we illustrate such inferences.

1.1 Examples of Inferences

A hospital initially has a dataset in Fig. 1 and publishes its 2-diverse version shown in Fig. 2. As previously discussed, in an ℓ-diverse dataset the probability of attribute disclosure is kept under $1/\ell$. For example, even if an attacker knows that the record of Tom, who is a 21-year-old male, is in the published dataset, he cannot be sure about Tom's disease with greater than $1/2$ probability (although he learns that Tom has either asthma or flu). At a later time, three more patient records (shown in *Italic*) are inserted into the dataset, resulting the dataset in Fig. 3. The hospital then publishes a new 2-diverse version in Fig. 4. Observe that Tom's privacy is still protected in the newly published dataset. However, not every patient is protected from the attacker.

Example 1. Suppose the attacker knows that Alice, who is in her late twenties, has recently been admitted to the hospital. Thus, he knows that Alice is not in the old dataset in Fig. 2, but in the new dataset in Fig. 4. From the new dataset, he learns only that Alice has one of {Asthma, Flu, Cancer}. However, by consulting the previous dataset, he can easily infer that Alice has neither asthma nor flu. He concludes that Alice has cancer.

Example 2. The attacker knows that Bob is 52 years old and has long been treated in the hospital. Thus, he is sure that Bob's record is in both datasets. First, by studying the old dataset, he learns that Bob suffers from either alzheimer or diabetes. Now the attacker checks the new dataset and learns that Bob has either alzheimer or heart disease. He thus concludes that Bob suffers from alzheimer. Note that three other records in the new dataset are also vulnerable to similar inferences.

1.2   Contributions and Paper Outline

As shown in the previous section, anonymizing datasets statically (i.e., without considering previously released datasets) may lead to various inferences. In this paper, we present an approach to securely anonymizing a continuously growing dataset in an efficient manner while assuring high data quality. The key idea underlying our approach is that one can efficiently anonymize a current dataset by directly inserting new records to the previously anonymized dataset. This implies, of course, that both new records and anonymized records may have to be modified, as the resulting dataset must satisfy the imposed privacy requirements (e.g., k-anonymity or ℓ-diversity). Moreover, such modifications must be cautiously made as they may lead to poor data quality and/or enable undesirable inferences. We thus describe several inference attacks where attacker tries to undermine the imposed privacy protection by comparing a multiple number of anonymized datasets. We analyze various inference channels that attacker may exploit and discuss how to avoid such inferences. In order to address the issue of data quality, we introduce a data quality metric, called *Information Loss* (IL) metric, which measures the amount of data distortion caused by generalization. Based on our analysis on inference channels and IL metric, we develop an algorithm that securely and efficiently inserts new records into an anonymized dataset while assuring high data quality.

The remainder of this paper is organized as follows. We review the basic concepts of the k-anonymity and ℓ-diversity models in Section 2. In Section 3, we describe several inference attacks and discuss possible inference channels and how to prevent such inferences. Then we describe our algorithm that securely and efficiently anonymizes datasets in Section 4 and evaluate our techniques in Section 5. We review some related work in Section 6 and conclude our discussion in Section 7.

2 k-Anonymity and ℓ-Diversity

The k-anonymity model assumes that person-specific data are stored in a table (or a relation) of columns (or attributes) and rows (or records). The process of anonymizing such a table starts with removing all the explicit identifiers, such as name and SSN, from it. However, even though a table is free of explicit identifiers, some of the remaining attributes in combination could be specific enough to identify individuals. For example, as shown by Sweeney [22], 87% of individuals in the United States can be uniquely identified by a set of attributes such as {ZIP, gender, date of birth}. This implies that each attribute alone may not be specific enough to identify individuals, but a particular group of attributes could be. Thus, disclosing such attributes, called *quasi-identifier*, may enable potential adversaries to link records with the corresponding individuals.

Definition 1. (Quasi-identifier) A quasi-identifier of table T, denoted as Q_T, is a set of attributes in T that can be potentially used to link a record in T to a real-world identity with a significant probability. □

The main objective of the k-anonymity problem is thus to transform a table so that no one can make high-probability associations between records in the table and the corresponding entity instances by using quasi-identifier.

Definition 2. (k-anonymity requirement) Table T is said to be k-*anonymous* with respect to quasi-identifier Q_T if and only if for every record r in T there exist at least $(k - 1)$ other records in T that are indistinguishable from r with respect to Q_T. □

By enforcing the k-anonymity requirement, it is guaranteed that even though an adversary knows that a k-anonymous table T contains the record of a particular individual and also knows the quasi-identifier value of the individual, he cannot determine which record in T corresponds to the individual with a probability greater than $1/k$. The k-anonymity requirement is typically enforced through generalization, where real values are replaced with "less specific but semantically consistent values" [22]. Given a domain, there are various ways to generalize the values in the domain. Commonly, numeric values are generalized into intervals (e.g., $[12-19]$), and categorical values into a set of distinct values (e.g., {USA, Canada}) or a single value that represents such a set (e.g., North-America). A group of records that are indistinguishable from each other is often referred to as an *equivalence class*.

Although often ignored in most k-anonymity techniques, a private dataset typically contains some sensitive attribute(s) that are not quasi-identifier attributes. For instance, in the patient records in Fig. 3, *Diagnosis* is considered a sensitive attribute. For such datasets, the key consideration of anonymization is the protection of individuals' sensitive attributes. Observe, however, that the k-anonymity model does not provide sufficient security in this particular setting, as it is possible to infer certain individuals' attributes without precisely re-identifying their records. For instance, consider a k-anonymized table where all records in an equivalence class have the same sensitive attribute value. Although none of these records can be matched with the corresponding individuals, their sensitive attribute value can be inferred with a probability of 1. Recently, Machanavajjhala et al. [16] pointed out such inference issues in the k-anonymity model and proposed the notion of ℓ-*diversity*.

Definition 3. (ℓ-diversity requirement) Table T is said to be ℓ-*diverse* if records in each equivalence class have at least ℓ distinct sensitive attribute values. □

As the ℓ-diversity requirement ensures that every equivalence class contains at least ℓ distinct sensitive attribute values, the risk of attribute disclosure is kept under $1/\ell$. Note that the ℓ-diversity requirement also ensures ℓ-anonymity, as the size of every equivalence class must be greater than equal to ℓ.

3   Incremental Data Release and Inferences

In this section, we first describe our assumptions on datasets and their releases. We then discuss possible inference channels that may exist among multiple data releases and present requirements for preventing such inferences.

3.1   Incremental Data Release

We assume that a private table T, which contains a set of quasi-identifier attributes Q_T and a sensitive attribute S_T, stores person-specific records, and that only its ℓ-diverse[1] version $\widehat{T}$ is released to public. As more data are collected, new records are inserted into T, and $\widehat{T}$ is updated and released periodically to reflect the changes of T. Thus, users, including potential attackers, are allowed to read a sequence of ℓ-diverse tables, $\widehat{T}_0, \widehat{T}_1, \ldots$, where $|\widehat{T}_i| < |\widehat{T}_j|$ for $i < j$. As previously discussed, this type of data release is necessary to ensure high data quality in anonymized datasets.

As every released table is ℓ-diverse, by observing each table independently, one cannot gain more information than what is allowed. That is, the risk of attribute disclosure in each table is at most $1/\ell$. However, as shown in Section 1, it is possible that one can increase the probability of attribute disclosure by observing changes made to the released tables. For instance, if one can be sure that two (anonymized) records in two different versions indeed correspond to the same individual, then he may be able to use this knowledge to infer more information than what is allowed by the ℓ-diversity protection.

Definition 4. (Inference channel) Let $\widehat{T}_i$ and $\widehat{T}_j$ be two ℓ-diverse versions of a private table T. We say that there exists an inference channel between $\widehat{T}_i$ and $\widehat{T}_j$, denoted as $\widehat{T}_i \rightleftharpoons \widehat{T}_j$, if observing $\widehat{T}_i$ and $\widehat{T}_j$ together increases the probability of attribute disclosure in either $\widehat{T}_i$ or $\widehat{T}_j$ to a probability greater than $1/\ell$.   □

Thus, for a data provider, it is critical to ensure that there is no inference channel among the released tables. In other words, the data provider must make sure that a new anonymized table to be released does not create any inference channel with respect to the previously released tables.

Definition 5. (Inference-free data release) Let $\widehat{T}_0, \ldots, \widehat{T}_n$ be a sequence of previously released tables, each of which is ℓ-diverse. A new ℓ-diverse table $\widehat{T}_{n+1}$ is said to be *inference-free* if and only if $\nexists \, \widehat{T}_i, i = 1, \ldots, n$, s.t. $\widehat{T}_i \rightleftharpoons \widehat{T}_{n+1}$.   □

---

[1] Although we focus on ℓ-diverse data in this paper, one can easily extend our discussion to k-anonymous data.

It is worth noting that the above definitions do not capture possible inference channels completely. For instance, it is possible that some inference channels exist across more than two versions of a private table (e.g., $\widehat{T}_i, \widehat{T}_j \rightleftharpoons \widehat{T}_k$). Although such inferences are also plausible, in this paper we focus on simple "pairwise" inference channels.

3.2   Inference Attacks

We first describe a potential attacker and illustrate how the attacker may discover inference channels among multiple anonymized tables. We then describe various inference channels and discuss how to prevent them.

Attacker's knowledge.   Before discussing possible inference channels, we first describe a potential attacker. We assume that the attacker has been keeping track of all the released tables; he thus possesses a set of released tables $\{\widehat{T}_0, \ldots, \widehat{T}_n\}$, where $\widehat{T}_i$ is a table released at time i. We also assume that the attacker has the knowledge of who is and who is not contained in each table. This may seem to be too farfetched at first glance, but such knowledge is not always hard to acquire. For instance, consider medical records released by a hospital. Although the attacker may not be aware of all the patients, he may know when target individuals (in whom he is interested) are admitted to the hospital. Based on this knowledge, the attacker can easily deduce which tables include such individuals and which tables do not. Another, perhaps the worst, possibility is that the attacker may collude with an insider who has access to detailed information about the patients; e.g., the attacker could obtains a list of patients from a registration staff. Thus, it is reasonable to assume that the attacker's knowledge includes the list of individuals contained in each table as well as their quasi-identifier values. However, as all the released tables are ℓ-diverse, the attacker cannot infer the individuals' sensitive attribute values with a significant probability. That is, the probability that an individual with a certain quasi-identifier has a particular sensitive attribute is bound to $1/\ell$; $P(S_T = s | Q_T = q) \leq 1/\ell$. Therefore, the goal of the attacker is to increase this probability of attribute disclosure (i.e., above $1/\ell$) by comparing the released tables all together.

Comparing anonymized tables.   Let us suppose that the attacker wants to know the sensitive attribute of a particular individual, say Tom, whose quasi-identifier value is q. There are two types of comparisons that may help the attacker: 1) comparison of table $\widehat{T}_i$ that does not contain Tom and table $\widehat{T}_j$ that does, and 2) comparison of $\widehat{T}_i$ and $\widehat{T}_j$, that both contain Tom. In both cases, $i < j$. Let us call these types $\delta(\neg\widehat{T}_i, \widehat{T}_j)$ and $\delta(\widehat{T}_i, \widehat{T}_j)$, respectively. Note that in either case the attacker only needs to look at the records that may relate to Tom. For instance, if Tom is a 57 years old, then records such as $\langle [10-20], Female, Flu \rangle$ would not help the attacker much. In order to find records that may help, the attacker first finds from $\widehat{T}_i$ an equivalence class e_i, where $q \subseteq e_i[Q_T]$. In the case of $\delta(\neg\widehat{T}_i, \widehat{T}_j)$, the attacker knows that Tom's record is not in e_i; thus, none of the records in e_i corresponds to Tom. Although such information may not seem useful, it could help the attacker as he may be able to eliminate such records when he looks for Tom's record from $\widehat{T}_j$. In the case of $\delta(\widehat{T}_i, \widehat{T}_j)$, however, the attacker knows that one of the records in e_i must be Tom's. Although he cannot identify Tom's record or infer his sensitive attribute at this point (as e_i must contain at least ℓ number of

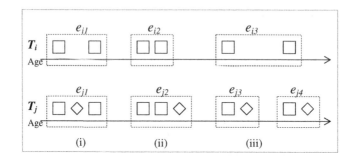

Fig. 5. Compatible equivalence classes

records that are all indistinguishable to each other and also at least ℓ number of distinct sensitive attribute values), this could be useful information when he examines $\widehat{T}_j$.

After obtaining e_i, the attacker needs to identify in $\widehat{T}_j$ the records that possibly correspond to the records in e_i, that is, equivalence class(es) that are *compatible* to e_i.

Definition 6. (Compatibility) Let $Q = \{q_1, \ldots, q_m\}$ be a set of quasi-identifier attributes. Let $e[q_i]$ be the q_i-value of an equivalence class e, where $q_i \in Q$. We say that two equivalence classes e_a and e_b are *compatible* with respect to Q if and only if any of the following conditions holds.

1. $\forall q_i \in Q,\ e_a[q_i] = e_b[q_i]$: the quasi-identifer values of e_a and e_b are identical to each other; we denote it as $e_a \cong e_b$.
2. $e_a \not\cong e_b$ and $\forall q_i \in Q,\ e_a[q_i] \subseteq e_b[q_i]$: the quasi-identifer value of e_b is a more generalized form of the quasi-identifier of e_a; we denote it as $e_a \prec e_b$.
3. $e_a \not\cong e_b, e_a \not\prec e_b$, and $\forall q_i \in Q,\ e_a[q_i] \cap e_b[q_i] \neq \emptyset$: the quasi-identifier values of e_a and e_b overlap with each other; we denote it as $e_a \leftrightsquigarrow e_b$.   □

Example 3. Consider Fig. 5, where the records of two tables T_i and T_j are spatially represented along the dimension of the quasi-identifier, *Age*. For simplicity, we do not show their sensitive attribute values. Table T_i contains six records (shown as '□'), and its 2-diverse version, $\widehat{T}_i$, consists of three equivalence classes, e_{i1}, e_{i2}, and e_{i3}. On the other hand, table T_j contains four additional records (shown as '◇'), and its 2-diverse version, $\widehat{T}_j$, consists of four equivalence classes, e_{j1}, e_{j2}, e_{j3}, and e_{j4}. Given $\widehat{T}_i$ and $\widehat{T}_j$, the following compatible equivalences can be found.

1. $e_{i1} \cong e_{j1}$ (Fig. 5 (i))
2. $e_{i2} \prec e_{j2}$ (Fig. 5 (ii))
3. $e_{i3} \leftrightsquigarrow e_{j3}$ and $e_{i3} \leftrightsquigarrow e_{j4}$ (Fig. 5 (iii))

The fact that two equivalence classes are compatible implies that there exist some records present in both equivalence classes, although their quasi-identifiers may have been modified differently. In what follows, we show how matching such records between compatible equivalence classes could enable the attacker to make high probability inferences.

Inference channels between compatible equivalence classes. As previously discussed, there are three cases of compatible equivalence classes. We now examine these cases in conjunction with each of $\delta(\neg \widehat{T_i}, \widehat{T_j})$ and $\delta(\widehat{T_i}, \widehat{T_j})$, illustrating how the attacker may infer Tom's sensitive attribute, s_T.

1. $e_i \cong e_j$ or $e_i \prec e_j$: In these cases, the attacker can reason that all the records in e_i must also appear in e_j, and the attacker only needs to look at the sensitive attribute values. Let $e_i[S]$ and $e_j[S]$ be the multisets (i.e., duplicate-preserving sets[2]) of sensitive attribute values in e_i and e_j, respectively.

   (a) In the case of $\delta(\neg \widehat{T_i}, \widehat{T_j})$, the attacker knows that Tom's sensitive attribute value is not in $e_i[S]$, but in $e_j[S]$; i.e., $s_T \notin e_i[S]$ and $s_T \in e_j[S]$. As he knows that all the values in $e_i[S]$ must also appear in $e_j[S]$, he can conclude that $s_T \in (e_j[S] \setminus e_i[S])$. Therefore, the attacker can infer s_T with a probability greater than $1/\ell$ if $(e_j[S] \setminus e_i[S])$ contains less than ℓ number of distinct values.

   (b) In the case of $\delta(\widehat{T_i}, \widehat{T_j})$, $s_T \in e_i[S]$ and $s_T \in e_j[S]$. However, as both sets are ℓ-diverse, the attacker does not gain any additional information on s_T.

2. $e_i \leftrightsquigarrow e_{j1}$ and $e_i \leftrightsquigarrow e_{j2}$[3]: In this case, the attacker reasons that the records in e_i must appear in either e_{j1} or e_{j2}. Moreover, as the attacker knows Tom's quasi-identifier is q, he can easily determine which of e_{j1} and e_{j2} contains Tom's record. Let us suppose e_{j1} contains Tom's record; i.e., $q \subseteq e_{j1}[Q_T]$. Let $e_i[S]$, $e_{j1}[S]$, and $e_{j2}[S]$ be the multisets of sensitive attribute values in e_i, e_{j1}, and e_{j2}, respectively.

   (a) In the case of $\delta(\neg \widehat{T_i}, \widehat{T_j})$, the attacker knows that Tom's sensitive attribute value is included in neither $e_i[S]$ nor $e_{j2}[S]$, but in $e_{j1}[S]$; i.e., $s_T \notin e_i[S]$, $s_T \notin e_{j2}[S]$, and $s_T \in e_{j1}[S]$. Note that unlike the previous cases, he cannot simply conclude that $s_T \in (e_{j1}[S] \setminus e_i[S])$, as not all the records in e_i are in e_{j1}. However, it is true that Tom's record is in $e_{j1} \cup e_{j2}$, but not in e_i; thus $s_T \in (e_{j1}[S] \cup e_{j2}[S]) \setminus e_i[S]$. As Tom's record must be in e_{j1}, the attacker can finally conclude that $s_T \in ((e_{j1}[S] \cup e_{j2}[S]) \setminus e_i[S]) \cap e_{j1}[S]$. Therefore, if this set does not contain at least ℓ distinct values, the attacker can infer s_T with a probability greater than $1/\ell$.

   (b) In the case of $\delta(\widehat{T_i}, \widehat{T_j})$, the attacker knows that Tom's sensitive attribute value appears in both $e_i[S]$ and $e_{j1}[S]$. Based on this knowledge, he can conclude that $(s_T \in e_i[S] \cap e_{j1}[S])$. Thus, attacker can infer s_T with a probability greater than $1/\ell$ if $(e_i[S] \cap e_{j1}[S])$ contains less than ℓ distinct values.

We summarize our discussion on possible inference-enabling sets in Fig. 6. Intuitively, a simple strategy that prevents any inference is to ensure that such sets are all ℓ-diverse. Note that with current static anonymization techniques, this could be a daunting task as inference channels may exist in every equivalence class and also with respect

---

[2] Therefore, set operations (e.g., $\cap$, $\cup$, and $\setminus$) used in our discussion are also multiset operations.

[3] It is possible that $\widehat{T_j}$ contains more than two equivalence classes that are compatible to e_i. However, we consider two compatible equivalence classes here for simplicity.

	$e_i \cong e_j$	$e_i \prec e_j$	$e_i \rhd e_{j1}$ and $e_i \rhd e_{j2}$
$\delta(\neg \widehat{T}_i, \widehat{T}_j)$	$e_j[S] \setminus e_i[S]$	$e_j[S] \setminus e_i[S]$	$((e_{j1}[S] \cup e_{j2}[S]) \setminus e_i[S]) \cap e_{jk}[S],\ k = 1,2$
$\delta(\widehat{T}_i, \widehat{T}_j)$	$e_i[S],\ e_j[S]$	$e_i[S],\ e_j[S]$	$e_i[S] \cap e_{jk}[S],\ k = 1,2$

Fig. 6. Summary of inference-enabling sets

to every previously released dataset. In the following section, we address this issue by developing an efficient approach to preventing inferences during data anonymization.

4   Secure Anonymization

In this section, we present an approach to securely anonymizing a dataset based on previously released datasets. We first describe a simple ℓ-diversity algorithm and propose a novel quality metric that measures the amount of data distortion in generalized data. Based on the algorithm and the quality metric, we then develop an approach where new records are selectively inserted to a previously anonymized dataset while preventing any inference.

4.1 ℓ-Diversity Algorithm and Data Quality

Data anonymization can be considered a special type of optimization problem where the cost of data modification must be minimized (i.e., the quality of data must be maximized) while respecting anonymity constraints (e.g., k-anonymity or ℓ-diversity). Thus, the key components of anonymization technique include generalization strategy and data quality metric.

ℓ-diversity algorithm.   In [16], Machanavajjhala et al. propose an ℓ-diversity algorithm by extending the k-anonymity algorithm in [13] to ensure that every equivalence class is ℓ-diverse. In this paper, we present a slightly different ℓ-diversity algorithm which extends the *multidimensional* approach described in [14]. The advantage of the multidimensional approach is that generalizations are not restricted by pre-defined generalization hierarchies (DGH) and thus more flexible. Specifically, the algorithm consists of the following two steps. The first step is to find a partitioning scheme of the d-dimensional space, where d is the number of attributes in the quasi-identifier, such that each partition contains a group of records with at least ℓ number of distinct sensitive attribute values. In order to find such a partitioning, the algorithm recursively splits a partition at the median value (of a selected dimension) until no more split is allowed with respect to the ℓ-diversity requirement. Then the records in each partition are generalized so that they all share the same quasi-identifier value, thereby forming an equivalence class. Compared to the technique based on DGH in [16], this multidimensional approach allows finer-grained search and thus often leads to better data quality.

Data quality metric.   The other key issue is how to measure the quality of anonymized datasets. To date, several data quality metrics have been proposed for k-anonymous datasets [3,10,14,11,21]. Among them, Discernibility Metric (DM) [3] and Average Equivalence Class Size Metric [14] are two data quality metrics that do not depend on generalization hierarchies. Intuitively, DM measures the effect of k-anonymization

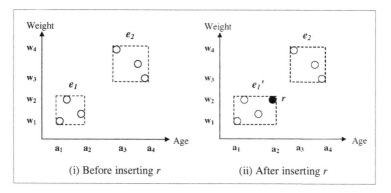

Fig. 7. Generalization and data distortion

process by measuring how much records are indistinguishable from each other. However, DM does not consider the actual transformation of data values. For instance, suppose that there are more than k records that already have the identical quasi-identifer value and that they are all in the same equivalence class. Even though these records are not generalized at all, DM penalizes each of these un-generalized records. The same issue arises for the average equivalence class size metric, which measures the quality of anonymization directly based on the size of the equivalence classes.

To address this shortcoming, we propose a data quality metric that captures the amount of data distortion by measuring the expansion of each equivalence class (i.e., the geometrical size of each partition). For instance, consider Fig. 7 (i), where the records are spatially represented in 2-dimensional space for quasi-identifier, {*Age, Weight*}. In the figure, the dotted regions group the records into two 3-diverse equivalence classes, e_1 and e_2. Note that as all the records in an equivalence class are modified to share the same quasi-identifer, each region indeed represents the generalized quasi-identifier of the records contained in it. For instance, the generalized records in e_1 may share the identical quasi-identifier $\langle[a_1 - a_2], [w_1 - w_2]\rangle$. Thus, data distortion can be measured naturally by the size of the regions covered by equivalence classes. Based on this idea, we now define a new data quality metric, referred to as *Information Loss* metric (IL) as follows.

Definition 7. (Information loss) Let $e = \{r_1, \ldots, r_n\}$ be an equivalence class where $Q_T = \{a_1, \ldots, a_m\}$. Then the amount of data distortion occurred by generalizing e, denoted by $IL(e)$, is defined as:

$$\text{IL}(e) = |e| \times \sum_{j=1,\ldots,m} \frac{|G_j|}{|D_j|}$$

where $|e|$ is the number of records in e, and $|D_j|$ represents the domain size of attribute a_j. $|G_j|$ represents the amount of generalization in attribute a_j (e.g., the length of an interval which contains all the attribute values existing in e). □

4.2 Updates of Anonymized Datasets

As previously described, our goal is to produce an up-to-date anonymized dataset by inserting new records into a previously anonymized dataset. Note that in our discussion below, we assume that all ℓ-diverse tables are maintained internally as partitioned, but unmodified tables. That is, each ℓ-diverse table consists of a set of equivalent groups, $\{e_1, \ldots, e_m\}$, which contain un-generalized records. This is a practical assumption as generating actual ℓ-diverse records for publication from a partitioned table is a relatively simple task. Consequently, given such a partitioned table and a new set of records, our insertion algorithm produces a new partitioned table which includes the new records.

Suppose that an anonymized table $\widehat{T}$, which is an ℓ-diverse version of a private table T, has been published. Suppose that at a later time, a new set of records $R = \{r_1, \ldots, r_n\}$ has been inserted into T. Let us denote the updated T as T'. Intuitively, a new ℓ-diverse version $\widehat{T}'$ can be generated by inserting R into $\widehat{T}$. The key requirements for such insertions are: 1) $\widehat{T}'$ must be ℓ-diverse, 2) the data quality of $\widehat{T}'$ should be maintained as high as possible, and 3) $\widehat{T}'$ must be inference-free.

We now briefly describe such an insertion algorithm which ensures the first two requirements. A key idea is to insert a record into a "closest" equivalence class so that the necessary generalization is minimized. For instance, let us revisit Fig. 7, which (i) depicts six records partitioned into two 3-diverse equivalence classes, and (ii) shows revised equivalence classes after record r is inserted. Observe that as r is inserted into e_1 resulting in e_1', the information loss of the dataset is increased by $IL(e_i') - IL(e_i)$. However, if r were inserted into e_2, then the increase of the information would have been much greater. Based on this idea, we devise an insertion algorithm that ensures high data quality as follows.

1. **(Add)** If a group of records in R forms an ℓ-diverse equivalence class which does not overlap with any of existing equivalence classes, then we can simply *add* such records to $\widehat{T}$ as a new equivalence class.
2. **(Insert)** The records which cannot be added as a new equivalence class must be *inserted* into some existing equivalence classes. In order to minimize the data distortion in $\widehat{T}'$, each record r_i is inserted into equivalent group e_j in $\widehat{T}$ which minimizes $IL(e_j \cup \{r_i\}) - IL(e_j)$.
3. **(Split)** After adding or inserting all the records in R into $\widehat{T}$, it is possible that the number of distinct values in some equivalence class exceeds 2ℓ. If such an equivalence class exists, then we may be able to *split* it into two separate equivalence classes for better data quality. Note that even if an equivalence class is large enough, splitting it may or may not be possible, depending on how the records are distributed in the equivalence class.

Clearly, the algorithm above do not consider the possibility of inference channels at all. In the following section, we enhance this algorithm further to ensure that an updated dataset does not create any inference channel.

4.3   Preventing Inference Channels

In Section 3, we discussed that in order to prevent any inference channel, all the inference-enabling sets (see Fig. 6) must be ℓ-diverse. We now discuss how to enhance our unsecure insertion algorithm to ensure such sets are all ℓ-diverse. Specifically, we examine each of three major operations, *add*, *insert*, and *split*, and describe necessary techniques to achieve inference-free updates.

Clearly, the add operation does not introduce any inference channel, as it only adds new ℓ-diverse equivalence classes that are not compatible to any previously released equivalence class. However, the insert operation may introduce inference channels (i.e., $e_j[S] \setminus e_i[S]$). That is, if the new records inserted into an equivalence class contain less than ℓ number of distinct sensitive values, then the equivalence class becomes vulnerable to inference attacks through $\delta(\neg \widehat{T_i}, \widehat{T_j})$. Thus, such insertions must not be allowed. In order to address this issue, we modify the insertion operation as follows. During the insertion phase, instead of inserting records directly to equivalence classes, we insert records into the waiting-lists of equivalence classes. Apparently, the records in a waiting-list can be actually inserted into the corresponding equivalence class if they are ℓ-diverse by themselves; until then, they are suppressed from the anonymized dataset. Note that as more records are continuously inserted into the table (and into the waiting-lists), for most records, the waiting period would not be too significant. However, to expedite the waiting period, we also check if the records in the waiting-lists can be added as an independent equivalence class which does not overlap with any other existing equivalence class.

There are two kinds of possible inference channels that may be introduced when an equivalence class e_i is split into e_{j1} and e_{j2}. The first possibility is: $((e_{j1}[S] \cup e_{j2}[S]) \setminus e_i[S]) \cap e_{jk}[S]$, $k = 1, 2$. Clearly, if such sets are not ℓ-diverse, then they become vulnerable to inference attacks through $\delta(\neg \widehat{T_i}, \widehat{T_j})$. Thus, the condition must be checked before splitting e_i. The other possible inference channel is: $e_i[S] \cap e_{jk}[S]$, $k = 1, 2$. This implies that if there are not enough overlapping sensitive values between the original equivalence class and each of the split equivalence classes, then split equivalence classes become vulnerable to inference attacks through $\delta(\widehat{T_i}, \widehat{T_j})$. Thus, unless such condition is satisfied, e_i must not be split. The tricky issue in this case is, however, that inference channels may exist between any of the compatible equivalence classes that were previously released. For instance, if there exists equivalence class e'_i that was released before e_i, then the splitting condition must be satisfied with respect to e'_i as well. This means that the system needs to maintain the information about the previous releases. Although this approach leads to extra computational overhead, it is necessary to maintain data privacy. In order to facilitate this, we store such information for each equivalence class; that is, each equivalence class keeps the information about its previous states. Note that it does not require a huge storage overhead, as we need to keep only the information about the sensitive attribute (not all the records). We also purge such information when any previous equivalence class becomes no longer compatible to the current equivalence class.

Clearly, inference preventing mechanisms may decrease the quality of anonymized data. Although it is a drawback, it is also the price to pay for better data privacy.

5   Experimental Results

In this section, we describe our experimental settings and report the results in details.

Experimental setup. The experiments were performed on a 2.66 GHz Intel *IV* processor machine with 1 GB of RAM. The operating system on the machine was Microsoft Windows XP Professional Edition, and the implementation was built and run in Java

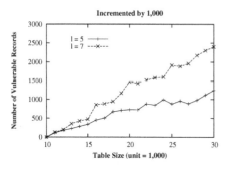
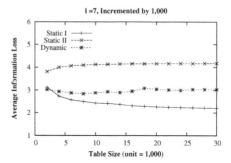

Fig. 8. Vulnerabilities   **Fig. 9.** Data quality

2 Platform, Standard Edition 5.0. For our experiments, we used the Adult dataset from the UC Irvine Machine Learning Repository [18], which is considered a de facto benchmark for evaluating the performance of anonymization algorithms. Before the experiments, the Adult data set was prepared as described in [3,11,14]. We removed records with missing values and retained only nine of the original attributes. In our experiments, we considered {*age*, *work class*, *marital status*, *occupation*, *race*, *gender*, *native country*, *salary*} as the quasi-identifier, and *education* attribute as the sensitive attribute.

For the experiments, we implemented three different ℓ-diversity approaches: *Static I*, *Static II*, and *Dynamic*. Static I is an approach where the entire dataset is anonymized whenever new records are inserted, while Static II anonymizes new records independently and merges the result with the previously anonymized dataset. Dynamic implements our approach, where new records are directly inserted into the previously anonymized dataset while preventing inference channels.

Vulnerability. The first question we investigated was how vulnerable datasets were to inferences when they were statically anonymized (i.e., Static I). In the experiment, we first anonymized 10K records and generated the first "published" dataset. We then generated twenty more subsequent datasets by anonymizing 1,000 more records each time. Thus, we had the total of twenty-one ℓ-diverse datasets with different sizes ranging from 10K to 30K. After obtaining the datasets, we examined the inference-enabling sets existing between the datasets. For instance, we examined the inference-enabling sets of the 12K-sized dataset with respect to the 10K- and 11K-sized datasets. Whenever we found an inference channel, we counted how many records were vulnerable by it. Fig. 8 shows the results where $\ell = 5, 7$. As expected, more records become vulnerable to inferences as the size of dataset gets larger; for the 30K-sized dataset with $\ell = 7$, about 8.3% of records are vulnerable to inferences. Note that there were no vulnerable records in datasets generated by Static II and Dynamic.

Data Quality. Next, we compared the data quality resulted by Static I, Static II, and Dynamic. For each approach, we generated different sizes of ℓ-diverse datasets, ranging from 1K to 30K, with increment of 1,000 records. For the data quality measure, we used the average cost of IL metric (described in Section 4.1). That is, the quality of an anonymized dataset $\widehat{T}$ was computed as: $\sum_{e \in \mathcal{E}} IL(e) \, / \, |\widehat{T}|$, where $\mathcal{E}$ is a set of all equivalence classes in $\widehat{T}$. Intuitively, this measure indicates the degree to which each

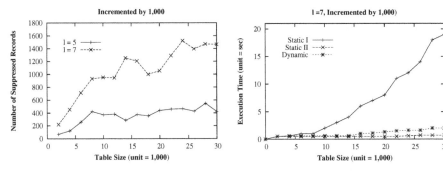

Fig. 10. Suppression   **Fig. 11.** Execution Time

record is generalized. Our experiment results are shown in Fig. 9. Although Dynamic results in lower data quality when compared to Static I, it produces much higher quality data than Static II. Moreover, the quality is maintained regardless of the data size. Fig. 10 shows the number of suppressed records in Dynamic approach. Note that each number shows the total number of suppressed records with respect to the entire dataset. For instance, when $\ell = 5$, only 421 records needed to be suppressed for the 30K-sized dataset.

Execution Time. Fig. 11 shows the execution times of anonymizing various sizes of datasets. As shown, the execution time of Static I increases linearly with respect to the size of the dataset, while Static II and Dynamic produce anonymized datasets almost constantly. Note that in the cases of Static II and Dynamic, the reported numbers are the total execution times which include the management of waiting-lists.

6   Related Work

In this section, we briefly survey existing literature that addresses data privacy. Instead of providing a comprehensive survey, we discuss various aspects of data privacy. Note that we do not include the k-anonymity or ℓ-diversity work here as detailed discussion can be found in Section 2.

Ensuring privacy in published data has been a difficult problem for a long time, and this problem has been studied in various aspects. In [12], Lambert provides informative discussion on the risk and harm of undesirable disclosures and discusses how to evaluate a dataset in terms of these risk and harm. In [4], Dalenius poses the problem of re-identification in (supposedly) anonymous census records and firstly introduces the notion of "quasi-identifier". He also suggests some ideas such as suppression or encryption of data as possible solutions.

Data privacy has been extensively addressed in statistical databases [1,5], which primarily aim at preventing various inference channels. One of the common techniques is data perturbation [15,17,23], which mostly involves swapping data values or introducing noise to the dataset. While the perturbation is applied in a manner which preserves statistical characteristics of the original data, the transformed dataset is useful only for statistical research. Another important technique is query restriction [6,8], which restricts queries that may result in inference. In this approach, queries are restricted by various criteria such as query-set-size, query-history, and partitions. Although this approach can be effective, it requires the protected data to remain in a dedicated database at all time.

Today's powerful data mining techniques [7,9,19] are often considered great threats to data privacy. However, we have recently seen many privacy-preserving data mining techniques being developed. For instance, Evfimievski et al. in [2] propose an algorithm which randomizes data to prevent association rule mining [20]. There has also been much work done addressing privacy-preserving information sharing [24,2], where the main concern is the privacy of databases rather than data subjects.

7   Conclusions

In this paper, we presented an approach to securely anonymizing a continuously growing dataset in an efficient manner while assuring high data quality. In particular, we described several inference attacks where attacker tries to undermine the imposed privacy protection by comparing a multiple number of anonymized datasets. We analyzed various inference channels and discussed how to avoid such inferences. We also introduced Information Loss (IL) metric, which measures the amount of data distortion caused by generalization. Based on the discussion on inference channels and IL metric, we then developed an algorithm that securely and efficiently inserts new records into an anonymized dataset while assuring high data quality.

Acknowledgements

This material is based upon work supported by the National Science Foundation under Grant No. 0430274, the sponsors of CERIAS, and the Korea Research Foundation Grant funded by the Korean Government (MOEHRD) under KRF- 2005-214-D00360.

References

1. N. Adam and J. Wortmann. Security-control methods for statistical databases: A comparative study. *ACM Computing Surveys*, 21, 1989.
2. R. Agrawal, A. Evfimievski, and R. Srikant. Information sharing across private databases. In *ACM International Conference on Management of Data*, 2003.
3. R. J. Bayardo and R. Agrawal. Data privacy through optimal k-anonymization. In *the 21st International Conference on Data Engineering*, 2005.
4. T. Dalenius. Finding a needle in a haystack. *Journal of Official Statistics*, 2, 1986.
5. D. E. Denning. *Cryptography and Data Security*. Addison-Wesley, 1982.
6. D. Dobkin, A. K. Jones, and R. J. Lipton. Secure databases: Protection against user influence. *ACM Transactions on Database systems*, 4, 1979.
7. X. Dong, A. Halevy, J. Madhavan, and E. Nemes. Reference reconciliation in complex information spaces. In *ACM International Conference on Management of Data*, 2005.
8. I. P. Fellegi. On the question of statistical confidentiality. *Journal of the American Statistical Association*, 1972.

9. I. P. Fellegi and A. B. Sunter. A theory for record linkage. *Journal of the American Statistical Association*, 1969.

10. B. C. M. Fung, K. Wang, and P. S. Yu. Top-down specialization for information and privacy preservation. In *the 21st International Conference on Data Engineering*, 2005.

11. V. S. Iyengar. Transforming data to satisfy privacy constraints. In *ACM Conference on Knowledge Discovery and Data mining*, 2002.

12. D. Lambert. Measures of disclosure risk and harm. *Journal of Official Statistics*, 9, 1993.

13. K. LeFevre, D. DeWitt, and R. Ramakrishnan. Incognito: Efficient full-domain k-anonymity. In *ACM International Conference on Management of Data*, 2005.

14. K. LeFevre, D. DeWitt, and R. Ramakrishnan. Mondrian multidimensional k-anonymity. In *the 22nd International Conference on Data Engineering*, 2006.

15. C. K. Liew, U. J. Choi, and C. J. Liew. A data distortion by probability distribution. *ACM Transactions on Database Systems*, 10, 1985.

16. A. Machanavajjhala, J. Gehrke, D. Kifer, and M. Venkitasubramaniam. ℓ-diversity: Privacy beyond *k*-anonymity. In *the 22nd International Conference on Data Engineering*, 2006.

17. S. P. Reiss. Practical data-swapping: The first steps. *ACM Transactions on Database Systems*, 9, 1980.

18. C. B. S. Hettich and C. Merz. UCI repository of machine learning databases, 1998.

19. S. Sarawagi and A. Bhamidipaty. Interactive deduplication using active learning. In *ACM International Conference on Knowledge Discovery and Data Mining*, 2002.

20. R. Srikant and R. Agrawal. Mining quantitative association rules in large relational tables. In *ACM International Conference on Management of Data*, 1996.

21. L. Sweeney. Achieving k-anonymity privacy protection using generalization and suppression. *International Journal on Uncertainty, Fuzziness and Knowledge-based Systems*, 2002.

22. L. Sweeney. K-anonymity: A model for protecting privacy. *International Journal on Uncertainty, Fuzziness and Knowledge-based Systems*, 2002.

23. J. F. Traub and Y. Y. H. Wozniakowski. The statistical security of statistical database. *ACM Transactions on Database Systems*, 9, 1984.

24. J. Vaidya and C. Clifton. Privacy preserving association rule mining in vertically partitioned data. In *ACM International Conference on Knowledge Discovery and Data Mining*, 2002.

Difference Set Attacks on Conjunctive Keyword Search Schemes*

Hyun Sook Rhee[1], Ik Rae Jeong[2], Jin Wook Byun[1], and Dong Hoon Lee[1]

[1] Center for Information Security Technologies (CIST),
Korea University, Anam Dong, Sungbuk Gu, Seoul, Korea
[2] Electronics and Telecommunications Research Institute (ETRI),
Gajeong-dong, Yuseong-gu, Daejeon, Korea
[1]{math33, byunstar, donghlee}@korea.ac.kr, [2]jir@etri.re.kr

Abstract. In a keyword search scheme a user stores encrypted data on an untrusted server and gives a database manager a capability for a keyword which enables a database manager to find encrypted data containing the keyword without revealing the keyword to the database manager. *Conjunctive* keyword search scheme enables a user to obtain data containing *all* of several keywords through only one query. One of the security requirements of conjunctive keyword search schemes is that a malicious adversary should not be able to generate new valid capabilities from the observed capabilities. In this paper we show that conjunctive keyword search schemes are not secure. In particular, given two capabilities corresponding two sets of keywords, an adversary is able to generate a new capability corresponding to the difference set of two keywords sets.

Keywords: Privacy; keyword search; conjunctive keyword search; difference set attacks.

1 Introduction

As the amount of information to be stored and managed on the Internet rapidly increases, the importance of storage system such as database is increasingly growing. As a result, ensuring privacy for the stored data on the storage system becomes one of the most urgent challenges in database research and industry.

A user of database systems such as e-mail and on-line storage systems normally believes that the managers of systems are trustworthy. However, serious damages caused by the abuse of personal data have often occurred by the system managers. Hence, the data need to be protected even from the system managers if the database systems can not be trusted. When the storage system is not trustful, users may ensure the privacy of their data by storing it in an encrypted form. However, encryption makes it hard to find specific data in the encrypted database. To resolve this hardness, various keyword search schemes have been

---

* This research was supported by the MIC(Ministry of Information and Communication), Korea, under the ITRC(Information Technology Research Center) support program supervised by the IITA(Institute of Information Technology Assessment).

W. Jonker and M. Petkovic (Eds.): SDM 2006, LNCS 4165, pp. 64–74, 2006.

suggested in the various encrypted database systems such as web-based storage system, e-mail system, and pay-per-view system [5,8,11,18,19,22,23].

The database systems may be classified into three types. The first type is *Storage system*, where a user stores his encrypted data to an untrusted server, and later searches data containing a keyword chosen by the user [8,11,13,23]. Song *et al.* studied an efficient and secure keyword search scheme by using a symmetric cipher [23]. Goh suggested a keyword search scheme using a Bloom filter [11].

The second type is *Transfer system*, where a data suplier may store encrypted data with a user's public key in the untrusted server, and later the user searches data containing a keyword such as e-mail system. Boneh *et al.* suggested public key encryption keyword search schemes in [5], and Park *et al.* suggested a conjunctive keyword search scheme in [19].

The third type is *Vendor system*, where a database manager becomes a data supplier and a user retrieves data containing a keyword without revealing to the database manager which contents the user receives [18]. For this type of database systems, Rhee *et al.* suggested a conjunctive keyword search scheme using an oblivious transfer [22].

1.1 Our Work and Motivation

The naive approach for conjunctive keyword search is that a user iteratively gives a capability for each keyword and receives data containing the keyword. In this naive approach, a database manager searches the set of data containing each keyword by executing a keyword search scheme for each keyword and finally return the intersection of all the sets. This approach allows the database manager to obtain the encrypted data containing a specific keyword.

For the more useful and secure conjunctive keyword search scheme, a user gives only one capability and receives data containing all keywords. The usefulness of this approach is from the followings: (1) If we do not query iteratively, the computational and communicational complexity may be reduced. (2) In this approach, a database manager can not know the encrypted data related to a specific keyword.

Note that the database manager does not know keywords themselves directly from given capabilities in both approaches. However, it may be still possible for the manager to link data from the given capabilities.

For example, suppose that $SI_i(Alice)$ and $SI_j(Bob)$ are the randomized searchable informations of keywords *Alice* and *Bob*, respectively. D_k is the encrypted data. Assume that the database manager has the following encrypted database.

	Keyword Field 1	Keyword Field 2
D_1	$SI_1(Alice)$	...
D_2	...	$SI_1(Bob)$
D_3	$SI_2(Alice)$	...
D_4	...	$SI_2(Bob)$
D_5	$SI_3(Alice)$	$SI_3(Bob)$

Let $K_1 = \{\text{Alice}, \text{Bob}\}$ and $K_2 = \{\text{Alice}\}$ be the sets of keywords, and $C_1 = Cap(K_1)$ and $C_2 = Cap(K_2)$ be the capabilities of K_1 and K_2, respectively. If the database manager has seen the capabilities C_1 and C_2, the manager can know the fact that C_1 is a capability which makes the manager search data $\{D_5\}$ and C_2 is a capability which makes the manager to search data $\{D_1, D_3, D_5\}$. The manger can know that $K_2 \subseteq K_1$ from $\{D_5\} \subseteq \{D_1, D_3, D_5\}$. Thus the information which the database manager gets is as follows:

(1) K_1 is related to $\{D_5\}$.
(2) K_2 is related to $\{D_1, D_3, D_5\}$.
(3) $K_2 \subseteq K_1$

In a secure conjunctive keyword search scheme, the database manager should not learn any more information except the above information. But in some conjunctive keyword search schemes, the database manager can know that a difference set $K_1 - K_2$ is related to $\{D_2, D_4\}$. That is, some conjunctive keyword search schemes do not provide "*unlinkability*" of data.

In this paper we show that the conjunctive keyword search schemes in [13,19,22] do not satisfy unlinkability. The above attack, "*difference set*" attack, is generalized in the following definition.

Definition 1. Let $\mathcal{A}$ be a malicious database manager of a conjunctive keyword search scheme CKS. Let $(K_1, ..., K_l)$ be the sets of keywords. Let $(C_1, ..., C_l)$ be the capabilities of $(K_1, ..., K_l)$, respectively, which are given to $\mathcal{A}$. If $\mathcal{A}$ can make a new capability C for a set of keywords $K = K_i - K_j$, where $K \notin \{K_1, ..., K_l\}$, $K_j \subset K_i$, $1 \leq i, j \leq l (i \neq j)$ then CKS is not secure against *difference set* attacks.

In the following sections, we show that the conjunctive keyword search schemes in [13,19,22] are not secure against the difference set attacks.

2 Attacks on Golle *et al.*'s Conjunctive Keyword Search Schemes

Golle *et al.* proposed two conjunctive keyword search schemes for storage system in [13]. For convenience, we call the first scheme as Golle I and the second scheme as Golle II. In this section, we briefly review Golle I and Golle II and show that they are not secure against difference set attacks.

2.1 Difference Set Attacks on Golle I Scheme

We first briefly review Golle I. A user manages his own data in the database. A user sends the following message:

$$E(m_i) \parallel \mathsf{CSI}_i = \{I_i, \mathsf{CSI}_{i,1}(W_{i1}, \rho, K), ..., \mathsf{CSI}_{i,m}(W_{im}, \rho, K)\}$$

where m_i is a message, E is a secure encryption algorithm, and m is the number of the keyword fields. CSI_i does not reveal any information about the message, whereas it enables the database manager to search for a set of keywords. The protocol works as follows:

- Param(1^k) : It takes as an input a security parameter k, and outputs parameters $\rho = (G, g, f(\cdot, \cdot), h(\cdot))$, where G is a group of order q in which decisional Diffie-Hellman (DDH) problem is hard, g is a generator of G, $f : \{0,1\}^k \times \{0,1\}^* \longrightarrow Z_q^*$ is a keyed function and h is a hash function.
- KeyGen(1^k) : It takes as an input a security parameter k, and outputs a secret key $(sk = K)$ for the function f, and we denote $f(K, \cdot)$ by $f_K(\cdot)$.
- CSI$(\rho, K, \{W_{i,1}, ..., W_{i,m}\})$: It takes as inputs ρ, K and $\{W_{i,1}, ..., W_{i,m}\}$, and outputs conjunctive searchable information $\mathsf{CSI}_i = \{I_i, \mathsf{CSI}_{i,1}(W_{i,1}, \rho, K), ..., \mathsf{CSI}_{i,m}(W_{i,m}, \rho, K)\}$. Let $V_{i,j} = f_K(W_{i,j})$ for $1 \le j \le m$. Let a_i be a value randomly chosen from Z_q^*. The output CSI_i is:

$$\mathsf{CSI}_i = (g^{a_i}, g^{a_i V_{i,1}}, ..., g^{a_i V_{i,m}})$$

where I_i is an additional information needed for conjunctive keyword search, and $\mathsf{CSI}_{i,j}(W_{i,j}, \rho, K)$ is the corresponding searchable information of $W_{i,j}$ for $1 \le j \le m$.
- TCK$(\rho, K, p_1, ..., p_l, Q_l)$: For $1 \le l \le m$, it takes as inputs a secret key sk, a list of names of target keyword fields in the database, and the corresponding l conjunctive keywords $\{W_{p_1}, ..., W_{p_l}\}$. It outputs a query $T_l = \{Q, C, p_1, ..., p_l\}$, where $Q = (h(g^{a_1 s}), ..., h(g^{a_n s}))$ and $C = s + \sum_{\omega=1}^{t} f_K(W_{j\omega})$.
- Test(CSI_i, T) : It takes as inputs the conjunctive searchable information CSI_i and query T. It outputs "yes" if the condition $(W_{i,p_1} = W_{p_1}) \wedge ... \wedge (W_{i,p_l} = W_{p_l})$ holds, and "no" otherwise. The server computes $R_i = g^{a_i C} \cdot g^{-a_i(\sum_{\omega=1}^{t} V_{ij\omega})}$, and returns "true" if $h(R_i) = h(g^{a_i s})$ or "false" otherwise.

Lemma 1. Golle I scheme is not secure against difference set attacks.

Proof. We show that a malicious database manager $\mathcal{S_A}$ can make a new capability from the two queried capabilities if some conditions hold. $\mathcal{S_A}$ works as follows:

- **Step 1.** Assume that $\mathcal{S_A}$ has been asked with two queries, $T_1 = \{Q_1, C_1, 1, 2, 3\}$ and $T_2 = \{Q_2, C_2, 1, 2\}$, such that:

$$Q_1 = \{h(g^{a_1 s_1}), ...h(g^{a_n s_1})\}$$
$$C_1 = s_1 + f_K(W_1) + f_K(W_2) + f_K(W_3)$$
$$Q_2 = \{h(g^{a_1 s_2}), ..., h(g^{a_n s_2})\}$$
$$C_2 = s_2 + f_K(W_1) + f_K(W_2)$$

Note that $\mathcal{S_A}$ can not know the secret information s_1 and s_2 which are randomly selected from a querier, but can know that the keyword fields of the first query are $(1, 2, 3)$ and the keyword fields of the second query are $(1, 2)$.
- **Step 2.** Suppose that a set of data collected from the first query is $\{D_1\}$ and a set of data collected from the second query is $\{D_1, D_2\}$. Since two sets contain the same data D_1 and $\{1, 2\} \subset \{1, 2, 3\}$, $\mathcal{S_A}$ can know that the keywords of two queries T_1 and T_2 are same in the keyword fields 1 and 2,

respectively. From this fact, $\mathcal{S}_A$ can make a new capability $T_3 = \{Q_3, C_3, 3\}$ using T_1 and T_2 as follows:

$$C_3 = C_1 - C_2 = s_1 - s_2 + f_K(W_3)$$

$$R_i = \frac{g^{a_i C_1}}{g^{a_i(V_{i1})} \cdot g^{a_i(V_{i2})} \cdot g^{a_i(V_{i3})}}$$

$$R'_i = \frac{g^{a_i C_2}}{g^{a_i(V'_{i1})} \cdot g^{a_i(V'_{i2})}}$$

$$Q_3 = (h(\frac{R_1}{R'_1}), ..., h(\frac{R_n}{R'_n}))$$

$\mathcal{S}_A$ makes a new valid query $T_3 = \{C_3, Q_3, 3\}$, and thus can find the encrypted data related to an unknown keyword W_3 by using Test algorithm. For every $1 \leq i \leq n$, $\mathcal{S}_A$ computes as follows:

$$h(g^{a_i C_3}/g^{a_i V_{i3}}) = h(g^{a_i(s_1-s_2)})$$
$$= h(\frac{R_i}{R'_i})$$

Hence, this scheme is not secure against difference set attacks.   □

2.2   Difference Set Attacks on Golle II Scheme

Golle II Scheme works as follows.

- Param(1^k) : It takes as an input a security parameter k, and outputs parameters $\rho = (G_1, G_2, \hat{e}, g, f(\cdot, \cdot))$, where G_1 and G_2 are two groups of order q, g is a generator of G_1, $\hat{e} : G_1 \times G_1 \rightarrow G_2$ is an admissible bilinear map and a keyed function $f : \{0,1\}^k \times \{0,1\}^* \longrightarrow Z_q^*$. The security parameter k is used implicitly in the choice of the groups G_1 and G_2.
- KeyGen(1^k) : It takes as an input a security parameter k, and outputs a secret value α and a secret key $(sk = K)$ for the function f, and we denotes $f(K, \cdot)$ by $f_K(\cdot)$, and $\{f_K(\cdot)\}_K$ forms a pseudorandom function family.
- CSI(ρ, K, D_i): It takes as inputs ρ, K and document $D_i = \{W_{i1}, ..., W_{im}\}$, and outputs conjunctive searchable information $\mathsf{CSI}_i = \{I_i, \mathsf{CSI}_{i,1}(W_{i,1}, \rho, K), ..., \mathsf{CSI}_{i,m}(W_{i,m}, \rho, K)\}$. Let $V_{i,j} = f_K(W_{i,j})$ for $1 \leq j \leq m$. Let a_i be a value chosen uniformly at randomly at random from Z_q^*. The output CSI_i is:

$$\mathsf{CSI}_i = (g^{a_i}, g^{a_i(V_{i,1}+R_{i,1})}, ..., g^{a_i(V_{i,m}+R_{i,m})}, g^{a_i \alpha R_{i,1}}, ..., g^{a_i \alpha R_{i,m}})$$

- TCK($\rho, K, j_1, ..., j_t, Q_l$) : For $1 \leq l \leq m$, it takes as inputs a secret key sk, a list of names of target keyword fields in the database, and the corresponding l conjunctive keywords $Q_t = \{W_{j_1}, ..., W_{j_t}\}$. It outputs a trapdoor $T_t = \{Q, C, H, j_1, ..., j_t\}$, where $Q = g^{\alpha r}$ and $C = g^{\alpha r(\sum_{\omega=1}^{t} f_K(W_{j\omega}))}$ and $H = g^r$.

- Test(ρ, CSI$_i$, T) : It takes as inputs the conjunctive searchable information CSI$_i$ and the trapdoor T. The algorithm checks whether the following equality holds:

$$\hat{e}(g^{\alpha r(\sum_{\omega=1}^t f_K(W_{j\omega})}, g^{a_i}) = \prod_{k=1}^t \frac{\hat{e}(g^{\alpha r}, g^{a_i(V_{i,j_k}+R_{i,j_k})})}{\hat{e}(g^r, g^{a_i \alpha R_{i,j_k}})}$$

and returns "true" if the equality holds, and "false" otherwise.

Lemma 2. Golle II scheme is not secure against difference set attacks.

Proof. The environment of Golle II scheme is the same as Golle I scheme. $\mathcal{S}_{\mathcal{A}}$ works as follows:

- **Step 1.** $\mathcal{S}_{\mathcal{A}}$ first captures two valid trapdoor $T_1 = \{Q_1, C_1, H_1, 1, 2, 3\}$ and $T_2 = \{Q_2, C_2, H_2, 1, 2\}$ as follows:

$$Q_1 = g^{\alpha r_1}, \quad H_1 = g^{r_1}, \quad C_1 = g^{\alpha r_1(f_K(W_1)+f_K(W_2)+f_K(W_3))}$$

$$Q_2 = g^{\alpha r_2}, \quad H_2 = g^{r_2}, \quad C_2 = g^{\alpha r_2(f_K(W_1)+f_K(W_2))}$$

$\mathcal{S}_{\mathcal{A}}$ cannot know the secret information r_1 and r_2 which are randomly selected from Z_q^*, but $\mathcal{S}_{\mathcal{A}}$ sufficiently can know the fact that the keyword fields of first capability are $(1, 2, 3)$ and the keyword fields of second capability are $(1, 2)$.

- **Step 2.** For every $1 \leq i \leq n$, $\mathcal{S}_{\mathcal{A}}$ computes V_i and V_i' and V_i/V_i' as follows:

$$V_i = \hat{e}(g^{\alpha r_1(\sum_{\omega=1}^3 f_K(W_\omega)}, g^{a_i})$$

$$V_i' = \hat{e}(g^{\alpha r_2(\sum_{\omega=1}^2 f_K(W_\omega)}, g^{a_i})$$

$$\frac{V_i}{V_i'} = \frac{\hat{e}(g^{\alpha r_1(f_K(W_1)+f_K(W_2)+f_K(W_3))}, g^{a_i})}{\hat{e}(g^{\alpha r_2(f_K(W_1)+f_K(W_2))}, g^{a_i})}$$

- **Step 3.** Suppose that the result data from the first Test algorithm is a D_1 and the resulted data from the second Test algorithm are D_1, D_2. Since two results simultaneously contain the data D_1 in the common keyword fields 1and 2 and $\{1, 2\} \subset \{1, 2, 3\}$, $\mathcal{S}_{\mathcal{A}}$ sufficiently can know the fact that the keyword fields of first capability are $(1, 2, 3)$ and the keyword fields of second capability are $(1, 2)$. From this fact, $\mathcal{S}_{\mathcal{A}}$ makes a new valid query $T_3 = \{Q_3 = Q_1, C_3 = \bar{V}_i, H_3 = H_3, 3\}$. For every $1 \leq i \leq n$, $\mathcal{S}_{\mathcal{A}}$ computes $\bar{V}_i$ as follows:

$$\bar{V}_i = \frac{V_i}{V_i'} \times \prod_{k=1}^2 \frac{\frac{\hat{e}(g^{\alpha r_2}, g^{a_i(V_{i,k}+R_{i,k})})}{\hat{e}(g^{r_2}, g^{a_i \alpha R_{i,k}})}}{\frac{\hat{e}(g^{\alpha r_1}, g^{a_i(V_{i,k}+R_{i,k})})}{\hat{e}(g^{r_1}, g^{a_i \alpha R_{i,k}})}}$$

- **Step 4.** Let's define ds_Q as follows. For every $1 \leq i \leq n$, $\mathcal{S}_{\mathcal{A}}$ compares $\bar{V}_i$ with ds_Q as follows:

$$ds_Q = \frac{\hat{e}(g^{\alpha r_1}, g^{a_i(V_{i,3}+R_{i,3})})}{\hat{e}(g^{r_1}, g^{a_i \alpha R_{i,3}})}$$

$\mathcal{S}_{\mathcal{A}}$ can find the encrypted data related to an unknown keyword W_3 by using Test algorithm:

$$\bar{V}_i = d s_Q$$

Hence, this scheme is not secure against difference set attacks   □

3   Attack on Park *et al.*'s Conjunctive Keyword Search Scheme

In this section, we briefly review Park *et al.*'s CKS scheme and show that it is not secure against difference set attacks. Park I scheme is as follows:

- KeyGen(1^k) : It takes as an input a security parameter k, and determines two groups $\mathbb{G}_1$ and $\mathbb{G}_2$, and chooses $s_1, s_2 \in Z_q^*$ and a generator P of $\mathbb{G}_1$. It outputs are a public key $pk = (P, y_1 = s_1 P, y_2 = s_2 P)$ and the corresponding secret key $sk = (s_1, s_2)$.
- CSI(pk, D) : It selects a random number $r \in Z_q^*$, and outputs $S = (A_1, ..., A_m, B, C) = [e(rH(W_1), y_1), e(rH(W_2), y_1), ..., e(rH(W_m), y_1), ry_2, rP]$.
- TCK($sk, p_1, ...p_t, Q_t = \{W_1, .., W_t\}$) : It takes as an input $sk, p_1, ...p_t, Q_t = \{W_1, .., W_t\}$ and chooses a random $u \in Z_q^*$ and outputs $T_Q = [T_1, T_2, p_1, ..., p_t]$ where $T_1 = (\frac{s_1}{s_2+u} mod\ q)(H(W_{i,p_1}) + ... + H(W_{i,p_t}))$, $T_2 = u$, and $p_1, ..., p_t$ are positions of keyword fields.
- Test(pk, S, T_t) : It checks the equation $A_{I_1} \times A_{I_2} \times ... \times A_{I_t} = e(T_1, B + T_2 C)$. If so, outputs "yes". Otherwise, outputs "no".

Lemma 3. Park I scheme is not secure against difference set attacks.

Proof. We show that a malicious database manager $\mathcal{S}_{\mathcal{A}}$ can make a new capability from the two queried capabilities if some conditions hold, and thus a new valid query. $\mathcal{S}_{\mathcal{A}}$ works as follows:

- **Step 1.** $\mathcal{S}_{\mathcal{A}}$ first captures two valid trapdoor $\{T_1, T_2, 1, 2, 3\}$ and $\{T_1', T_2', 1, 2\}$ as follows:

$$T_1 = \{(\frac{s_1}{s_2 + u})(H(W_1) + H(W_2) + H(W_3))\}$$
$$T_2 = u$$
$$T_1' = \{(\frac{s_1}{s_2 + u'})(H(W_1) + H(W_2))\}$$
$$T_2' = u'$$

- **Step 2.** For $1 \le i \le n$, $\mathcal{S}_{\mathcal{A}}$ can get the following information.

$$\hat{e}(T_1, B_i + T_2 C_i) = A_{i1} \times A_{i2} \times A_{i3}$$
$$\hat{e}(T_1', B_i + T_2' C_i) = A_{i1} \times A_{i2}$$

- **Step 3.** Suppose that the first search result is D_1 and the second search result is D_1, D_2. $\mathcal{S}_{\mathcal{A}}$ can know the fact that the first and the second capability has the same keyword in 1 and 2 keyword fields, respectively. Although $\mathcal{S}_{\mathcal{A}}$ cannot know the fact that the third keyword is W_3, he can search data related keyword W_3 without Test algorithm using the capabilities $\{T_1, T_2, 1, 2, 3\}$ and $\{T_1', T_2', 1, 2\}$. This is because:

$$\frac{\hat{e}(T_1, B_i + T_2 C_i)}{\hat{e}(T_1', B_i + T_2' C_i)} = \hat{e}(H(W_3), P)^{r_i s_1}.$$

- **Step 4.** For every $1 \leq i \leq n$, $\mathcal{S}_{\mathcal{A}}$ compares A_{i3} with $\hat{e}(H(W_3), P)^{r_i s_1}$. $\mathcal{S}_{\mathcal{A}}$ can get the data related keyword W_3. Hence, this scheme is not secure against difference set attacks. $\qquad\square$

4 Attack on Rhee *et al.*'s Conjunctive Keyword Search Scheme

In this section, we briefly review Rhee *et al.*'s scheme and show that it is not secure against difference set attacks. Rhee *et al.*'s OCKS scheme is as follows:

- **[Commitment Phase]** $\mathcal{T}$ generates a public key (N, e) and a secret key d of RSA. We assume that the value k_i is a decryption key of encrypted data $c_i = E_{k_i}(D_i)$, where $D_i = \{w_{i1}, ..., w_{im}\}$. Let $keygen_i(x) = (x - r_{i1}) \times \cdots \times (x - r_{im}) + k_i$ be a key generation function which provides a decryption key k_i corresponding to data c_i, where m is the number of keyword fields. Let leng : $Z_N \longrightarrow Z_q$ is an ideal hash function and $f_k : Z_N \longrightarrow Z_N$ is a pseudo random function. For every $i = 1, ..., n$ and $j = 1, ..., m$, $\mathcal{T}$ computes the followings.
  (**Step 1**) $\mathcal{T}$ randomly chooses $r_i' \in Z_N$.
  (**Step 2**) $\mathcal{T}$ makes $\mathsf{OCSI}_{ij} = f_k(w_{i,j})^d r_i' \mod N$, where OCSI_{ij} is the oblivious conjunctive keyword searchable information for w_{ij}.
  (**Step 3**) $\mathcal{T}$ computes $\mathsf{leng}(r_i'^j) = r_{ij}$ and sets $y_{ij} = g^{r_{ij}}$.
  (**Step 4**) $\mathcal{T}$ constructs $B_i = c_i \parallel y_{i1}, y_{i2}, ..., y_{im} \parallel keygen_i(x) \parallel \mathsf{OCSI}_{i1}, ..., \mathsf{OCSI}_{im}$. $\mathcal{T}$ commits $B_1, B_2, \cdots, B_n$.
- **[Transfer Phase]** The transfer phase consists of k subphases. $\mathcal{U}$ learns a conjunctive keyword search result $\bigcap_{t=1}^{d_j} search(w_{jt}^*)$ as follows.
  (**Step 1**) $\mathcal{U}$ choose d_j keywords $\boldsymbol{w^*} = w_{j1}^*, w_{j2}^*, ..., w_{jd_j}^*$ on W adaptively
  (**Step 2**) $\mathcal{U}$ chooses a random element $r \in Z_N$ and computes Y as follows. $\mathcal{U}$ sends Y to $\mathcal{T}$.

$$Y = r^e \times f_k(w_{j1}^*) \times \cdots \times f_k(w_{jd_j}^*).$$

  (**Step 3**) $\mathcal{T}$ computes $K' = Y^d \mod N$ and sends it to $\mathcal{U}$.
  (**Step 4**) $\mathcal{U}$ computes $K = K'/r$.
  (**Step 5**) For every i from 1 to n, $\mathcal{U}$ computes r_{id_j} as follows.

$$\begin{cases} \mathsf{OCSI}_{ij_1} \times \cdots \times \mathsf{OCSI}_{ij_{d_i}}/K \Longrightarrow (r_i')^{d_j} \\ \mathsf{leng}((r_i')^{d_j}) \Longrightarrow r_{id_j} \end{cases}$$

If the following equation (1) is satisfied, then we determine that the data D_i contains the keywords $w_{j1}^*, w_{j2}^*, ..., w_{jd_j}^*$.

$$g^{r_{id_j}} = y_{id_j} \tag{1}$$

And $\mathcal{U}$ can get a decryption key k_i for c_i by the equation (2).

$$k_i = keygen_i(r_{id_j}) \tag{2}$$

User $\mathcal{U}$ can get data D_i as decrypting the data c_i with k_i.

Lemma 4. Rhee *et al.*'s OCKS scheme is not secure against difference set attacks.

Proof. We show that a malicious user $\mathcal{U}_A$ can make a new capability from the two queried capabilities if some conditions hold. $\mathcal{U}_A$ works as follows:

- **Step 1.** If $\mathcal{U}_A$ got the data related keywords $\{W_1, W_2\}$ and a data related keywords $\{W_1, W_2, W_3, W_4\}$ then the user can get an extra information that is a data related keywords $\{W_3, W_4\}$ without the transfer phase with the database supplier. $\mathcal{U}_A$ randomly picks r_1, r_2 and computes the followings and transfers to the database supplier:

$$Y_1 = r_1^e \cdot (f_K(W_1) + f_K(W_2) + f_K(W_3) + f_K(W_4))$$
$$Y_2 = r_2^e \cdot (f_K(W_1) + f_K(W_2))$$

- **Step 2.** The database supplier computes the followings and sends them to $\mathcal{U}_A$:

$$Y_1^d = r_1 \cdot (f_K(W_1)^d \times f_K(W_2)^d \times f_K(W_3)^d \times f_K(W_4)^d)$$
$$Y_2^d = r_1 \cdot (f_K(W_1)^d \times f_K(W_2)^d)$$

- **Step 3.** $\mathcal{U}_A$ computes the followings and can get the following extra information EI:

$$Y_1^d/r_1 = (f_K(W_1)^d \times f_K(W_2)^d \times f_K(W_3)^d \times f_K(W_4)^d)$$
$$Y_2^d/r_2 = (f_K(W_1)^d \times f_K(W_2)^d)$$

$$EI = \frac{Y_1^d/r_1}{Y_2^d/r_2} = f_K(W_3)^d \times f_K(W_4)^d$$

- **Step 4.** For $1 \leq i \leq n$, $\mathcal{U}_A$ computes the following values and compares $g^{r_{i2}}$ and y_{i2}:

$$OCSI_{i3} \times OCSI_{i4}/EI \Longrightarrow (r_i')^2$$
$$leng((r_i')^2) \Longrightarrow r_{i2}$$

If $g^{r_{i2}} = y_{i2}$ is satisfied, then $k_i = keygen_i(r_{i2})$ is the decryption key and so $\mathcal{U}_A$ can get the data related keywords W_3, W_4 without processing the transfer phase. Hence, this scheme is not secure against difference set attacks. $\quad \square$

5   Conclusion

In this paper, we have reviewed Golle *et al.*'s scheme, Park *et al.*'s scheme, and Rhee *et al.*'s scheme and showed that these schemes are vulnerable to difference set attacks. It would be a good future work to design a security model considering difference set attacks and a secure conjunctive keyword search scheme to be secure against such attacks.

References

1. Michel Abdalla, Mihir Bellare, Dario Catalano, Eike Catalano, Tanja Lange, John Malone-Lee, Gregory Neven, Pascal Paillier, Haixia Shi, "Searchable Encryption Revisited: Consistency Properties, Relation to Anonymous IBE, and Extions.", *Crypto'05*, LNCS Vol3621. , pp205-222 , 2005.
2. R. Agrawal and R. Srikant, "Privacy-Preserving Data Mining", *In Proceedings of the 2000 ACM SIGMOD International Conference on Management of Data*, pp. 439-450, 2000.
3. M. Balze, "A Cryptographic file system for UNIX.", *Processings of 1st ACM Conference om Communications and Computing Security*, 1993.
4. S. Bellovin , W. Cheswick, "Privacy-enhanced searches using encrypted bloom filters", *Cryptology ePrint Archive*, Report 2004/022, Feb 2004.
5. D. Boneh, G. D. Crescenzo, R. Ostrovsky, and G. Persiano, "Public key Encryption with Keyword Search", *EUROCRYPT'04*, 2004.
6. D. Brassard, C. Crepeau, and J. M. Robert, "All-or-Nothing Disclosure of Secrets", *Crypto'86*, Springer-Verlag, 1987, pp. 234-238.
7. M. Bellare, C. Namprempre, and D. Pioncheval, "The Power of RSA Onversion Oracles and the Security of Chaum's RSA-Based Blind Signature Scheme", *Proc. of Finandcial Cryptography 2001*, LNCS vol. 2339, pp. 319-338.
8. Y. C. Chang, M. Mitzenmacher, "privacy preserving keyword searches on remote encrypted data", *ePrint*, October 7th 2003.
9. G. Cattaneo, G. Persiano, A. Del Sorbo, A. Cozzolino, E. Mauriello, and R. Pisapia, "Design and implementation of a transparent cryptographic file system for UNIX", *Techincal Report, University of Salerno*, 1997.
10. S. Even, O. Goldreich, and A. Lempel, "A Randomized Protocol for Signing Contracts", *comm. of ACM*, 28:637-647, 1985.
11. E. J. Goh, "secure index", *ePrint*, October 7th 2003.
12. P. Golle, M. Jakobsson, A. Juels, and Paul Syverson, "Universal Re-encryption for Mixnets", *In proceedings of CT-RSA 2004*, 2004.
13. P. Golle, J. Staddon and B. Waters, "Secure Conjunctive Keyword Search Over Encrypted Data", *Proceedings of the Second International Conference on ACNS:Applied Cryptography and Network Security*, 2004.
14. J. Hughes and D. Corcoran, "A nuiversal access, smart-card-based, secure fiel system.", *Atlanta Linux Showcase* , October 1999.
15. A. John , R. Peter, "Electric Communication Development", *Communications of the ACM* ,40,May 1997, pp. 71-79. 48-63, 2002.
16. K. Kurosawa, "Multi-recipient Public-Key Encryption with Shortened Ciphertext", *In proceedings of PKC 2002*, LNCS 2274, pp. 48-63, 2002.
17. M. Noar and B. Pinkas, "Efficient Oblivious trnasfer protocols", *12th Annual Symposium on Discrete Algorithms(SODA)*, pp 448-457(2001).

18. W. Ogata and K. Kurosawa, "Oblivious Keyword Search", *Journal of complexity'04*, Vol 20. April/Jun 2004.
19. D. Park, K. Kim, and P. Lee, "Public key Encryption with Conjunctive Field Keyword Search", *WISA'04*, LNCS 3325, pp73-86, 2004.
20. D. Pointcheval and J. P. Stern, "Provably secure blind signature schemes", *Proc. of Asiacrypt'96*, LNCS Vol. 1163, pp 252-265, 1996.
21. M. Rabin, "How to exchange secrets by oblivious transfer", *Technical Report TR 81*, Aiken computation Lab, Harvard University.
22. H.S. Rhee, J. W. Byun, D. H. Lee, J. I. Lim, "Oblivious Conjunctive Keyword Search", *WISA 2005*, LNCS Vol3786. , pp318-327 , 2005.
23. D. Song, D. Wagner, and A. Perrige, "Practical Techniques for searches on Encrypted Data", *In Proc. of the 2000 IEEE Security and Privacy Symposium*, May 2000.
24. B. R. Waters, D. Balfanz, G. Durfee, and D. K. Smetters, "Building an Encrypted and Searchable Audit Log",*11th Annual Network and Distributed Security Symposium (NDSS '04)*; 2004.
25. E. Zadok, I. Badulescu, and A. Shender, "Cryptfs : A stackable vnode level encryption fiel system.", *Technical Report CUCS-021-98*: 1998.

Off-Line Keyword Guessing Attacks on Recent Keyword Search Schemes over Encrypted Data*

Jin Wook Byun, Hyun Suk Rhee, Hyun-A Park, and Dong Hoon Lee

Center for Information Security Technologies (CIST),
Korea University, Anam Dong, Sungbuk Gu, Seoul, Korea
{byunstar, math33, kokokzi, donghlee}@korea.ac.kr

Abstract. A keyword search scheme over encrypted documents allows for remote keyword search of documents by a user in possession of a trapdoor (secret key). A data supplier first uploads encrypted documents on a storage system, and then a user of the storage system searches documents containing keywords while insider (such as administrators of the storage system) and outsider attackers do not learn anything else about the documents.

In this paper, we firstly raise a serious vulnerability of recent keyword search schemes, which lies in the fact that keywords are chosen from much smaller space than passwords and users usually use well-known keywords for search of document. Hence this fact sufficiently gives rise to an off-line keyword guessing attack. Unfortunately, we observe that the recent public key-based keyword search schemes are susceptible to an off-line keyword guessing attack. We demonstrated that anyone (insider/outsider) can retrieve information of certain keyword from any captured query messages.

Keywords: Keyword search on encrypted data, off-line keyword guessing attack, database security and privacy.

1 Introduction

With rapid developments of Internet technologies, the amount of personal information to be stored and managed on web-based storage systems rapidly increases. Thus, protecting personal data stored on the database from outsider/insider has been hot issues in a secure storage system. The most instinctive solution to prevent theft and misuse of personal data from an outsider/insider attacker is that a user of database system simply encrypts personal data with his own private key, and stores the encrypted results on the storage system. The user should also manage his encryption and decryption keys securely without revealing it to the outsider/insider attackers. However, secure encryption makes be unreadable to anyone other than the users holding the encryption

---

* This research was supported by the MIC(Ministry of Information and Communication), Korea, under the ITRC(Information Technology Research Center) support program supervised by the IITA(Institute of Information Technology Assessment).

W. Jonker and M. Petkovic (Eds.): SDM 2006, LNCS 4165, pp. 75–83, 2006.

keys, hence the server is unable to determine which encrypted documents contain specific keywords. Thus, in recent years, efficient and secure search of data using user's specific keywords has received a lot of attentions in the literature [1,3,5,6,8,9,11,12,13,14].

A keyword search protocol over encrypted documents consists of three entities: a data supplier, a storage system such as database, and a user of storage system. A data supplier uploads encrypted documents on a storage system, and then a user of the storage system searches documents containing keywords. For a more practical scenario, let's consider a common e-mail system such as *hotmail*. In this e-mail system, a data supplier is an e-mail sender, a storage system is an e-mail server, and a user of storage system is a user of an e-mail server. An e-mail sender first encrypts an e-mail with user's (receiver's) public key and sends the encrypted e-mail to an e-mail server. Actually, e-mails are encrypted by secure e-mail protocol such as PGP (pretty good privacy) protocol [15]. A legitimate user of e-mail server logs in the system, and searches for the encrypted e-mails by using specific keywords. In this setting, recently, Boneh *et al.* firstly proposed public key encryption keyword search (for short, PEKS) schemes and formally proved its security under the random oracle model [3]. However, as mentioned in the literature [8,13], the PEKS schemes are inappropriate for conjunctive keywords search such as searching on the conjunction of "Urgent", "Bob" and "Finance". Very recently, Park *et al.* presented two conjunctive keyword search protocols [13] based on the PEKS, and showed the protocols are secure under the random oracle model [2].

1.1   Our Contributions

Generally, off-line guessing or dictionary attacks arise when an attacker exploits the fact that certain weak secrets (such as passwords) may have low entropy, i.e. stem from a small set of values. Our main motivation of this paper starts from a simple fact that keywords are also chosen from much smaller space than passwords and users usually use well-known keywords (low entropy) for search of document.

In particular, let's suppose an e-mail system which is a major application area of keyword search scheme based on public key encryption [3,13]. In the e-mail search system, users are interested to search for their e-mails sent by "Supervisor" or "Lover" in the From field or they may concern well-known keywords such as "Urgent", "Exam", and "Hello" in the Title fields. Usually, when users fill in a title of e-mail, they use a simple and representative sentence composed of very short keywords to make receivers easily grasp the content of e-mail. Sufficiently, this fact can give rise to keyword guessing attacks where an malicious attacker is able to guess some candidate keywords, and verify his guess is correct or not in an off-line manner. By performing this off-line keyword guessing attack, malicious outsider/insider attacker can get relevant information of encrypted e-mail, and intrude on a users' e-mail privacy.

Actually, keywords are chosen from much smaller space than the space of passwords. Surprisingly, we note that the latest Merriam-Webster's colegiate dictionary contains only 225000 ($\approx 2^{18}$) keyword definitions [7,10], hence the probability of guessing a correct keyword in a brute force way is $\frac{1}{2^{18}}$. However, the probability of guessing a correct password is $(\frac{1}{62})^8 \approx \frac{1}{2^{48}}$ if we assume that every password has 8 character length and consists of alphabetic characters (52 characters : 'a' to 'z' and 'A' to 'Z') and numeric characters (10 characters : 0 to 9). Thus, we should give more careful attention on an off-line keyword guessing attack when we design a keyword search scheme, as we have carefully designed password-based authentication scheme to be secure against off-line password guessing attack.

In this paper, we firstly point out security vulnerabilities on recent keyword search schemes [3,13] by performing off-line keyword guessing attacks. We demonstrate that anyone (insider/outsider) can retrieve information of certain keyword from any captured query message of the protocol.

1.2   Organization

In Section 2, we explain security models of keyword search schemes. In Section 3,4 we overview two public key-based keyword search schemes and perform off-line keyword guessing attacks on the schemes, respectively. In Section 5, we conclude and present future works.

2   Keyword Search Schemes and Their Security Definitions

2.1   Keyword Search Schemes

[**Single Keyword Search Scheme**]. Let's consider a following setting where a sender encrypts its documents with a user's (i.e., the intended receiver's) public key and stores it on database of an untrusted server. First, a sender encrypts his e-mail (or sensitive document) with a user's public key (pk) and appends searchable information (SI) to the encryption, and then sends the appending result to the database of the untrusted server. We assume that the documents are encrypted by a standard public key encryption which is semantically secure against chosen ciphertext attacks. The user makes a trapdoor query for a keyword (TQ) using his private key, and sends the query to the server. After receiving the value of TQ from the user, the server is able to determine which encrypted documents contain queried keyword by checking the received TQ and all the values of SI in the database, but without learning anything else about the document from the received TQ and the SI. The server sends the corresponding encrypted documents (for example, $E_{pk}(D_1), .., E_{pk}(D_l)$, for $l \leq m$) to the requesting user. The keyword search protocols based on the public key encryption consists of the following polynomial time algorithms. We illustrate the framework of single keyword search scheme in Fig. 1.

- Key generation algorithm KeyGen(1^k) : Takes as an input a security parameter k, and outputs a public/private key pair (pk, sk).

- $\mathsf{SI}(pk, W)$: Takes as inputs a user's public key pk and a keyword W, and outputs searchable information.
- Trapdoor generation algorithm $\mathsf{TQ}(sk, W)$: Takes as inputs a secret key sk and a keyword W, outputs a trapdoor T_W for W.
- Test algorithm $\mathsf{Test}(pk, S, T_W)$: Takes inputs as searchable information $S = \mathsf{SI}(pk, W')$, and trapdoor T_W, and outputs 'Yes' if $W = W'$, and 'No' otherwise.

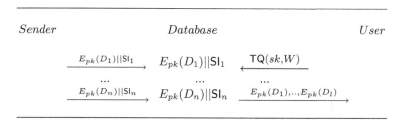

Fig. 1. The framework of single keyword search protocol

[Conjunctive Keyword Search Scheme]. A conjunctive keyword search scheme allows users to search on the conjunction of multiple keywords, hence searchable information generation and trapdoor generation algorithms of the scheme require the several keywords. To deal several keywords, we consider an actual database which has several records, each of which contains fields. Let n be the total number of documents, and we have n rows and m keyword fields in the database. For each row R_i ($1 \leq i \leq n$), we define i-th document by $D_i = \{W_{i,1}, ..., W_{i,m}\}$. The row R_i consists of encrypted document $E_{pk}(D_i)$ and conjunctive searchable information CSI_i where $\mathsf{CSI}_i = \{\mathsf{CSI}_{i,1}(W_{i,1}), ..., \mathsf{CSI}_{i,m}(W_{i,m})\}$ for m keyword fields. For $1 \leq j \leq m$, the $\mathsf{CSI}_{i,j}(W_{i,j})$ is the corresponding searchable information of the $W_{i,j}$ and it is stored on the j-th keyword field of i-th row in the database.

- Key generation algorithm $\mathsf{KeyGen}(1^k)$: Takes as an input a security parameter k, and outputs a public/private key pair (pk, sk).
- $\mathsf{CSI}(pk, D_i)$: Takes as inputs a user's public key pk and a document D_i, and outputs conjunctive searchable information CSI_i.
- Trapdoor generation algorithm for conjunctive keywords queries $\mathsf{TCK}(sk, p_1, ..., p_t, Q_t)$: For $1 \leq t \leq m$, takes inputs as a secret key sk, a list of names of target keyword fields such as "Name", "Date", and "address" (for simplicity, we denote these names by $p_1, .., p_t$), and the corresponding t conjunctive keywords $Q_t = \{W_1, ..., W_t\}$. Output is a trapdoor T_t for conjunctive Q_t.
- Test algorithm $\mathsf{Test}(pk, \mathsf{CSI}_i, T_t)$: Takes inputs as the public key pk, conjunctive searchable information $\mathsf{CSI}_i = \{\mathsf{CSI}_{i,1}(W_{i,1}, pk), ..., \mathsf{CSI}_{i,m}(W_{i,m}, pk)\}$, and trapdoor $T_t = \mathsf{TCK}(sk, p_1, ..., p_t, Q_t = \{W_1, ..., W_t\})$, and outputs 'Yes' if the condition $(W_{i,p_1} = W_1) \wedge ... \wedge (W_{i,p_t} = W_t)$ holds, and 'No' otherwise.

We illustrate the framework of conjunctive keyword search scheme in Fig. 2.

Sender	Database	User
$\xrightarrow{E_{pk}(D_1)\|\mathsf{CSI}_1}$	$R_1 = \{E_{pk}(D_1)\|\mathsf{CSI}_1\}$	$\xleftarrow{\mathsf{TCK}(sk,p_1,..,p_l,Q_t=\{W_1,..,W_l\})}$
...	...	...
$\xrightarrow{E_{pk}(D_n)\|\mathsf{CSI}_n}$	$R_n = \{E_{pk}(D_n)\|\mathsf{CSI}_n\}$	$\xrightarrow{E_{pk}(D_1),..,E_{pk}(D_t)}$

Fig. 2. The framework of conjunctive keyword search protocol

Definition 2.1 [Bilinear Maps]. Let $\mathbb{G}_1$ and $\mathbb{G}_2$ be two groups of order q for some large prime q. A bilinear map is defined $\hat{e} : \mathbb{G}_1 \times \mathbb{G}_1 \to \mathbb{G}_2$. The map has the following properties: (1) Bilinearity : $\hat{e}(g^a, g^b) = \hat{e}(g, g)^{ab}$ where $a, b \in Z_q^*$; (2) Non-degeneracy : $\hat{e}$ does not send all pairs of points in $\mathbb{G}_1 \times \mathbb{G}_1$ to the identity in $\mathbb{G}_2$. If g is a generator of $\mathbb{G}_1$ then $\hat{e}(g, g)$ is a generator of $\mathbb{G}_2$; (3) Computation : for all $P, Q \in \mathbb{G}_1$, the map $\hat{e}(P, Q)$ is efficiently computable.

3   Keyword Guessing Attacks on Boneh *et al.*'s Scheme

Boneh *et al.* firstly suggested a single keyword search scheme based on the identity based public key encryption scheme [4]. In this section, we show that the scheme is susceptible to an off-line keyword guessing attack.

3.1   A Brief Description of Boneh *et al.*'s Scheme

Two hash functions $H_1 : \{0,1\}^* \to \mathbb{G}_1$ and $H_2 : \mathbb{G}_2 \to \{0,1\}^{\log_2 q}$ are used in the scheme.

- KeyGen(1^k) : Takes a security parameter k, and determines two groups $\mathbb{G}_1$ and $\mathbb{G}_2$, and chooses $\alpha \in Z_q^*$ and a generator g of $\mathbb{G}_1$. Outputs are a public key $pk = (g, y = g^\alpha)$ and the corresponding secret key $sk = \alpha$.
- SI(pk, W) : Computes $t = e(H_1(W), h^r)$ for a random $r \in Z_q^*$, outputs $S = (A, B) = (g^r, H_2(t))$.
- TQ(sk, W) : Outputs $T_W = H_1(W)^\alpha$.
- Test(pk, S, T_W) : Checks whether $H_2(e(T_W, A))$ is B or not. If so, outputs 'Yes'. Otherwise, outputs 'No'.

3.2   Security Vulnerability

Lemma 1. Boneh *et al.*'s scheme is vulnerable to an off-line keyword guessing attack.

Proof. An attacker $\mathcal{A}_s$ performs the following steps.

- **Step 1:** $\mathcal{A}_s$ first captures a valid trapdoor $H_1(W)^\alpha$. $\mathcal{A}_s$ guesses an appropriate keyword W', and computes $H_1(W')$
- **Step 2:** $\mathcal{A}_s$ checks whether $e(y, H_1(W'))$ is $e(g, H_1(W)^\alpha)$ or not. If so, the guessed keyword is a valid keyword. Otherwise, go to Step 1.   □

4   Keyword Guessing Attacks on Park *et al.*'s Schemes

Park *et al.* suggested two conjunctive keyword search schemes Park I and Park II. For a conjunctive keyword search, $\mathsf{CSI}(pk, D)$ algorithm is used to generate conjunctive keyword searchable information. D is a document consisting of m keywords $\{W_1, ..., W_m\}$. A hash function $H : \{0,1\}^* \rightarrow \mathbb{G}_1$ is used in the protocol.

4.1   A Brief Description of Park *et al.*'s Scheme I

- $\mathsf{KeyGen}(1^k)$: Takes as an input a security parameter k, and determines two groups $\mathbb{G}_1$ and $\mathbb{G}_2$, and chooses $s_1, s_2 \in Z_q^*$ and a generator P of $\mathbb{G}_1$. Outputs are a public key $pk = (P, y_1 = s_1P, y_2 = s_2P)$ and the corresponding secret key $sk = (s_1, s_2)$.
- $\mathsf{CSI}(pk, D)$: Selects a random number $r \in Z_q^*$, outputs $S = (A_1, ..., A_m, B, C)$ $= [e(rH(W_1), y_1), e(rH(W_2), y_1), ..., e(rH(W_m), y_1), ry_2, rP]$.
- $\mathsf{TCK}(sk, p_1, ...p_t, Q_t = \{W_1, .., W_t\})$: Chooses a random $u \in Z_q^*$ and outputs $T_Q = [T_1, T_2, p_1, ..., p_t]$ where $T_1 = \left(\frac{s_1}{s_2 + u}\right)(H(W_{i,p_1}) + ... + H(W_{i,p_t}))$, $T_2 = u$, and $p_1, ..., p_t$ are positions of keyword fields.
- $\mathsf{Test}(pk, S, T_t)$: Checks the equation $A_{I_1} \times A_{I_2} \times ... \times A_{I_t} = e(T_1, B + T_2C)$. If so, outputs 'Yes'. Otherwise, outputs 'No'.

4.2   Security Vulnerability

Lemma 2. Park *et al.*'s scheme I is vulnerable to an off-line keyword guessing attack.

Proof. An attacker $\mathcal{A}_c$ performs the following steps.

- **Step 1:** When the number of queries is one (i.e., the number of keyword fields is one), an attacker $\mathcal{A}_c$ captures the trapdoor $T_1 = \left(\frac{s_1}{s_2 + u}\right)(H(W_{i,p_l}))$, $T_2 = u$, p_l for some position l.
- **Step 2:** $\mathcal{A}_c$ guesses an appropriate keyword W', and computes $H(W')$.
- **Step 3:** $\mathcal{A}_c$ computes $y_2 \cdot uP = (s_2 + u)P$ from public key and trapdoor.
- **Step 4:** $\mathcal{A}_c$ first computes $\lambda = e(y_1, H(W'))$, and checks the equality as follows.

$$e\left((s_2 + u)P, T_1\right) = e\left((s_2 + u)P, \left(\frac{s_1}{s_2 + u}\right)H(W_{i,p_l})\right)$$
$$= e\left(P, s_1H(W_{i,p_l})\right)$$
$$= e\left(s_1P, H(W_{i,p_l})\right)$$
$$= e\left(y_1, H(W_{i,p_l})\right)$$
$$= \lambda$$

If so, the guessed keyword is a valid keyword. Otherwise, go to Step 2.   □

4.3   A Brief Description of Park *et al.*'s Scheme II

Two hash functions $H_1 : \{0,1\}^* \rightarrow \{0,1\}^{\log_2 q}$ and $H_2 : \{0,1\}^* \rightarrow \{0,1\}^{\log_2 q}$ are used in the protocol.

- KeyGen(1^k) : Takes as an input a security parameter k, and determines two groups $\mathbb{G}_1$ and $\mathbb{G}_2$, and chooses $s_1, s_2, ..., s_{m+1}, s_{m+2} \in Z_q^*$ and a generator P of $\mathbb{G}_1$. Outputs are a public key $pk = (P, y_1 = s_1 P, y_2 = s_2 P, ..., y_{m+1} = s_{m+1}P, y_{m+2} = s_{m+2}P)$ and the corresponding secret key $sk = (s_1, s_2, ..., s_{m+1}, s_{m+2})$.
- CSI(pk, D) : Chooses m random numbers $r_0, r_1, r_2, ...r_m \in Z_q^*$, and outputs $S = (A_1, ..., A_m, B_1, ..., B_m, C, D) = [r_0(y_1 + H_1(W_1)P) + r_1 P, ..., r_0(y_m + H_1(W_m)P) + r_m P, r_1 y_{m+1}, ..., r_m y_{m+1}, r_0 y_{m+2}, H_2(g^{r_0})]$.
- TCK($sk, p_1, ...p_t, Q_t = \{W_1, .., W_t\}$) : Chooses a random $u \in Z_q^*$ and outputs $T_Q = [T_1, T_2, T_3, p_1, ..., p_t]$ where $p_1, ..., p_t$ are positions of keyword fields and

$$T_1 = \frac{1}{s_{p_1} + ... + s_{p_t} + H_1(W_{i,p_1}) + ... + H_1(W_{i,p_t}) + s_{m+2}u} P,$$

$$T_2 = \left(\frac{1}{s_{m+1}}\right) T_1,$$

$$T_3 = u.$$

- Test(pk, S, T_t) : Checks the following equation.

$$H_2 \left(\frac{e\left(A_{p_1} + ... + A_{p_t} + T_3 C, T_1\right)}{e\left(B_{p_1} + ... + B_{p_t}, T_2\right)}\right) = D$$

If so, outputs 'Yes'. Otherwise, outputs 'No'.

4.4   Security Vulnerability

Lemma 3. Park *et al.*'s scheme II is vulnerable to an off-line keyword guessing attack.

Proof. An attacker $\mathcal{A}_c$ performs the following steps.

- **Step 1:** When the number of queries is one, an attacker $\mathcal{A}_c$ captures the trapdoor $T_1 = \left(\frac{1}{s_{p_l} + H(W_{i,p_l}) + s_{m+2}u}\right) P, T_2 = \left(\frac{1}{s_{m+1}}\right) T_1, T_3 = u, p_l$ for some position l.
- **Step 2:** $\mathcal{A}_c$ guesses an appropriate keyword W', and computes $H(W')$.
- **Step 3:** $\mathcal{A}_c$ computes $\lambda = y_{p_l} + H_1(W')P + u \cdot y_{m+2}$
- **Step 4:** $\mathcal{A}_c$ checks the following equation.

$$e(T_1, \lambda) = 1$$

If so, the guessed keyword is a valid keyword. Otherwise, go to Step 2.   □

5   Conclusion and Open Problem

Up until now, there have been a great deal of research related to the privacy of database. Especially, in recent years, efficient and secure search of encrypted documents using keywords have received a lot of attentions in the literature. However, all the schemes have not taken account of a simple fact that keywords have low entropy and are chosen from much smaller size than the size of passwords. In this paper, we demonstrated vulnerabilities on the recent keyword search schemes by performing off-line keyword guessing attacks. We have the following future works.

- [**Designing a scheme secure against off-line keyword guessing attacks**]. The vulnerabilities of keyword guessing attack come from that trapdoors are simply generated by just combining keywords and secret key. That is, any insider/outsider attacker can relate the combination with the public keys by using pairing operation, which finally cause off-line keyword guessing attack. It is not an easy task to remove a redundancy from trapdoor queries and public keys to be strong against off-line keyword guessing attacks still keeping its original security.
- [**Security Model**]. Over the years, keyword search schemes based on public key encryption have been studied in viewpoint of how to efficiently design single or conjunctive protocols with provable security [7,8,9,11,12,13,14]. However, all works have not taken account of any security definition against an *off-line keyword guessing attack*. It still remains to establish a new security model including an off-line keyword guessing attack.

Acknowledgement

The authors would like to thank anonymous reviewers of SDM 2006 for their invaluable comments and suggestions.

References

1. M. Abdalla, M. Bellare, D. Catalano, E. Kiltz, T. Kohno, T. Lange, J. Malone-Lee, G. Neven, P. Paillier, and H. Shi, "Encryption with keyword search, revisited: consistency conditions, relations to anonymous IBE, and extensions". *This paper will be appear in Crypto05.*
2. M. Bellare and P. Rogaway, "Random oracles are practical: a paradigm for designing efficient protocols", *In Proceedings of the First ACM Conference on Computer and Communications Security, ACM*, 1995
3. D. Boneh, G. D. Crescenzo, R. Ostrovsky, and G. Persiano, "Public Key Encryption with Keyword Search", *In Proceedings of Eurocrypt '04*, LNCS Vol. 3089, pp. 31-45, Springer-Verlag, 2004.
4. D. Boneh and M. Franklin, "Identity-Based Encryption from the Weil Pairing", *SIAM J. of Computing*, Vol. 32, No. 3, pp. 586-615, 2003.
5. B. Chor, O. Goldreich, E. Kushilevitz, and M. Sudan, "Private Information Retrieval", *In Proceedings of 29th STOC*, 1997.

6. G. Di. Crescenzo, Y. Ishai, and R. Ostrovsky, "Universal Servie-providers for Dtabase Private Information Retrieval", *In Proceedings of 17th PODC*, 1998.
7. Y. Chang and M. Mitzenmacher, "Privacy preserving keyword searches on remote encrypted data", This paper will be appeared in ACNS 2005. An early version of this paper is appeared on Cryptology ePrint Archieve. Availabe at http://eprint.iacr.org/2004/051
8. P. Golle, J. Staddon, and B. Waters, "Secure Conjunctive keyword search over encrytped data", *In Proceedings of ACNS '04*, LNCS Vol. 3089, pp. 31-45, Springer-Verlag, 2004.
9. E. Goh, "Secure Indexes", In Cryptology ePrint Archieve on March 16, 2004, This paper is availabe at http://eprint.iacr.org/2003/216
10. F. Mish, "Merriam-Webster's Collegiate Dictionary", 11th edition, Merriam-Webser, Inc., 2003. Refer to `http://www.m-w.com/help/`
11. R. Ostrovsky and W. Skeith, "Private keyword search on streaming data", *This paper will be appear in Crypto05*.
12. W. Ogata and K. Kurosawa, "Oblivious keyword search" *Journal of Complexity* Vol. 20, Issues 2-3, pp. 356-371, 2004.
13. D. J. Park, K. Kim, and P. J. Lee, "Public Key Encryption with Conjunctive Field Keyword Search", *In Proceedings of WISA '04*, LNCS Vol. 3325, pp. 73-86, Springer-Verlag, 2004.
14. D. Song, D. Wagner, and A. Perrig, "Practical Techniques for Searches on Encrypted Data", *In Proceedings of IEEE sysmposium on Security and Privacy*, 2000.
15. P. R. Zimmermann, "The official PGP User's Guide", MIT Press, Cambridge, Massachusetts, 1995.

Privacy Preserving BIRCH Algorithm for Clustering over Vertically Partitioned Databases

P. Krishna Prasad and C. Pandu Rangan

Department of Computer Science and Engineering
Indian Institute of Technology - Madras
Chennai - 600036, India
pkp@cse.iitm.ernet.in,
rangan@iitm.ernet.in

Abstract. BIRCH algorithm, introduced by Zhang et al. [15], is a well known algorithm for effectively finding clusters in a large data set. The two major components of the BIRCH algorithm are CF tree construction and global clustering. However BIRCH algorithm is basically designed as an algorithm working on a single database. We propose the first novel method for running BIRCH over a vertically partitioned data sets, distributed in two different databases in a privacy preserving manner. We first provide efficient solutions to crypto primitives such as finding minimum index in a vector sum and checking if sum of two private values exceed certain threshold limit. We then use these primitives as basic tools to arrive at secure solutions to CF tree construction and single link clustering for implementing BIRCH algorithm.

1 Introduction

Due to explosive growth in the volume of digital data, there is a need for automated tools to analyze and extract useful information from very large volumes of data. Data Mining is "the non trivial extraction of implicit previously unknown and potentially useful information from data." Data mining includes various algorithms for *classification, association rule mining, and clustering*. In this paper we focus on *clustering*.

Definition 1. (*Clustering Problem*) *Given a database $D = \{t_i\}_{i=1}^n$ of tuples and an integer value k, the clustering problem is to define a mapping $f : D \rightarrow \{1, 2, \cdots, k\}$ where each t_i is assigned to one cluster $K_j, 1 \leq j \leq k$. A Cluster K_j contains precisely those tuples mapped to it; that is, $K_j = \{t_i | f(t_i) = K_j, 1 \leq i \leq n, \text{ and } t_i \in D\}$.*

Most of the classical clustering algorithms such as $k-means$, assume that sufficient main memory exists to hold the data to be clustered and the data structures needed to support them. With large databases containing thousands of items(or more), these algorithms are not realistic. In addition, performing I/Os continuously through the multiple iterations of an algorithm is too expensive. Because of these restrictions, these types of algorithms do not scale up easily

W. Jonker and M. Petkovic (Eds.): SDM 2006, LNCS 4165, pp. 84–99, 2006.

for large data bases. In data mining literature there are some clustering methods like CLARANS, BIRCH, DBSCAN, CURE etc., which scale well for large databases. BIRCH is considered to be superior to CLARANS [15].

The data of interest is often distributed across several parties. Due to privacy rules and regulations such as HIPAA, GLBA and SOX [10], the data owning site is not supposed to give its data to other parties. Here the key challenge is to design clustering algorithms in a privacy preserving manner when the data is distributed in several databases. This issue was pointed by Agrawal and Srikant [2] and Lindell and Pinkas[9]. In this paper we consider vertically partitioned data which is also known as heterogeneously distributed data. This means that different sites gather information on different feature sets about the same set of entities [16].

Some of the applications of privacy preserving clustering of vertically partitioned data bases, are :

– Imagine two databases, one contains medical records and another contains cell phone data of the same set of people. Mining the joint global database may provide insight to questions such as "Do cell phones with *Lithium* batteries lead to brain tumors in diabetics patients?"
– Two organizations, an Internet marketing company and an on-line retail company, have datasets with different attributes for a common set of individuals. These organizations decide to share their data for clustering to find the optimal customer targets so as to maximize return on investments. How can these organizations learn about their clusters using each other's data without learning anything about the attribute values of each other?

In this paper we give a method for securely obtaining clusters by using BIRCH clustering method when the data is vertically partitioned between two parties. This is a first attempt in giving the solution for privacy preserving clustering for large databases when partitioned vertically.

Organization of the paper. In Section 2 we briefly survey the existing techniques for privacy preserving clustering. In Section 3 we discuss preliminaries that are used in developing the secure protocols. In Section 4 we give the building blocks that are used for finding the clusters securely. In order to keep the exposition self contained, we briefly describe BIRCH algorithm in Section 5. In Section 6 we give the method of obtaining clusters in secure way when the data is vertically partitioned.

2   Related Work

Privacy preserving data mining, introduced by Agrawal and Srikant [2] and Lindell and Pinkas [9] allows certain data mining computations to take place, while providing some protection for the underlying data. In general, there are two approaches for privacy preserving data mining algorithms. The first approach is, perturb the data and share the perturbed data for data mining applications. The other approach is based on multi-party computation which is based on cryptographic primitives. In perturbation approach, the idea of reconstructing the data distribution itself gives information about the original data values [1] . Our work is based on secure multi-party computation approach where there is a guarantee of privacy. In privacy preserving data mining people have looked into privacy preserving association rule mining [16], privacy preserving decision tree construction [9] and recently privacy preserving clustering [17,11,14,7] in vertically or horizontally or arbitrarily partitioned database.

Jagannathan and Wright [7] introduced the concept of arbitrarily partitioned data and they gave an efficient privacy preserving protocol for k-means clustering in the setting of arbitrarily partitioned data and it works only for small databases.

Jha et al. [14] gave a distributed privacy preserving algorithm for $k- means$ clustering when the data is horizontally partitioned. This algorithm works only for small databases when partitioned horizontally.

Vaidya and Clifton [17] introduced the problem of privacy preserving clustering when the data is vertically partitioned data. Their algorithm directly follows the standard $k - means$ algorithm. At each iteration of the algorithm, every point is assigned to the proper cluster by securely finding out the minimum distance for each point to the clusters formed in the previous iteration. They used Yao's circuit evaluation protocol to find the closest cluster. The number of database scans is dependent on the termination criteria. As the $k - means$ algorithm works only for small databases, their algorithm too suffers from the same limitation.

To our knowledge, till now there is only one privacy preserving algorithm which works for large databases. This is recently proposed by Jagannathan et al. [6]. This algorithm is known as *Recluster*. It works for horizontally partitioned databases. Their algorithm works based on divide, conquer, and combine fashion.

Till now there is no privacy preserving clustering algorithm which works for large databases when the database is vertically partitioned. In this paper we present a privacy preserving protocol for BIRCH clustering, which works for large databases when the data is vertically partitioned.

3   Preliminaries

In this paper we assume the participants who run the protocol are **semi honest**. A semi honest adversary is also known as passive adversary who follows correctly the protocol specification, yet attempts to learn additional information by analyzing the transcript of messages received during the execution. This assumption is often a realistic one [9].

Theorem 1. (*Composition theorem for the semi honest model*): *Suppose that g is privately reducible to f and that there exists a protocol for privately computing f. Then, the protocol defined by replacing each oracle-call to f by a protocol that privately computes f, is a protocol for privately computing g.*

Our protocol finds the clusters over vertically partitioned databases by running many invocations of secure computation of simpler functionalities. Loosely speaking, consider a hybrid model where the protocol uses a trusted party that computes the functionalities $f_1, f_2, \cdots, f_l$. The secure composition theorem states that we may replace the calls to the trusted party by calls to secure protocols computing $f_1, f_2, \cdots, f_l$, and still have a secure protocol. [9].

Homomorphic encryption scheme: The limitation of an ordinary encryption system is that an information system can only store and retrieve encrypted data for users. Any other operation on data requires decryption, and once the data is decrypted, Its privacy is lost. Rivest et al., [13] proposed a new encryption scheme that enables direct computation on encrypted data without decryption, which is called privacy homomorphism. We denote the encryption of a message m by $E_{k_p}(m)$ and decryption of a cipher text c by $D_{k_s}(c)$ where k_p and k_s are the public key and secret key respectively. A public-key crypto system is *homomorphic* when $E_{k_p}(m_1) \cdot E_{k_p}(m_2) = E_{k_p}(m_1 + m_2)$ where $+$ is a group operation and $\cdot$ is a groupoid operation. This means that a party can add two encrypted plain texts by doing simple computations with cipher texts, even without the knowledge of the secret key. One of the most widely used semantically secure homomorphic cryptosystem is Paillier cryptosystem [12] or improved version proposed by Damgard and Jurick [5].

Millionaire Problem: We use this primitive in one of our protocols. The purpose of this primitive is to compare two private numbers and decide which one is larger. This problem was first proposed by Yao in 1982 [18] and is widely known as Yao's Millionaire problem. Essentially the problem is Alice and Bob are two millionaires who want to find out who is richer without revealing the precise amount of their wealth. Cachin [4] proposed a solution based on the ϕ-hiding assumption. The communication complexity of Cachin's scheme is $O(l)$, where l is the number of bits of each input number and the computation complexity is also linear on the number of bits used to represent both the numbers.

Secure Scalar Product: We use this primitive in two of our protocols. The purpose of this primitive is to find securely $\overrightarrow{X} \cdot \overrightarrow{Y}$ where Alice has the private vector $\overrightarrow{X} = (x_1, x_2, \cdots, x_n)$ and Bob has the private vector $\overrightarrow{Y} = (y_1, y_2, \cdots, y_n)$ and $\overrightarrow{X} \cdot \overrightarrow{Y} = \sum_{i=1}^{n} x_i y_i$. We use the private homomorphic dot product protocol given by Goethals et al. [3].

4   Building Blocks

In this section we give two protocols that are used as building blocks for obtaining secure BIRCH algorithm. These protocols are used in,

1. constructing CF tree securely (ie., in secure CF tree insertion given in section 6.1),
2. secure single link clustering for global clustering and
3. labeling the data points securely.

Protocol 1. *Party A has private input $X = (x_1, x_2, \cdots, x_n)$ and party B has private input $Y = (y_1, y_2, \cdots, y_n)$. They wish to securely find out the index i*

such that $x_i + y_i = min(x_1 + y_1, x_2 + y_2, \cdots, x_n + y_n)$ *without A knowing Y and B knowing X.*

Private inputs : Private vectors $X, Y \in \mathbb{R}^n$. *That is* $X = (x_1, x_2, \cdots, x_n)$ *and* $Y = (y_1, y_2, \cdots, y_n)$

Output : index i such that $x_i + y_i = min(x_1 + y_1, x_2 + y_2, \cdots, x_n + y_n)$

1. *Party A does:*
   Generate a private and public key pair k_s, k_p *for* **homomorphic cryptosystem** *and send* k_p *to Bob.*

2. *Party A does :*
   Encrypt X ie., $E_{k_p}(X) = (E_{k_p}(x_1), E_{k_p}(x_2), \cdots, E_{k_p}(x_n))$ *and send* $E_{k_p}(X)$ *to B.*

3. *Party B does:*
   Generate a random value r and add r to each element of its vector Y.
   $Y' = (y_1', y_2', \cdots, y_n') = (y_1 + r, y_2 + r, \cdots, y_n + r)$.
   Find $E_{k_p}(Y') = (E_{k_p}(y_1'), E_{k_p}(y_2'), \cdots, E_{k_p}(y_n'))$.
   Find $E_{k_p}(X)E_{k_p}(Y')$
   $= (E_{k_p}(x_1)E_{k_p}(y_1'), E_{k_p}(x_2)E_{k_p}(y_2'), \cdots, E_{k_p}(x_n)E_{k_p}(y_n'))$
   $= (E_{k_p}(x_1 + y_1'), E_{k_p}(x_2 + y_2'), \cdots, E_{k_p}(x_n + y_n'))$.
   Use **random permutation** π *to permute* $E_{k_p}(X)E_{k_p}(Y')$ *and*
   Send $\pi(E_{k_p}(X)E_{k_p}(Y'))$ *to A.*

4. *Party A does:*
   Decrypt $\pi(E_{k_p}(X)E_{k_p}(Y'))$
   $D_{k_s}(\pi(E_{k_p}(X)E_{k_p}(Y'))) = \pi(x_1 + y_1', x_2 + y_2', \cdots, x_n + y_n')$.
   Find index j such that $x_j + y_j' = min(\pi(x_1 + y_1', x_2 + y_2', \cdots, x_n + y_n'))$.
   Send j to B.

5. *Party B does:*
   Send $\pi^{-1}(j)$ *to A, where* $\pi^{-1}(j)$ *is the required index i.*

Theorem 2. *Protocol 1 gives the index i such that* $x_i + y_i = \overset{min}{_j}(\{x_j + y_j\})$.

Proof. In Step 4 of the *protocol 1*, A gets all the decrypted values $x_j + y_j'$. Which is equal to $x_j + y_j + r$. As the same r is added to all $x_j + y_j$, the index for $min(\pi(\{x_j + y_j\}))$ is same as the index for $min(\pi(\{x_j + y_j'\}))$. Thus, party A can obtain the min index. Party B knows the permutation order. In Step 5, party B gets the original index corresponding to the permuted index, from which B can also obtain the min index.   □

Security analysis of Protocol 1

Security for A: B has the knowledge of only A's encrypted values while B doesn't have access to A's secret key. Hence A's privacy is preserved. *Security for B:* B uses a random value r and adds it to all of its values. A has access to only the random permutation of $\{x_j + y_j'\}$ where only B knows the random permutation π. At the end of the protocol A knows the min index i. Using min index i, A can obtain only y_i' which is $y_i + r$. A can not obtain y_i because r is known only to B. Hence the protocol is secure with respect to both A and B.

Computation and communication analysis: Vaidya and Clifton [17] and Jagannathan and Wright [7] gave a general solution for securely finding the index for minimum sum by using Yao's circuit evaluation protocol [19]. This approach is impractical for large inputs. In our approach the communication complexity is $2n + 2$ values. The computation complexity is n encryptions at both sides and n decryptions at A.

Protocol 2. *Party A has value* **a** *and party B has value* **b** *and they both know the value T. They both wish to find out securely whether* $\mathbf{a} + \mathbf{b} > T$. *The condition here is party A should not know the value* **b** *and B should not know the value* **a**.

1. *B generates a random value* **r**.
2. *A constructs its vectors as* $(\frac{a}{T}, 1)$ *and B constructs its vector as* $(r, r(\frac{b}{T}))$. *Now A invokes the* **secure scalar product protocol**[3] *and gets the scalar product of* $(\frac{a}{T}, 1)(r, r(\frac{b}{T}))^T = r(\frac{a+b}{T})$ *without B knowing the result.*
3. *Now A has the value* $r(\frac{a+b}{T})$ *and B has the value* **r**. *They both run Millionaire protocol to decide whether* $r(\frac{a+b}{T}) > r$
4. *If* $r(\frac{a+b}{T}) > r$ *then they decide that* $(a + b) > T$ *else they decide* $(a + b) \leq T$

The **Protocol 2** uses **secure scalar product** and Cachin's protocol for Yao's **Millionaire Problem** which are proved to be secure. Hence by composition theorem the **Protocol 2** is secure. The communication complexity for **Protocol 2** is $4l$ bits for secure scalar product and $O(l)$ bits for protocol for Yao's Millionaire Problem where l is the number of bits required to represent a number. Hence the total communication complexity is $O(l)$ bits.

5   Overview of BIRCH

In this section we give a brief review of distance metrics for clustering and BIRCH algorithm for clustering. The distance metrics are used for similarity measure for clusters. Given N, $d-$dimensional data points in a cluster: $\{\overrightarrow{X_i}\}$ where $i = 1, 2, \cdots, N$, the centroid $\overrightarrow{X_0}$, radius R and diameter D of the cluster are defined as:

$$\overrightarrow{X_0} = \frac{\sum_{i=1}^{N} \overrightarrow{X_i}}{N}, \quad R = \left(\frac{\sum_{i=1}^{N} \left(\overrightarrow{X_i} - \overrightarrow{X_0} \right)^2}{N} \right)^{\frac{1}{2}} \text{ and } D = \left(\frac{\sum_{i=1}^{N} \sum_{j=1}^{N} \left(\overrightarrow{X_i} - \overrightarrow{X_j} \right)^2}{N(N-1)} \right)^{\frac{1}{2}}.$$

Given the centroids of two clusters: $\overrightarrow{X}_{0_1}$ and $\overrightarrow{X}_{0_2}$, the centroid Euclidean distance D_0 and centroid Manhattan distance D_1 of the two clusters are defined as:

$$D_0 = \left(\left(\overrightarrow{X}_{0_1} - \overrightarrow{X}_{0_2} \right)^2 \right)^{\frac{1}{2}} \text{ and } D_1 = \left| \overrightarrow{X}_{0_1} - \overrightarrow{X}_{0_2} \right| = \sum_{i=1}^{d} \left| \overrightarrow{X}_{0_1}^{(i)} - \overrightarrow{X}_{0_2}^{(i)} \right|$$

Given N_1, d-dimensional data points in a cluster: $\{\overrightarrow{X_i}\}$ where $i = 1, \cdots, N_1$ and N_2, d-dimensional data points in another cluster: $\{\overrightarrow{X_j}\}$ where $j = N_1 + 1, N_1 + 2, \cdots, N_1 + N_2$, the average inter-cluster distance D_2, average intra-cluster distance D_3 of two clusters and variance increase distance D_4 of two clusters are defined as:

$$D_2 = \left(\frac{\sum_{i=1}^{N_1} \sum_{j=N_1+1}^{N_1+N_2} \left(\overrightarrow{X_i} - \overrightarrow{X_j} \right)^2}{N_1 N_2} \right)^{\frac{1}{2}} \tag{1}$$

$$D_3 = \left(\frac{\sum_{i=1}^{N_1+N_2} \sum_{j=1}^{N_1+N_2} \left(\overrightarrow{X_i} - \overrightarrow{X_j} \right)^2}{(N_1 + N_2)(N_1 + N_2 - 1)} \right)^{\frac{1}{2}} \tag{2}$$

$$D_4 = \sum_{k=1}^{N_1+N_2} \left(\overrightarrow{X}_k - \frac{\sum_{l=1}^{N_1+N_2} \overrightarrow{X_l}}{N_1 + N_2} \right)^2 - \sum_{i=1}^{N_1} \left(\overrightarrow{X}_i - \frac{\sum_{l=1}^{N_1} \overrightarrow{X_l}}{N_1} \right)^2$$

$$- \sum_{j=N_1+1}^{N_1+N_2} \left(\overrightarrow{X}_j - \frac{\sum_{l=N_1+1}^{N_1+N_2} \overrightarrow{X_l}}{N_2} \right)^2 \tag{3}$$

The concepts of Clustering Feature and CF Tree are core of the BIRCH's incremental clustering. Here we give brief description of these concepts and For complete information on CF Tree construction and BIRCH algorithm, refer [15]. A clustering feature is a triple summarizing the information that we maintain about a cluster and it is defined as follows:

Definition 2. *Given N d-dimensional data points in a cluster: $\{\overrightarrow{X_i}\}$ where $i = 1, 2, \cdots, N$, the clustering feature (CF) vector of the cluster is defined as a triple: $CF = (N, \overrightarrow{LS}, SS)$ where N is the number of data points in the cluster, $\overrightarrow{LS}$ is the linear sum of the N data points, i.e., $\sum_{i=1}^{N} \overrightarrow{X_i}$ and SS is the square sum of the N data points, ie., $\sum_{i=1}^{N} \overrightarrow{X_i}^2$.*

Theorem 3. *(CF additivity theorem): Assume that $CF_1 = (N_1, \overrightarrow{LS_1}, SS_1)$, and $CF_2 = (N_2, \overrightarrow{LS_2}, SS_2)$ are the CF vectors of two disjoint clusters. Then the CF vector of the cluster that is formed by merging the two disjoint clusters is: $CF_1 + CF_2 = (N_1 + N_2, \overrightarrow{LS_1} + \overrightarrow{LS_2}, SS_1 + SS_2)$.*

From **Definition 2** and **Theorem 3** , the CF vectors of clusters can be stored and calculated incrementally accurately as clusters are formed and merged. Given the CF vectors of clusters , the corresponding $\overrightarrow{X}_0, R, D, D_0, D_1, D_2$ and D_3, as well as the usual quality metrics can all be calculated easily. For example, The radius R of a cluster CF can be calculated as,

$$R = \left(\frac{SS - \frac{1}{N} \left(\overrightarrow{LS}\overrightarrow{LS}^T \right)}{N} \right)^{\frac{1}{2}} \tag{4}$$

The diameter D of the cluster is,

$$D = \left(\frac{2N(SS) - 2\overrightarrow{LS}\overrightarrow{LS}^T}{N(N-1)} \right)^{\frac{1}{2}} \tag{5}$$

The centroid Manhattan distance D_1 for two clusters is calculated as,

$$D_1 = \left| \sum_{i=1}^{d} \frac{1}{N_1} \overrightarrow{LS}_1^{(i)} - \frac{1}{N_2} \overrightarrow{LS}_2^{(i)} \right| \tag{6}$$

The inter-cluster distance D_2 for clusters CF_1 and CF_2 can be calculated as,

$$D_2 = \left(\frac{N_2(SS_1) - 2\overrightarrow{LS}_1 \overrightarrow{LS}_2^T + N_1(SS_2)}{N_1 N_2} \right)^{\frac{1}{2}} \tag{7}$$

The average intra-cluster distance D_3 can be calculated as

$$D_3 = \left(\frac{2(N_1 + N_2)(SS_1 + SS_2) - 2\left(\overrightarrow{LS}_1 \overrightarrow{LS}_1^T + \overrightarrow{LS}_2 \overrightarrow{LS}_2^T\right)}{(N_1 + N_2)(N_1 + N_2 - 1)} \right)^{\frac{1}{2}} \tag{8}$$

The variance increase distance D_4 of two clusters can be calculated as,

$$D_4 = \frac{\overrightarrow{LS}_1 \overrightarrow{LS}_1^T}{N_1} + \frac{\overrightarrow{LS}_2 \overrightarrow{LS}_2^T}{N_2} - \frac{\overrightarrow{LS}_1 \overrightarrow{LS}_1^T + \overrightarrow{LS}_2 \overrightarrow{LS}_2^T}{(N_1 + N_2)^2} \tag{9}$$

where $CF_1 = (N_1, \overrightarrow{LS}_1, SS_1)$ and $CF_2 = (N_2, \overrightarrow{LS}_2, SS_2)$.

Thus, the CF summary is not only efficient because it stores much less than the all the data points in the cluster, but also accurate because it is sufficient for calculating all the measurements that we need for making clustering decisions in BIRCH [15].

Given below is the definition of CF tree and the procedure for inserting an entry into the tree.

Definition 3. *A CF tree is a balanced tree with a branching factor (maximum number of children a node may have) B. Each internal node contains CF triple for each of its children. Each leaf node also represents a cluster and contains a CF entry for each sub cluster in it. A sub cluster in a leaf node must have a diameter no greater than a given threshold value T.*

Given below is an algorithm for inserting an entry into a CF Tree:

1. Identify the appropriate leaf.
2. Modify the leaf.
3. Modify the path to the leaf.
4. A Merge refinement.

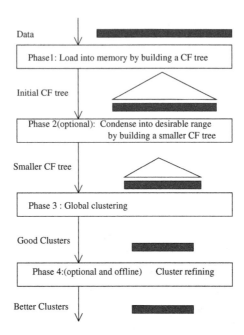

Fig. 1. Overview of BIRCH in single database case

The internal details of the steps of above algorithm can be found in [15]. Figure 1, gives an overview of the BIRCH algorithm in single database case [15].

6   Secure BIRCH Algorithm

Assume that the database DB is vertically partitioned between two parties A and B, where A has database DB_A with d_A attributes and B has database DB_B with d_B attributes.

The problem of clustering the vertically partitioned database is defined as follows:

Definition 4. *Given a vertically partitioned database $DB = DB_A \| DB_B = \{t_{1_A} \| t_{1_B}, t_{2_A} \| t_{2_B}, \cdots, t_{n_A} \| t_{n_B}\}$ of tuples and an integer value k, the clustering problem in vertically partitioned data base is to define a mapping $f : D_A \| D_B \to \{1, 2, \cdots, k\}$ where each $t_{i_A} \| t_{i_B}$ is assigned to one cluster $K_j, 1 \leq j \leq k$. This mapping should be done by both parties, without A knowing DB_B and without B knowing DB_A. cluster K_j, contains precisely those tuples mapped to it; that is, $K_j = \{t_{i_A} \| t_{i_B} \mid f(t_{i_A} \| t_{i_B}) = K_j, 1 \leq i \leq n, \text{ and } t_{i_A} \| t_{i_B} \in DB_A \| DB_B\}$.*

The clustering feature (CF) vector for vertically partitioned database is defined as follows :

Definition 5. *Given N $d-$dimensional points partitioned between two parties A and B where d_A dimensions are at party A and d_B dimensions are at party B and*

$d_A + d_B = d$ are in a cluster : $\{\vec{X}_{i_A}||\vec{X}_{i_B}\}$ where $i = 1, 2, \cdots, N$, the partitioned Clustering Feature (CF) vector of the cluster is defined as a triple: $CF_A||CF_B = (N, \vec{LS}_A||\vec{LS}_B, SS_A + SS_B)$, where N is the number of data points in the cluster, $\vec{LS}_A||\vec{LS}_B$ is the linear sum of the N data points, ie., $\sum_{i=1}^{N}(\vec{X}_{i_A}||\vec{X}_{i_B})$, and $SS_A + SS_B$ is the square sum of the data points, ie., $\sum_{i=1}^{N}(\vec{X}_{i_A}||\vec{X}_{i_B})^2$.

Theorem 4. (CF additivity theorem for partitioned data): Assume that $CF_{1_A}||CF_{1_B} = (N_1, \ \vec{LS}_{1_A}||\vec{LS}_{1_B}, \ SS_{1_A} + SS_{1_B})$ and $CF_{2_A}||CF_{2_B} = (N_2, \ \vec{LS}_{2_A}||\vec{LS}_{2_B}, \ SS_{2_A} + SS_{2_B})$ are the CF vectors of the two disjoint clusters. Then the CF vector of the cluster that is formed by merging the two disjoint clusters is: $CF_1 + CF_2 = (CF_{1_A}||CF_{1_B}) + (CF_{2_A}||CF_{2_B}) = (N_1 + N_2, (\vec{LS}_{1_A} + \vec{LS}_{2_A})||(\vec{LS}_{1_B} + \vec{LS}_{2_B}), (SS_{1_A} + SS_{2_A}) + (SS_{1_B} + SS_{2_B}))$.

Proof.

$$
\begin{aligned}
CF_1 + CF_2 &= CF_{1_A}||CF_{1_B} + CF_{2_A}||CF_{2_B} \\
&= (N_1, \vec{LS}_{1_A}||\vec{LS}_{1_B}, SS_{1_A} + SS_{1_B}) \\
&\quad + (N_2, \vec{LS}_{2_A}||\vec{LS}_{2_B}, SS_{2_A} + SS_{2_B}) \\
&= (N_1 + N_2, (\vec{LS}_{1_A}||\vec{LS}_{1_B}) + (\vec{LS}_{2_A}||\vec{LS}_{2_B}), \\
&\quad (SS_{1_A} + SS_{1_B}) + (SS_{2_A} + SS_{2_B})) \\
&= (N_1 + N_2, (\vec{LS}_{1_A} + \vec{LS}_{2_A})||(\vec{LS}_{1_B} + \vec{LS}_{2_B}), \\
&\quad (SS_{1_A} + SS_{2_A}) + (SS_{1_B} + SS_{2_B}))
\end{aligned}
$$

$\square$

Now we give the distance metrics similar to the metrics (4), (5), (7), (8) and (9) for vertical partitioned data base case.

$$
R = \left(\frac{SS_A - \frac{1}{N}\left(\vec{LS}_A\vec{LS}_A^T\right)}{N} + \frac{SS_B - \frac{1}{N}\left(\vec{LS}_B\vec{LS}_B^T\right)}{N} \right)^{\frac{1}{2}} \tag{10}
$$

$$
D = \left(\frac{2N(SS_A) - 2\left(\vec{LS}_A\vec{LS}_A^T\right)}{N(N-1)} + \frac{2N(SS_B) - 2\left(\vec{LS}_B\vec{LS}_B^T\right)}{N(N-1)} \right)^{\frac{1}{2}} \tag{11}
$$

$$
D_1 = \sum_{i=1}^{d_A} \left| \frac{1}{N_1}\vec{LS}_{1_A}^{(i)} - \frac{1}{N_2}\vec{LS}_{2_A}^{(i)} \right| + \sum_{i=1}^{d_B} \left| \frac{1}{N_1}\vec{LS}_{1_B}^{(i)} - \frac{1}{N_2}\vec{LS}_{2_B}^{(i)} \right| \tag{12}
$$

$$
D_2 = \left(\frac{N_2(SS_{1_A}) - \vec{LS}_{1_A}\vec{LS}_{2_A}^T + N_1(SS_{2_A})}{N_1 N_2} + \right.
$$

$$
\left. \frac{N_2(SS_{1_B}) - \vec{LS}_{1_B}\vec{LS}_{2_B}^T + N_1(SS_{2_B})}{N_1 N_2} \right)^{\frac{1}{2}} \tag{13}
$$

$$D_3 = (\frac{2(N_1+N_2)(SS_{1_A}+SS_{2_A})-2(\overrightarrow{LS}_{1_A}\overrightarrow{LS}_{1_A}^T+\overrightarrow{LS}_{2_A}\overrightarrow{LS}_{2_A}^T)}{(N_1+N_2)(N_1+N_2-1)}+$$

$$\frac{2(N_1+N_2)(SS_{1_B}+SS_{2_B})-2(\overrightarrow{LS}_{1_B}\overrightarrow{LS}_{1_B}^T+\overrightarrow{LS}_{2_B}\overrightarrow{LS}_{2_B}^T)}{(N_1+N_2)(N_1+N_2-1)})^{\frac{1}{2}} \quad (14)$$

$$D_4 = \frac{\overrightarrow{LS}_{1_A}\overrightarrow{LS}_{1_A}^T}{N_1} + \frac{\overrightarrow{LS}_{2_A}\overrightarrow{LS}_{2_A}^T}{N_2} - \frac{\overrightarrow{LS}_{1_A}\overrightarrow{LS}_{1_A}^T+\overrightarrow{LS}_{2_A}\overrightarrow{LS}_{2_A}^T}{(N_1+N_2)^2} +$$

$$\frac{\overrightarrow{LS}_{1_B}\overrightarrow{LS}_{1_B}^T}{N_1} + \frac{\overrightarrow{LS}_{2_B}\overrightarrow{LS}_{2_B}^T}{N_2} - \frac{\overrightarrow{LS}_{1_B}\overrightarrow{LS}_{1_B}^T+\overrightarrow{LS}_{2_B}\overrightarrow{LS}_{2_B}^T}{(N_1+N_2)^2} \quad (15)$$

We use the function $dist^2(CF_{i_A}||CF_{i_B}, CF_{j_A}||CF_{j_B})$ for the metrics (12), (13), (14) to reduce the square root effect.

For example, $dist^2(CF_{i_A}||CF_{i_B}, CF_{j_A}||CF_{j_B})$ for the metric D_2 is, D_2^2. The function $dist^2(CF_{i_A}||CF_{i_B}, CF_{j_A}||CF_{j_B})$ gives the metric in the form of $a+b$ where a can be calculated by A without the knowledge of the data of B and b can be calculated by B without the knowledge of the A's data. They have to share a and b to get the actual distance.

Below we give an algorithm to securely distribute the entries of a leaf node of CF tree.

Algorithm: NodeSplit

Input : Two private vectors of partitioned CFs of size p, $X = \{CF_{1_A}, CF_{2_A}, \cdots, CF_{p_A}\}$ and $Y = \{CF_{1_B}, CF_{2_B}, \cdots, CF_{p_B}\}$ by parties A and B respectively, where $CF_{i_A}||CF_{i_B} = CF_i$

Output: Two sets $node_1$ and $node_2$ of CFs based on minimum distance criteria.

1. Calculate distance for each pair of CFs.
   Get shares of $dist^2(CF_{i_A}||CF_{i_B}, CF_{j_A}||CF_{j_B})$ for $i = 1, 2, \cdots, p$, for $j = 1, 2, \cdots, p$ and $i \neq j$. The shares for all the distance pairs for A is $S_X = \{a_1, a_2, \cdots, a_{((p-1)p)/2}\}$ and the corresponding shares of distances for B is $S_Y = \{b_1, b_2, \cdots, b_{((p-1)p)/2}\}$.

2. Invoke **Protocol 1** with maximum index as the criteria instead of minimum index for the private input S_X from party A and for the private input S_Y from party B to get the index. Let $(CF_{m_A}||CF_{m_B}, CF_{n_A}||CF_{n_B})$ be the pair of partitioned CFs corresponding to the index. $CF_{m_A}||CF_{m_B}$ and $CF_{n_A}||CF_{n_B}$ are the two farthest clusters in the input.

3. For $i = 1, 2, \cdots, p$,

   (a) Get the shares for party A and party B
       for $dist^2(CF_{i_A}||CF_{i_B}, CF_{m_A}||CF_{m_B})$.
       Let the share of party A be a_1 and the share of party B be b_1. (ie., $a_1 + b_1 = dist^2(CF_{i_A}||CF_{i_B}, CF_{m_A}||CF_{m_B})$).

   (b) Get the shares for party A and party B
       for $dist^2(CF_{i_A}||CF_{i_B}, CF_{n_A}||CF_{n_B})$. Let the share for party A be a_2 and the share for party B be b_2.
       (ie., $a_2 + b_2 = dist^2(CF_{i_A}||CF_{i_B}, CF_{n_A}||CF_{n_B})$).

(c) Now A has $S = \{a_1, a_2\}$ and B has $T = \{b_1, b_2\}$ Now invoke **Protocol 1** with private inputs S and T. If the index is 1 put $CF_{i_A}||CF_{i_B}$ in the set $node1$ (ie., put CF_{i_A} in A's $node1$ and CF_{i_B} in B's $node1$) else put $CF_{i_A}||CF_{i_B}$ in $node2$ (ie., put CF_{i_A} in A's $node2$ and CF_{i_B} in B's $node2$).

6.1   Secure CF Tree Insertion

We now give the procedure for how to insert a new Ent securely in the CF tree in the partitioned case. The secure CF Tree insertion procedure is similar to the insertion procedure in single data base case but with invocation of secure protocols. Here the new entry Ent is partitioned into Ent_A and Ent_B where $Ent = Ent_A||Ent_B$ where A has Ent_A and B has Ent_B.

Both the parties learn the tree structure but the entries in the tree will be different for each party. Party A inserts its partitioned share of CF in its tree and at the same time party B inserts its partitioned share of CF in its tree at the corresponding node in its tree. Given below is the algorithm for inserting a new partitioned entry in to the CF tree securely.

1. *Identifying the appropriate leaf :* This step is same as the actual insertion in the tree for single database case. But choosing the closest child node is done as follows : (1) apply $dist^2()$ for $Ent_A||Ent_B$ to the entries of the current node to get the shares of distances for A as $X = \{a_1, a_2, \cdots, a_p\}$ and for B as $Y = \{b_1, b_2, \cdots, b_p\}$, where $\{dist^2(Ent_A||Ent_B, CF_{i_A}||CF_{i_B}) = a_i + b_i\}$ for $i = 1, 2, \cdots, p$ where p is the number of entries in the current node, (2) invoke **Protocol 1** with the input X by A and with the input Y by B to get the index **j** which is the closest child index for the new entry $Ent_A||Ent_B$ in the current node, and (3) both the parties share the index **j** and they descend through the corresponding branch from the current node at their respective trees.

2. *Modifying the leaf :* When the new entry $Ent_A||Ent_B$ reaches the leaf node, it finds the closest leaf entry say $L_{i_A}||L_{i_B}$ by using the same procedure described in the Step 1. The threshold violating condition is checked by the following procedure :

   (a) Let $Linew_A||Linew_B = L_{i_A}||L_{i_B} + Ent_A||Ent_B$. A has $Linew_A$ and B has $Linew_B$

   (b) Calculate D^2 by the formula (11) and let the shares of D^2 for A and B be **a** and **b** respectively.

   (c) Invoke **Protocol 2** with private inputs a and b and the threshold T^2 to check securely whether $a + b$ is greater than T^2 or not. (ie., if $a + b > T^2$ then $D > T$ else $D \leq T$).

   (d) If $D \leq T$, then $L_{i_A}||L_{i_B} \leftarrow Linew_A||Linew_B$. That is A updates L_{i_A} with $Linew_A$ and B updates L_{i_B} with $Linew_B$. If $D > T$, then a new entry for $Ent_A||Ent_B$ is added to the leaf. If there is a space for this new entry, we are done, otherwise we have to split the leaf node. Splitting is done by the algorithm for **NodeSplit** with the shares of leaf entries as inputs.

3. *Modifying the path to the leaf* : After inserting $"Ent_A||Ent''_B$ into a leaf, we must update the CF information for each non leaf entry on the path to the leaf. In absence of split it simply involves adding partitioned CF vector at each party in its tree to reflect the addition of $Ent_A||Ent_B$. If there is a leaf split, we have to insert a new non leaf entry in its parent node. If there is space in the parent node for this newly created leaf, at all higher levels we only need to update the shared CF vectors to reflect the addition of $Ent_A||Ent_B$. That is party A updates its share of CF vectors in its tree and party B updates its share of CF vectors in its tree. If there is no space for the new leaf in its parent, we have to split its parent as we did to split the leaf node and this change should be propagated up to root. If root is split, the tree height increases by one.

4. *A Merging Refinement* : Merging refinement has three main steps,
   (a) Identify node N_t such that the propagation of split of leaf stops.
   (b) Find the two closest entries in N_t as follows:
   Each party calculates its shares of distances for all the pairs of CFs in the node N_t: $\{dist^2(CF_{i_A}||CF_{i_B}, CF_{j_A}||CF_{j_B})\}$ for $i \neq j$. If there are p such pairs, shares of A is $X = \{a_1, a_2, \cdots, a_p\}$ and the shares of B is $Y = \{b_1, b_2, \cdots, b_p\}$ where $a_i + b_i = dist^2()$ for the ith pair. Use **Protocol 1** to find the minimum distance index and let the corresponding pair be $(CF_{m_A}||CF_{m_B}, CF_{n_A}||CF_{n_B})$.
   (c) If the pair $(CF_{m_A}||CF_{m_B}, CF_{n_A}||CF_{n_B})$ is not the pair corresponding to the split, merge them and corresponding child nodes (Each party can merge its share of CF entries in its corresponding tree). If there are more entries in the two child nodes than one page can hold, split the merging result again by using the **NodeSplit** algorithm.

Given below is the secure BIRCH clustering algorithm for vertically partitioned databases.

Algorithm: Secure BIRCH

Phase 1: Agree on the parameters $(\mathcal{B}, T, L)$ where $\mathcal{B}$ is the branching factor, T is the threshold factor and L is the maximum number of leaf entries in a leaf.

Phase 2: Load into each party's memory the CF tree of shared CF's that are formed by using the procedure **secure CF tree insertion** given in Section 6.1.

Phase 3: Condense the CF tree. This phase is same as the phase 2. Each party scans the leaf entries in the initial CF tree to rebuild a smaller CF tree by using the procedure **secure CF tree insertion** given in Section 6.1.

Phase 4: Use hierarchical clustering such as the single link clustering given in section 6.2 for the clusters formed in phase 2 or phase 3.

Phase 5 For each point in the partitioned database calculate the $dist^2()$ to the clusters formed in phase 4. Use **Protocol 1** to find out the minimum distance cluster and label the point with that cluster.

In **phase 4** of the the above algorithm, we can use any secure clustering algorithm such as **Secure Single Link Clustering Algorithm** given in section 6.2 that can work for CFs [15].

6.2   Secure Single Link Clustering

In this subsection we give the details of single link clustering which is used in
phase 4 of the secure BIRCH algorithm. The input to this algorithm is the
shares of CFs by A and by B that are the output of **phase 2** or **phase 3** of the
Secure BIRCH algorithm.

Single link clustering uses threshold graph $G(v)$ [8]. A threshold graph $G(v)$
is defined for each dissimilarity level v by inserting an edge (i, j) between nodes
i and j if object i and j are less dissimilar than v. That is, $(i, j) \in G(v)$ if and
only if $dist(i, j) \leq v$.

Algorithm: Secure Single Link Clustering for vertically partitioned
CF**s.**
Input : Shared CFs from **phase1** or **phase 2** of the secure BIRCH algorithm. If
there are N such shared CFs, $(CF_1, CF_2, \cdots, CF_N)$ where, $CF_i = CF_{i_A}||CF_{i_B}$
then, party A's input is $X = \{CF_{1_A}, \cdots, CF_{N_A}\}$ and party B's input is $Y = \{CF_{1_B}, \cdots, CF_{N_B}\}$.

1. Begin with disjoint clustering implied by threshold graph $G(0)$ which contains no edges. Each party will have $G(0)$ with its share of CFs. That is
   node i of $G(0)$ at A is CF_{i_A} where as node i of $G(0)$ at B is CF_{i_B}. Set $k \leftarrow 1$
2. Form threshold graph $G(k)$ at each site. (Each party knows the graph struc-
   ture of $G(k-1)$ that is each party knows the indices of CFs in each of the
   components of the graph. Each component of the graph $G(k-1)$ is a cluster
   formed at $(k-1)$th iteration.

   Find the components in the graph with distance $\leq k$. This can be done
   securely as follows :
   (a) Take two components of the graph.
   (b) Each party gets its shares of distance from these two components by
       getting the shares of distances between each CF in one component with
       CF in other component. Use $dist^2()$ to get the shares for square of the
       length of the distance and use **Protocol 2** with k^2 as the threshold to
       check if this is the pair with inter cluster distance $\leq k$ then list these
       two components as a single component.
   (c) Each party on its own checks whether the number of components in $G(k)$
       is less than the number of clusters in the current clustering. If it is true,
       re define the current clustering by naming each component of $G(k)$ as a
       cluster.
3. If $G(k)$ consists of a single connected graph, stop. Else set $k \leftarrow k+1$ and go
   to Step 2.

Communication and computation analysis of secure BIRCH algorithm
Communication complexity: In **phase 2** of the secure Birch algorithm, **Protocol
1** is executed $n \log_B K$ times, **Protocol 2** is executed n times and the procedure
NodeSplit is executed K times. Therefore the total communication complexity
for **phase 2** is $(O(nB \log_B K) + O(n) + O(KL^2))$ values. **Phase 4** requires K^2
executions of **Protocol 2**. Therefore the communication complexity for this phase

is $O(K^2)$ values. **Phase 5** requires n executions of **Protocol 1**. Therefore the communication complexity for this phase is $O(ng)$ values. In the above discussion n is the total number of records in the database, $\mathcal{B}$ is the branching factor of the CF tree, L is the number of leaf entries in a leaf node, K is the total number of leaf nodes in the CF tree and g is the total number of global clusters formed in **phase 4**. The total communication complexity for secure BIRCH algorithm is $O(n\mathcal{B}\log_{\mathcal{B}} K) + O(KL^2) + O(K^2) + O(ng)$ values. In reality the values for $\mathcal{B}, K, L, g$ are very small compared to the value for n.

Computation complexity: The major computation overhead is the computation of the encryption. Now we will see the total number of encryptions that are required for this algorithm. In **phase 2** each party does $n\log_{\mathcal{B}} K + 2n + 2KL$ encryptions, in **phase 4**, each party does $2K^2$ encryptions and in *phase 5* each party does ng encryptions. In total each party does $n\log_{\mathcal{B}} K + n(g+2) + 2KL + 2K^2$ encryptions.

Security analysis: In secure BIRCH algorithm we use **Protocols 1 and 2**. At any point of time, each party knows the min index or checks the threshold nothing more than that by using those two protocols. The **Protocols 1 and 2** are proved to be secure. Therefore by composition theorem [9] the proposed BIRCH algorithm is secure.

7   Conclusion and Future Work

While most existing privacy preserving algorithms work only on *k-means* algorithm which is suitable only for small data, our technique is applicable for large dataset. In *k-means*, for each iteration the database is scanned at least once. In entire BIRCH clustering the database is scanned at most two times which is less I/O. In our future work we wish to look into how this protocol can be extended to arbitrarily partitioned data. Also we wish to look into privacy preserving BIRCH or any clustering method for large databases either in horizontally or arbitrarily partitioned data.

References

1. Dakshi Agrawal, Charu C. Aggarwal. On the Design and Quantification of Privacy Preserving Data Mining Algorithms. In *Proceedings of the Twentieth ACM SIGACT - SIGMOD - SIGART Symposium on Principles of Database Systems*, pp. 247–255, Santa Barbara, CA, May 21-23 2001. ACM.
2. R. Agrawal and R. Srikant. Privacy preserving data mining. In *Proceedings of the 2000 ACM SIGMOD Conference on Management of Data*, Dallas, TX, May 14-19, 2000. ACM.
3. Bart Goethals and Sven Laur and Helger Lipmaa and Taneli Mielikainen. On private scalar product computation for privacy-preserving data mining. In *Proceedings of the 7th Annual International Conference in Information Security and Cryptology (ICISC 2004)*, December 2-3, 2004.

4. C. Cachin. Efficient private bidding and auctions with an oblivious third party. In*Proceedings of 6th ACM Computer and communications security* , pages 120-127. SIGSAC, ACM Press, 1999.

5. Ivan Damgard and Mads Jurik. A Generalisation, a Simplification and Some Applications of Paillier's Probabilistic Public-Key System. In*Proceedings of Public Key Cryptography 2001* , volume 1992 of Lecture Notes in Computer Science, pages 119-136, Cheju Island, Korea, 13-15 February 2001. Springer-Verlag.

6. Geetha Jagannathan, Krishnan Pillaipakkamnatt and Rebecca N. Wright. A New Privacy-Preserving Distributed k-Clustering Algorithm. In*Proceedings of the 2006 SIAM International Conference on Data Mining (SDM)* , 2006.

7. Geetha Jagannathan and Rebecca N. Wright. Privacy-preserving distributed k-means clustering over arbitrarily partitioned data. In*Proceedings of the 11th ACM SIGKDD International Conference on Knowledge Discovery and Data Mining, 2005* , Chicago, Illinois, USA., August 21-24 2005. ACM.

8. Anil K. Jain and Richard C. Dubes. Algorithms for Clustering Data. Chapter 3. Prentice-Hall Inc, 1988.

9. Yehuda Lindell and Benny Pinkas. Privacy preserving data mining. In*Proceedings of Advances in Cryptology - CRYPTO 2000* , pages 36-54. Springer-Verlag. Aug. 20-24 2000.

10. Ron Ben Natan. Implementing Database Security and Auditing, chapter 11. ELSEVIER, 2005.

11. S. Oliveira and O.R. Zaiane. Privacy preserving clustering by data transformation. In*Proceedings of the 18th Brazilian Symposium on Databases* ,pages 304-318, 2003.

12. Pascal Paillier. Public-key Cryptosystems Based on Composite Degree Residuosity Classes. In*Proceedings of Advances in Cryptology - EUROCRYPT'99* , volume 1592 of Lecture Notes in Computer Science, pages 223-238, Prague, Czeck Republic, 2-6 May 1999. Springer-Verlag.

13. R. Rivest, L. Adleman, and M. Dertouzos. On data banks and privacy homomorphisms. In*Foundations of Secure Computation* , pages 169-178. Academic Press, 1978.

14. Somesh Jha, Luis Kruger and Patrick McDaniel. Privacy Preserving Clustering. In*Proceedings of ESORICS 2005* , volume 3679 of Lecture Notes in Computer Science, pages 397-417, Milan, Italy, September 2005.

15. Tian Zhang, Raghu Ramakrishnan and Miron Livny. BIRCH: An efficient Data Clustering Method of Very Large Databases. In *Proceedings of the ACM SIGMOD Conference on Management of Data* , pages 103-114, Montreal, Canada, June 1996.

16. Jaideep Vaidya and Chris Clifton. Privacy preserving association rule mining in vertically partitioned data. In*Proceedings of the 8th ACM SIGKDD International Conference on Knowledge Discovery and Data Mining* , pages 639-644, Edmonton, Alberta, Canada, July 23-26 2002. ACM.

17. Jaideep Vaidya and Chris Clifton. Privacy-preserving k-means clustering over vertically partitioned data. In*Proceedings of the 9th ACM SIGKDD International Conference on knowledge Discovery and Data Mining* , Washington, DC, USA, August 24-27 2003. ACM.

18. A. C. Yao. Protocols for secure computation. In*Proceedings of 23rd IEEE Symposium on Foundations of Computer Science* , pages 160-164. IEEE Computer Society Press, 1982.

19. A. C. Yao. How to generate and exchange secrets. In*Proceedings of the 27th IEEE Symp. on Foundations of Computer Science* , pages 162-167, Toronto, Ontario, Canada, October 27 - 29, 1986.

Conflict of Interest in the Administrative Role Graph Model

Yunyu Song and Sylvia L. Osborn

Dept. of Computer Science
The University of Western Ontario
London, ON, Canada N6A 5B7
ysong7@csd.uwo.ca, sylvia@csd.uwo.ca

Abstract. The original role graph model for role-based access control assumed a centralized administrative model. Conflict of interest for the centralized model was previously discussed by Nyanchama and Osborn. More recently, a decentralized administrative model for role graphs has been introduced by Wang and Osborn. This paper investigates how considerations of conflict of interest interact with the decentralized administrative model, and the resulting impact on role graph operations.

Keywords: role-based access control, access control administration, conflict of interest.

1 Introduction

Role-based access control (RBAC) has been discussed since the mid 1990s [4,2,7]. There is now an ANSI standard for RBAC [1]. The role graph model [5] is one of the prominent RBAC models. In the role graph model there are three distinct entities: users, roles and privileges which are viewed as forming three planes. A group is a set of users who need to be considered as a unit, e.g. a department or a committee.. The user/group plane is where user and group subset relationships are modeled [6]. The role hierarchy or role graph is given on the role plane. Each node of the role graph represents a role, r, which consists of a name, *rname*, and set of privileges, *rpset*. The edges show the is junior relationship: when $r_1.rpset \subset r_2.rpset$, we say r_1 *is-junior* to r_2. The presence of an edge also indicates that all the privileges of the junior role are inherited by the senior role. Each role has *direct* privileges, which are the privileges directly assigned to the role, and *effective* privileges, which are the union of the direct privileges and the privileges inherited from the junior roles. We have given algorithms for operations on the role graph such as role addition and deletion [5]. Unlike the NIST or Sandhu models, our role graph algorithms add an edge from role r_i to r_j if the privilege set of r_i becomes a proper subset of the privilege set of r_j, say because of a privilege addition. All of the algorithms on role graphs must restore the *Role Graph Properties*, which are:

1. There is a single MaxRole, which inherits the privileges of all the roles in the role graph.

W. Jonker and M. Petkovic (Eds.): SDM 2006, LNCS 4165, pp. 100–114, 2006.

2. There is a single MinRole, which represents the minimum set of privileges available to the roles in the system. It can have an empty privilege set.
3. The role graph is acyclic.
4. For any two roles, r_i and r_j, in the graph, if $r_i.rpset \subset r_j.rpset$ then there must be a path from r_i to r_j.

We display a role graph with MaxRole at the top, MinRole at the bottom, and redundant edges removed. Privileges are modeled as a pair (x, m) where x refers to an object, and m is an access mode for object x. Implications can exist among privileges [3]. Figure 1 shows a role graph.

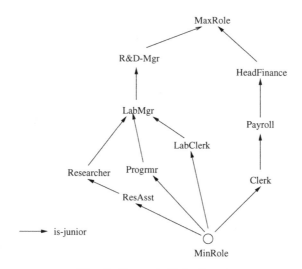

Fig. 1. Example Role Graph

1.1   Conflict of Interest in the Centralized Role Graph Model

In discussing access control, an important aspect is defining conflict of interest or separation of duty [9,2,8]. Conflict of interest is an inherent part of the ANSI RBAC standard [1]. In [5], several types of separation of duty (SOD) constraints, also called conflict of interest constraints, are identified with respect to the role graph model. They are: static SOD, dynamic SOD, user-role assignment conflict, and object-based SOD. The main conflicts are role-role conflicts and privilege-privilege conflicts. The algorithms given in [5] take these conflicts into account, assuming a centralized administration paradigm for the role graph.

In [5], it was observed that a role-role conflict (denoted by $r_i <<>> r_j$) is used to model static separation of duty, in that no user should be assigned to both roles. Privilege-privilege conflict (denoted $p_i <> p_j$), on the other hand, means that the two conflicting privileges should never be assigned to a single user. This has the implication that if two such privileges should appear in the same role, this role should not be assigned to any user. Since privileges are inherited in the role graph from junior to senior roles, all privileges are inherited by MaxRole. This gave the:

Privilege Conflict of Interest Constraint: No role (except MaxRole) may contain two privileges which have been declared to conflict.

There is a relationship between role-role conflicts and privilege-privilege conflicts. Indeed, privilege-privilege conflicts are a finer grained expression of the security policy. If two roles are defined to conflict, without any other information, we must assume that all the privileges of one of the roles are a problem if assigned to a user who can activate the other conflicting role. If this causes a problem, then the design of the roles should be modified so that a minimal set of privileges is present in roles declared to conflict. As noted in [5], if two roles are declared to conflict, then a user authorized to one of the roles must not be authorized to any of the privileges of the other role. The following theorem was proved, which we will call here the

Role Conflict of Interest Constraint: Conflicting roles must have no common seniors other than MaxRole.

The final constraint was:

User-Role Conflict of Interest Constraint: No user should be authorized to two roles which have been declared to conflict.

As just noted, if role-role conflict is to be used, then roles with the minimum conflicting privileges should be the ones declared to be in conflict, as all the seniors of one role will also be in conflict with the other and all of its seniors. If conflicting privileges are used, and, say p_i and p_j are assigned to roles r_1 and r_2 respectively, then r_1 and r_2 cannot be assigned to the same user.

1.2   Decentralized Administration in the Role Graph Model

A decentralized administrative model for role graphs has been proposed in [12]. The most important concept in the administrative role graph model (ARGM) is the administrative domain. An *administrative domain* is a set of roles that contains a top-most role, d, called the *domain identifier* or *domainID*, and all roles in the role graph, s, such that s is-junior d, except MinRole [12]. The domainID plays the rôle of MaxRole in a simple role graph, in that it is used to collect all the privileges that will be in any of the roles in the domain. A domain administrator can create arbitrary new roles within a domain using only the privileges present in the domainID. They cannot introduce new privileges to the domain; this is done by an administrator in a surrounding domain adding the new privileges to the domainID. In this way, domain administrators cannot create roles where edges must be added (in restoring role graph properties) going outside of the domain, which would possibly alter roles in another domain not under the control of this administrator.

An example role graph with administrative domains is given in Figure 2. In it, the domainIDs are R&D-Mgr, LabMgr, HeadFinance, R&DAdmin and MaxRole. The domain containing the whole graph, called the default domain, contains MinRole and MaxRole, and is administered by the highest administrative role, which we assume is the system security officer (SSO). Note that there is a many-to-many relationship between administrative roles and administrative domains. Administrative roles are treated as part of the role graph.

Administrative privileges include adding/deleting roles, adding/deleting edges, adding/deleting privileges, and adding/deleting users[12]. All but the last two dealing with user-role assignment can potentially alter the role graph. It is possible that administrative roles have only a subset of the administrative privileges governing an administrative domain; as we see in the example, LabHR can have the privileges governing user-role assignments, whereas LabRoles can deal with the role hierarchy and assignment of privileges. Also, by the inheritance (is-junior) edges shown in this example, SSO has no application privileges in the R&D domain nor in the Finance domain. In this example, only the SSO can alter the privileges in FinAdmin, MaxRole and MinRole, since they are all in the default domain. The design of the required administrative roles is ultimately under the control of the SSO, but the SSO can also design a situation where the control of domains and their structure is decentralized to subordinate administrative roles.

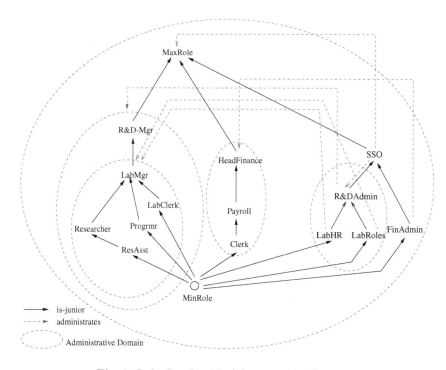

Fig. 2. Role Graph with Administrative Domains

With administrative domains added into the role graph model, dealing with conflicts must be revisited. In this paper, we will discuss how conflict of interest should be handled in the ARGM. Operations on administrative domains may also affect the conflicts, so we will also provide solutions for this.

The paper proceeds as follows: Section 2 discusses conflicts in a general way with respect to the administrative role graph model. Section 3 looks at changes required to the role graph algorithms. Section 4 considers operations on administrative domains and how they need to be modified to deal with conflict of interest constraints. Section 5 considers administration of constraints. Conclusions and suggestions for future work are found in Section 6.

2   Conflicts in the ARGM

In the ARGM, static separation of duty is modeled as a role-role conflict, privilege-privilege conflict or static user-role assignment conflict. Dynamic separation of duty is modeled by a dynamic user-role activation, and object-based separation of duty is modeled as a dynamic role-privilege assignment conflict [5]. Dynamic conflicts occur at run time, when there is a notion of sessions or workflow; this is beyond the scope of this paper. In the remainder of the paper, we will focus on design time conflicts, specifically role-role conflicts and privilege-privilege conflicts; since they are at design time, they represent static SOD.

In order to enforce declared conflicts, we need to consider which administrator controls the operations such as adding an edge, user-role assignment, etc. We also need to consider the relationship between administrative domains and conflict of interest. There are three different cases to consider for conflicting roles or privileges in the administrative role graph model:

1. The conflicting roles or privileges are in the same administrative domain. The local administrator can manage these conflicts.
2. The conflicting roles or privileges are in different administrative domains and their only common senior is MaxRole. The SSO must handle this conflict.
3. The conflicting roles or privileges are in different administrative domains which have common seniors besides MaxRole. Any higher level administrator who has administrative rights on all the domains in question can control these conflicts.

Any algorithms for operations on roles and privileges must check for and enforce the conflicts in all the situations above. With administrative domains in the role graph model, the constraints defined in [5] concerning conflict of interest need to be modified. They are all based on the premise that if a role r contains privileges that conflict, then r should not be assigned to a user. In the original formulation, if there are any conflicts, MaxRole would inherit conflicting privileges as it is senior to all roles in the role graph, and thus inherits conflicting privileges either from privilege-privilege conflicts or role-role conflicts. In the ARGM, domainIDs play the rôle of MaxRole within their domain, i.e. they collect privileges which are inherited from the junior roles in their domain, and really do not need to be assigned to a user. If there are any role-role or privilege-privilege conflicts within a domain, then the domainID will not be assignable to any users.

Based on this discussion, the constraints from [5] need to be modified; we restate them here with the necessary modifications in bold:

Privilege Conflict of Interest Constraint: No role (except MaxRole **and other domain identifiers**) may contain two privileges which have been defined to conflict.

Role Conflict of Interest Constraint: Conflicting roles must not have common seniors **except domain identifiers and** MaxRole.

User-Role Conflict of Interest Constraint: (This is the same as in [5].) No user should be authorized to two roles which have been declared to conflict.

3 Conflicts Arising from Role Graph Operations

An administrator of an administrative domain has the authority to perform operations on roles and privileges within his/her controlled domain. In this section, we will discuss how conflicts arise in performing role addition/deletion and privilege addition/deletion.

3.1 Role Addition

There are two algorithms given in [5] for role addition. The first algorithm takes as input the role graph, a new role with its direct privileges, its proposed immediate junior and senior roles and the set of privilege conflicts. The second algorithm takes the role graph, the effective privileges of the new role and the privilege conflicts as input; the algorithm determines the new role's immediate seniors and juniors. In both cases the role graph properties are restored (which means that edges may be added, and direct and effective privileges may be adjusted; after this, redundant edges are removed, which means that proposed immediate seniors and juniors may no longer be adjacent to the new role). In all the algorithms, if any properties would be violated, such as acyclicity or one of the conflict of interest properties, the algorithm aborts and no change is made to the role graph.

In Figure 3, conflicts Researcher <<>> Progrmr and LabClerk<<>> Head-Finance have been defined. The first conflict may arise because of the employment contract; the latter because the LabClerk prepares salary, expense forms, etc. which the HeadFinance role must approve. Figure 3 shows that role ProjMgr can be added into the administrative domain whose domainID is LabMgr between roles Researcher and LabMgr by someone in the LabRoles role (or by someone assigned to R&DAdmin or SSO). This operation follows the role conflict constraints and is permitted. Suppose R&DAdmin tries to add role ResSupervisor between roles LabMgr and R&D-Mgr. Roles R&D-Mgr and LabMgr are both domain identifiers; they can contain conflicting privileges. However, ResSupervisor which is not a domain identifier will inherit conflicting privileges from roles Researcher and Progrmr. This is not allowed, so this operation is aborted.

3.2 Role Deletion

Role deletion is another operation that may affect conflict of interest defined in the administrative domains. In the original role graph model, roles can be deleted with propagation or without propagation. As well, the rules defined in

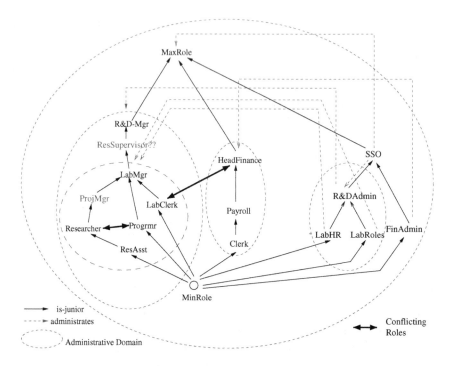

Fig. 3. Adding roles ResSupervisor and ProjMgr to the role graph

[11] still remain: if the role is a domain identifier, the deletion of the role is not allowed. A higher level administrator has to delete the domain first. For role deletion with propagation, the algorithm deletes the direct privileges of this role along the path of its senior roles until it reaches the domainID. For role deletion without propagation, the privileges of this role are passed to its immediate senior roles. If this role is defined to have a conflict with other roles, the algorithm will initiate a user dialog to let the domain administrator decide whether to keep the constraint or not. We take Figure 3 as an example to see what will happen if role Researcher is deleted from the role graph. If the operation is role deletion with propagation, the direct privileges of role Researcher will be removed from ProjMgr (its immediate senior) and remain in LabMgr which is the domainID. If the administrator performs the deletion without propagation, the direct privileges of role Researcher will remain in role ProjMgr, now as direct privileges rather than inherited privileges. The conflict between Researcher and Progrmr no longer exists; however the administrator can decide if the privilege conflicts still exist between their privileges.

3.3   Privilege Administration

Privilege-privilege conflicts can exist within the same domain or across different domains. We must emphasize that the local administrator is allowed to add the privileges which are contained in the domainID to a role within the domain. Only

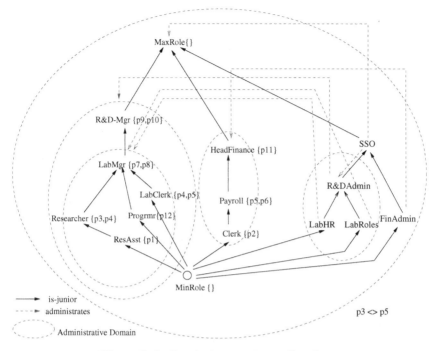

Fig. 4. Role Graph showing Direct Privileges

the administrator of a surrounding domain can add or delete the privileges in a domainID. Figure 4 shows the example with some direct privileges displayed, and with a privilege-privilege conflict between $p3$ and $p5$. There are several situations where privilege-privilege conflict needs to be checked by the algorithms such as role addition, privilege addition etc. We examine the cases here using the example.

- Adding a new role: suppose the administrator of domain LabMgr creates a new role ProjMgr which contains privilege $p3$ and $p5$ as its direct privileges. Suppose $p3$ is (equipment, order) and $p5$ is (equipment, approve), and they have been declared to conflict. The proposed role contains conflicting privileges, so the operation has to be aborted.
- Adding a privilege to an existing role: suppose an administrator of the domain with ID LabMgr tries to add privilege $p5$ to role Researcher. Since Researcher contains $p3$ which conflicts with $p5$, the operation is aborted.
- Adding an edge between two roles: suppose, the administrator of the domain with ID LabMgr tries to add an edge between ResAsst and LabClerk. There are no conflicts between them and no roles inherit conflicting privileges as a result. The operation is successful.
- Deleting an existing privilege from a role may change the conflict of interest defined in the domain. There are two cases: deletion with propagation and deletion without propagation. For example, suppose the local administrator of the domain with ID LabMgr deletes privilege $p3$ from role Researcher without propagation. Privilege $p3$ will remain in the senior role LabMgr since it is

a domainID, and only the administrator of a surrounding domain can delete privileges from domainIDs. The algorithm will prompt the administrator to decide if privilege $p3$ still conflicts with privilege $p5$.

The basic role graph algorithms have thus been modified to work with administrative domains and conflicts. Details can be found in [10].

4   Conflicts and Operations on Administrative Domains

In [12], the authors presented several new operations to administer administrative domains. In order to maintain separation of duty in the administrative role graph model, we need to consider these operations as well. These operations include domain creation, domain deletion, domain modification, splitting a domain, merging domains and testing for the overlap of two domains. We will discuss domain creation and domain deletion in this section.

4.1   Creating a Domain

Every role in the administrative role graph model belongs to at least one domain; the administrator who controls this domain or any surrounding domain has the right to define separation of duty constraints in this domain. When creating an administrative domain, domain overlapping must be checked [12]. Domain creation may cause a change with respect to what conflicts are allowed. The conflicting roles originally in one domain may sometimes be split into two different domains. However, creating a new domain will not lead to new conflicts.

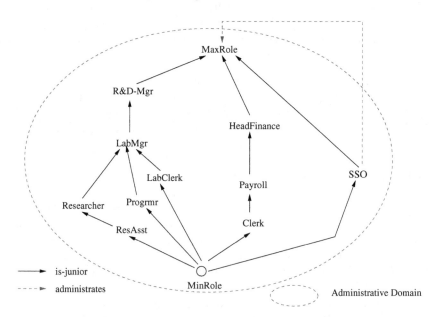

Fig. 5. Original Role Graph

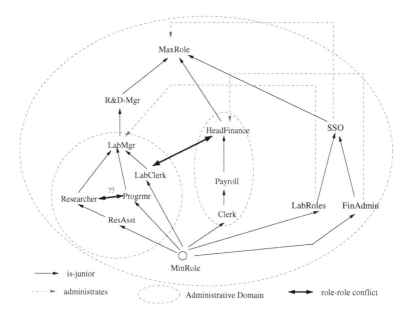

Fig. 6. Role Graph with domains LabMgr and HeadFinance created

Figure 5 shows the original role graph with only the default administrative domain controlled by the SSO. The SSO would like to define LabClerk and HeadFinance to be conflicting roles. Their only common senior role is MaxRole which satisfies the constraints for conflicting roles in the role graph, so this operation is successful. When the SSO wants to define conflicting roles between Researcher and Progrmr, the operation is aborted since their common senior roles are LabMgr, R&D-Mgr and MaxRole, and LabMgr and R&D-Mgr are not domainIDs, which would violate the Role Conflict of Interest Constraint. After the domain for LabMgr has been created, as shown in Figure 6, the conflict between Researcher and Progrmr can still not be created since R&DMgr is not a domainID. Finally, when the domain is created with ID R&DMgr, as shown previously in Figures 2 or 3, this conflict can be created since all the common seniors of Researcher and Progrmr are now domainIDs or MaxRole. The conflicting roles LabClerk and HeadFinance defined by the SSO are now in two different domains; the conflict still exists and is controlled by an administrator higher than LabMgr and HeadFinance (SSO in this case).

4.2   Deleting a Domain

Deleting a domain involves removing the domain but not any of the roles contained in the domain. If we delete a domain D but try to retain a role-role conflict which has domain D's domainID as a common senior of the two roles in conflict, such a domain deletion must be rejected. Thus, going back to Figure 3, deleting the domain for HeadFinance would be allowed with the role-role conflicts defined, but deleting either R&DMrg or LabMgr domains would be rejected. If

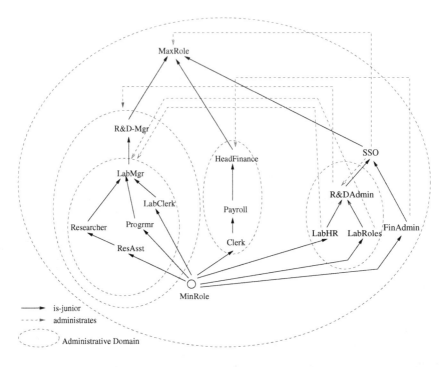

Fig. 7. After creating domain R&D-Mgr

we delete both domains LabMgr and R&D-Mgr at the same time, the operation will be successful. An alternative is to delete the conflict between Researcher and Progrmr first.

4.3 Other Operations on Administrative Domains

Other operations on administrative domains, defined in [11], are splitting of a domain, and merging two domains. Splitting a domain makes other roles become domainIDs; it cannot create new problems with respect to existing conflicts. Merging domains involves constructing a new domainID for the two domains which will be the domain identifier of the new domain. The operation for merging two domains includes deleting the old domains and creating a new domain. We can follow the rules defined for creating and deleting domains to enforce the separation of duty in the domains.

The algorithm to remove a domain is given in [10]. Since domain creations does not introduce new conflicts, a revised algorithm is not needed.

5   Administration of Constraints

Since we have introduced conflict of interest constraints into the administrative role graph model, we need to discuss operations on constraints. These operations

Algorithm DefinePrivilegeConstraint(**RG**, Privilege P1, Privilege P2)
    input: a role graph **RG**, Privilege P1 and P2 (P1 $\neq$ P2)
    output: true if successful, false otherwise
    Begin:
        ConstrainPairList PConstraintList
            $\longleftarrow$ get the privilege constraintList of the role graph
        ConstraintPair pconstraint
            $\longleftarrow$ create new privilege constraint with P1 and P2
        if find pconstraint in PConstrainList
            Display "the constraint is already in the constraintList"
            return false
        v1 $\longleftarrow$ get all the roles in RG which contain privilege P1
        v2 $\longleftarrow$ get all the roles in RG which contain privilege P2
        v $\longleftarrow$ get the common roles in v1 and v2
        for every role r_i in v
            if r_i is not a DomainID
                Display "conflicting privileges are together in non-DomainID"
                return false
        add pconstraint to PConstraintList
        return true
    End

Fig. 8. Algorithm to Define Privilege-privilege Constraint

include defining and removing a constraint. The constraints are modeled as lists of pairs; one contains privilege-privilege constraints and the other stores role-role constraints. Administrators who have control over an administrative domain can perform the operations on constraints within that domain.

When a role-role conflict is introduced, say $r_1 <<>> r_2$, we assume that all the privileges of r_1 and r_2 conflict. This has two implications: first that we need to add derived privilege-privilege conflicts between all the privileges of r_1 and r_2. The second is more subtle. If, for example, r_1's privileges are $\{p_1, p_2\}$ and r_2's are $\{p_3, p_4\}$, we need to add derived privilege-privilege conflicts $p_1 <> p_3, p1 <> p_4$, etc. Suppose somewhere in the graph there is a role r with privilege set $\{p_1, p_3\}$. All of our algorithms abort if the new thing being done to the graph creates a situation which would not be allowed with respect to the existing graph. Since adding this role-role conflict makes another role violate the Privilege Conflict of Interest Constraint, this new operation must be rejected. This logic is found in the algorithm in Figure 9, which also shows the derived privilege-privilege conflicts being constructed.

To enforce the Privilege Conflict of Interest Constraint, the algorithm for defining a privilege-privilege constraint checks if two privileges which will be defined as conflicting privileges exist in the same roles other than MaxRole or other Domain identifiers. The algorithm to remove a privilege-privilege constraint removes the constraint from the list. The algorithm for defining a role-role constraint is based on the Role Conflict of Interest Constraint. It uses a breadth first search to generate a senior role list of the given two roles. The common senior roles of the two role lists are generated next. The algorithm checks if

Algorithm DefineRoleConstraint (RG, Role r1, Role r2)
   input: a role graph **RG**, Role r1 and r2 (r1 $\neq$ r2)
   output: true if successful, false otherwise
   Begin:
        effr1 $\longleftarrow$ get all effective privileges of r1
        effr2 $\longleftarrow$ get all effective privileges of r2
        seniorr1 $\longleftarrow$ get all senior roles of r1
        seniorr2 $\longleftarrow$ get all senior roles of r2
        commonsenior $\longleftarrow$ take intersection of seniorr1 and seniorr2
        for every r_i in commonsenior
           if r_i is not a DomainID
               Display "r_i, not a domainID, contains conflicting privileges"
               return false
       /*check if other roles become invalid because of derived
          privilege constraints*/
        for every p_i in effr1
           for every p_j in effr2
               for every r_i in R, not equal to r_1 or r_2
                  if both p_i and p_j are in r_i
                     Display "conflicting privileges are in role r_i"
                     return false
        add r1 <<>> r2 to role constraintList of the role graph
        for every p_i in effr1
           for every p_j in effr2
               add p_i <> p_j to the derived privilege conflicts list
        return true
   End

Fig. 9. Algorithm Define Role-role Constraint

every role in the common senior role list is a domain identifier. If not, the operation is aborted and an error message is returned. The algorithm to remove a role-role constraint removes the constraint of the two given roles in the role-role constraint list. Since the role-role constraint between the two roles no longer exists, the privilege-privilege constraints derived by the role-role constraint need to be removed from the privilege-privilege constraint list of the role graph. The algorithms for defining/removing a role-role constraints and adding a privilege-privilege constraint are given in Figures 8 to 10. Removing a privilege-privilege constraint is very straightforward and can be found in [10].

6   Conclusions

In this paper we have added conflict of interest into the administrative role graph model. The relationship between conflict of interest and administrative domains has been explored. We have discussed role-role conflict, and privilege-privilege conflict in detail. We discussed revised algorithms for role addition, role deletion, privilege addition and privilege deletion that take into account the above conflicts. Operations on administrative domains such as administrative domain

Algorithm removeRoleConstraint (RG, Role r1, Role r2)
   input: a role graph **RG**, Role r1 and r2 (r1 $\neq$ r2)
   output: true if successful, false otherwise
   Begin:
         ConstraintPairList RConstraintList
            $\longleftarrow$ get the Role constraintList of the role graph
         ConstraintPairList PConstraintList
            $\longleftarrow$ get the Privilege constraintList of the role graph
         if constraint r1 $<<>>$ r2 is not in RConstraintList
            Display message that no such constraint in the role constraintlist
            return false
         else
            /* remove derived privilege-privilege Constraints caused by r1 $<<>>$ r2
            effr1 $\longleftarrow$ get all effective privileges of r1
            effr2 $\longleftarrow$ get all effective privileges of r2
            for every p_i in effr1
               for every p_j in effr2
                  update derived Privilege Constraint p_i $<>$ p_j
            /*update Role ConstraintList*/
            remove role constraint r1 $<<>>$ r2 from role ConstraintList
            return true
   End

Fig. 10. Algorithm Remove Role-role Constraint

creation and deletion which involve the conflicts have been discussed. Algorithms for dealing with constraints directly have been given. These, and the other revised algorithms mentioned, which appear in [10], all run in time polynomial in the number of roles, number of privileges and number of constraints. Future work would include adding more constraint types.

References

1. American National Standards Institute, Inc. *Role-Based Access Control.* ANSI INCITS 359-2004. Approved Feb. 3, 2004.
2. D. Ferraiolo, J. Cugini, and D. Kuhn. Role-based access control (RBAC): Features and motivations. In *Proceedings 11th Annual Computer Security Applications Conference*, 1995.
3. C. M. Ionita and S. L. Osborn. Privilege administration for the role graph model. In *Research Directions in Data and Applications Security*, pages 15–25. Kluwer Academic Publishers, 2003.
4. M. Nyanchama and S. L. Osborn. Access rights administration in role-based security systems. In J. Biskup, M. Morgenstern, and C. E. Landwehr, editors, *Database Security, VIII, Status and Prospects WG11.3 Working Conference on Database Security*, pages 37–56. North-Holland, 1994.
5. M. Nyanchama and S. L. Osborn. The role graph model and conflict of interest. *ACM TISSEC*, 2(1):3–33, 1999.
6. S. Osborn and Y. Guo. Modeling users in role-based access control. In *Fifth ACM RBAC Workshop*, pages 31–38, Berlin, Germany, July 2000.

7. R. Sandhu, E. Coyne, H. Feinstein, and C. Youman. Role-based access control models. *IEEE Computer*, 29:38–47, Feb. 1996.

8. R. S. Sandhu. Transaction control expressions for separation of duties. In *Proceedings of 4th Annual Computer Security Application Conference*, pages 282–286, Orlando, FL, December 1988.

9. R. Simon and M. Zurko. Separation of duty in role-based environments. In *Proceedings of 10th IEEE Computer Security Foundations Wo rkshop*, pages 183–194, Rockport, Mass., June 1997.

10. Y. Song. Conflict of interest in the administrative role graph model. Master's thesis, Dept. of Computer Science, The University of Western Ontario, Apr. 2006.

11. H. Wang. Role graph administration in an enterprise environment. Master's thesis, Dept. of Computer Science, The University of Western Ontario, 2003.

12. H. Wang and S. Osborn. An administrative model for role graphs. In *Data and Applications Security XVII, Status and Prospects. De Capitani di Vimercati, S, I. Ray and I. Ray, eds.* Estes Park, Colorado, Kluwer, pages 302–315, 2004.

Two Phase Filtering for XML Access Control

Changwoo Byun and Seog Park

Department of Computer Science, Sogang University,
Seoul, 121-742, South Korea
{chang, spark}@dblab.sogang.ac.kr

Abstract. We propose two phase filtering scheme to develop an efficient mechanism for XML databases to control query-based access. An access control environment for XML documents and some techniques to deal with fine-grained authorization priorities and conflict resolution issues are proposed. Despite this, relatively little work has been done to enforce access controls particularly for XML databases in the case of query-based access. The basic idea utilized is that a user query interaction with only necessary access control rules is modified to an alternative form which is guaranteed to have no access violations using tree-awareness metadata of XML schemas and set operations supported by XPath 2.0. The scheme can be applied to any XML database management system and has several advantages such as small execution time overhead, fine-grained controls, and safe and correct query modification. The experimental results clearly demonstrate the efficiency of the approach.

1 Introduction

As XML [1] is becoming a *de facto* standard for distribution and sharing of information, the need for an efficient yet secure access of XML data has become very important[4-13, 16-18]. Despite this, relatively little work has been done to enforce access controls particularly for XML databases in the case of query access.

We propose two phase filtering scheme for access control enforcement mechanism. The first phase filtering is to abstract only necessary access control rules based on a user query. The traditional access control enforcement mechanism for XML documents uses all access control rules corresponding to a query requester. In contrast, our scheme uses only the necessary access control rules that are related to an ancestor-or-self (or parent) or a descendant-or-self (or child) relation against the user query. As a result, these necessary access control rules are used in rewriting unsafe query into a safe one.

The second phase filtering is to modify an unsafe query into a safe one. Query modification is the development of an efficient query rewriting mechanism that transforms an unsafe query into a safe yet correct one that keeps the user access control policies. In NFA approaches [16,18], the process of rewriting queries may be particularly slower and incorrect because more states are being traversed to process "*" and "//".

We conducted an extensive experimental study, which shows that our approach improves access decision time and generates a more exact rewritten query.

W. Jonker and M. Petkovic (Eds.): SDM 2006, LNCS 4165, pp. 115–130, 2006.
© Springer-Verlag Berlin Heidelberg 2006

The rest of the paper is organized as follows: Section 2 briefly reviews related works and describes their weaknesses. Section 3 gives the metadata of the Document Type Definition (DTD) and the basic notations for two phase filtering scheme. In Section 4, we present two phase filtering scheme and the construction algorithms used. Section 5 presents the results of our experiments, which reveal the effective performance compared to the Q-Filter [18]. Finally, Section 6 summarizes our work.

2   Related Works

Traditional authorizations for XML documents should be associated with protection objects at different granularity levels. In general, existing XML access control models assume access control rules, which are identified as quintuple (Subject, Object, Access-type, Sign, Type) [4-13]. The subject refers to the user or user group with authority, the object pertains to an XML document or its specific portion, access-type means the kind of operations, the sign could either be positive (+) or negative (-), and the type shows 'R(ecusive)' or 'L(ocal)'. S. De Capitani *et al.* [19] propose an access control model handling the XQuery and an query rewriting process by using EXCEPT operation. The access control enforcement mechanism of these authorizations is view-based enforcement mechanism. The semantics of access control to a user is a particular view of the documents determined by the relevant access control rules. It provides a useful algorithm for computing the view using tree labeling. However, aside from its high cost and maintenance requirement, this algorithm is also not scalable for a large number of users.

To remedy view-based problem, M. Murata *et al.* [16] simply focused on filtering out queries that do not satisfy access control policies. J. M. Jeon *et al.* [17] proposed access control method that produces the access-granted XPath expressions from the query XPath expression by using access control tree (XACT), where the edges are structural summary of XML elements and the nodes contain access control XPath expressions. Since XACT includes all users' access control rules it is very complicated and leads to computation time overhead. B. Luo *et al.* [18] took extra steps to rewrite queries in combination with related access control policies before passing these revised queries to the underlying XML query system for processing. However, the shared Nondeterministic Finite Automata (NFA) of access control rules is made by a user (or a user role). Thus, the shared NFA involves many unnecessary access control rules from the user query point of view, which further result in a time-consuming decision during which the user query should have already been accepted, denied, or rewritten. In addition, although the proposed NFA-based algorithm is useful for rewriting queries with path expressions starting from the root, this approach is very inefficient for rewriting queries with the descendant-or-self axis("//") because of the exhaustive navigation of NFA. The many queries on XML data have path expressions with "//" axes because users may not be concerned with the structure of data and intentionally make path expressions with "//" axes to get intended results. The NFA-based method results in performance degradation and the generation of unsafe queries.

3   Background

3.1   XPath and Access Control Rule

XML specification defines two types of document: well-formed and valid ones. A well-formed document must conform to the three rules [1]. Valid documents, on the other hand, should not only be well-formed; they should also have a Document Type Definition (DTD) or XML Schema, which the well-formed document conforms to. Although we use a valid XML with a DTD, the following content may be applied to a valid XML with an XML Schema or a well-formed XML.

To enforce the fine-level granularity requirement, in general, authorization models proposed for regulating access to XML documents use XPath expressions to delineate the scope of each access control rule. XPath is a path expression language of a tree representation of XML documents. A typical path expression consists of a sequence of steps. Each step works by following a relationship between nodes in the document: child, attribute, ancestor, descendant, etc. Any step in a path expression can also be qualified by a predicate, which filters the selected nodes.

[**Assumption 1**]. *We consider XPath expressions with predicates for describing query and object parts of XML access control rules, which specify elements (including wildcard ('*') and a sequence of parent-child ('/') and ancestor-descendant ('//') steps.*

Meanwhile, XPath 2.0 [2] supports operations (*i.e.*, UNION, INTERSECT, and EXCEPT) that combine two sets of node. Although these operations are technically non-path expressions, they are invariably used in conjunction with path expressions, so they are useful in transforming unsafe queries into safe queries. We confirm these operations by using XML spy 2006 version[1].

3.2   Access Control Policies

In general, some hierarchical data models (e.g., Object-Oriented Data Model, XML Data Model, and etc.) exploit implicit authorization mechanism combining positive and negative authorizations [3]. The propagation policy by implicit authorizations leads to the situation that a node is defined as 'access-granted' and 'access-denied' at the same time. In addition, the decision policy determines when a node is neither access-granted nor access-denied. Open policy grants a query for a node whose access control information is not defined. Closed policy, on the other hand, denies a query for a node whose access-control information is not defined.

[**Assumption 2**]. *For the strict data security, we use 'most specific precedence' for the propagation policy, 'denials take precedence' for the conflict resolution policy, and 'closed policy' for decision policy to keep data in safety.*

---

[1] http://www.altova.com

Recall the implicit authorization mechanism combining the positive and negative authorizations. The combination of a negative authorization with positive authorizations allows the definition of positive authorizations as exceptions to a negative authorization at a higher level in granularity hierarchy. M. Murata *et al.* [16] calls this combination 'valid read accessibility views'. Similarly, the combination of a positive authorization with negative authorizations specifies exceptions to a positive authorization. This combination calls 'invalid read accessibility views'.

In this paper, we select 'valid read accessibility views'. To ensure that an access control policy is 'valid read accessibility views' in a positive/negative authorization mechanism we propose a new concept of generating access control rules. We define this as 'Integrity Rules of Access Control Rules'.

Definition 1. [Three Integrity Rules of ACRs]:

1. It is impossible for any node to have both a negative and a positive ACR.
2. If a conflict occurs between positive and negative ACRs, the negative ACR takes precedence.
3. We also assume "denial downward consistency" [2] [16].
4. It is impossible for any node, which is not in the scope of positive ACRs, to have negative ACRs.

Integrity rules 1 and 2 of ACRs are the result of 'denials take precedence'. Integrity rules 3 and 4 of ACRs are newly added into an XML access control policy. Any security specification model must ensure that access control policies are enforced correctly and efficiently. Given a query over a secured XML document tree, it is important that returned answers do not contain any data that violate access control policies. They are called safe answers [18].

Definition 2. [Safe Query]: If a query is assured to retrieve only safe answers, it is called a *safe query*, otherwise, it is an unsafe query.

Generally speaking, an XPath expression [2] declares the query requirement by identifying the node of interest via the path from the root of the document to the elements which serve as the root of the sub-trees to be returned [20]. The QFilter [18] defines these semantics as *'answer-as-sub-trees'*. We call the root of sub-trees to be returned as **target nodes**.

Definition 3. [Target Node]: A *target node* of a given XPath is the last node except for the predicates.

For example, the target node of an XPath, /site/people/person is a *person* node. Another example, the target node of an XPath, /site/regions/aisa/item[@id = "xxx"] is an *item* node.

---

[2] The combination of a negative authorization with positive authorizations allows the definition of positive authorizations as exceptions to a negative authorization at a higher level in granularity hierarchy.

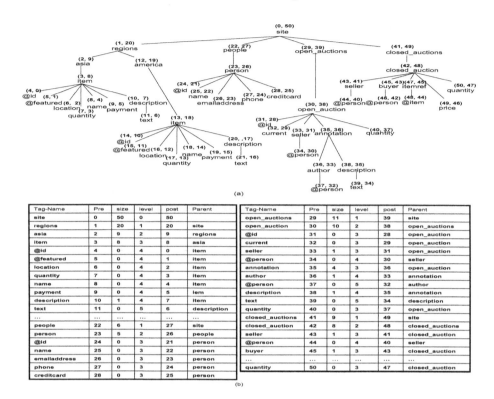

(a)

Tag-Name	Pre	size	level	post	Parent
site	0	50	0	50	
regions	1	20	1	20	site
asia	2	9	2	9	regions
item	3	8	3	8	asia
@id	4	0	4	0	item
@featured	5	0	4	1	item
location	6	0	4	2	item
quantity	7	0	4	3	item
name	8	0	4	4	item
payment	9	0	4	5	lem
description	10	1	4	7	item
text	11	0	5	6	description
...	...	...	...	...	...
people	22	6	1	27	site
person	23	5	2	26	people
@id	24	0	3	21	person
name	25	0	3	22	person
emailaddress	26	0	3	23	person
phone	27	0	3	24	person
creditcard	28	0	3	25	person

Tag-Name	Pre	size	level	post	Parent
open_auctions	29	11	1	39	site
open_auction	30	10	2	38	open_auctions
@id	31	0	3	28	open_auction
current	32	0	3	29	open_auction
seller	33	1	3	31	open_auction
@person	34	0	4	30	seller
annotation	35	4	3	36	open_auction
author	36	1	4	33	annotation
@person	37	0	5	32	author
description	38	1	4	35	annotation
text	39	0	5	34	description
quantity	40	0	3	37	open_auction
closed_auctions	41	9	1	49	site
closed_auction	42	8	2	48	closed_auctions
seller	43	1	3	41	closed_auction
@person	44	0	4	40	seller
buyer	45	1	3	43	closed_auction
...	...	...	...	...	...
quantity	50	0	3	47	closed_auction

(b)

Fig. 1. (a) DTD PRE/POST Structure of auction.dtd, (b) Relational Storage of (a)

3.3   PRE/POST Structure

In this section, we introduce our proposed metadata of a DTD, PRE/POST structure.

Figure 1(a) shows that the nodes of the DTD[3] tree are assigned with PRE(order) and POST(order) ranks, as seen when parsing the DTD tree sequentially. We adopt the PRE/POST plane concept of the query processor for the XML query language [14,15]. We call this as PRE/POST Structure (PPS) of the DTD tree. Figure 1(b) shows the actual relational DTD representation. LEVEL refers to a DTD tree level, and SIZE is the sub-tree size of any node. This PRE/SIZE/LEVEL encoding is equivalent to PRE/POST since $POST = PRE + SIZE - LEVEL$ [14,15]. PARENT refers to the parent node of the Tag-Name node in the DTD tree. We avoid any unnecessary ACRs through PPS information. PARENT information enable efficient finding the nodes for XPath expressions with "//" axes. Further details are provided in Section 4.

---

[3] It is a portion of an auction.dtd source extracted from the XMark [21], which we consider as a running example in our paper.

4   Two Phase Filtering

The objective of Two Phase Filtering is to select only the necessary ACRs for processing a user query, and to rewrite the unsafe query into a new safe query. Before describing each filtering technique in detail, we introduce information of a user query and access control rules.

Positive ACRs
(R1): /site/regions/*/item[location="LA"]
(R2): /site/people/person[name = "chang"]
(R3): /site/open_auctions/open_auction
(R4): //open_auction[quantity]/seller

Negative ACRs
(R5): /site/regions/*/item/payment
(R6): /site/people/person/creditcard
(R7): /site/*/open_auction[@id>50]/seller[@person="chang"]

(a)

ACR⁺-base

rule	path	Pre	Post	P_link
R1	/site/regions/*/item	3, 13	8, 18	P1
R2	/site/people/person	23	26	P2
R3	/site/open_auctions/open_auction	30	38	
R4	//open_auction[quantity]/seller	33	31	p3

ACR⁻-base

rule	path	Pre	Post	P_link
R5	/site/regions/*/item/payment	9, 19	5, 15	
R6	/site/people/person/creditcard	28	25	
R7	/site/*/open_auction[@id>50]/seller[@person="chang"]	33	31	p4, p5

PREDICATES-base

P-id	Parent-PRE	property	operator	value
P1	3, 13	location	=	LA
P2	23	name	=	chang
P3	30	quantity		
P4	30	@id	>	50
p5	33	@person	=	chang

(b)

Fig. 2. (a) Sample positive/negative ACRs, (b) Sample *ACRs* and *PREDICATES* databases

After a security officer determines the ACRs of which each object part uses an XPath expression in Figure 2(a), each ACR information is stored into *ACRs* and *PREDICATES* databases in Figure 2(b) at compile time. Note that the entity of PRE and POST columns may be more than two. For example, the target node of *R1* is *item*. The (PRE, POST) value set of the *item* is (3, 8) and (13, 18). This value set is stored into the PRE and POST columns, respectively. Moreover, *R1* has one predicate ([location="xxxx"]). The parent element of the predicate is *item*. The entity of Parent-PRE column is (3, 13), and the entities of property, operator, and value columns are 'location', '=', and 'xxxx', respectively. Finally, P1 as Predicate ID is stored into the P_link column in the *ACRs* database. In a similar way, other ACRs are stored into the *ACRs* and *PREDICATES* databases.

Meanwhile, if a user query is inputted, we get some information about the user query. Given a query *Q1*, the target node of *Q1* is *phone* node.

Q1: /site/people/person[name="chang"]/phone/

We looks up the PPS(in Figure 1(b)) and gets the (27, 24) value of the target node *phone*. We also obtains the predicate information of *Q1*. Note that there may also be more than two (PRE, POST) pairs. However, all (PRE, POST) pairs may not be the (PRE, POST) pairs of the user's query. Let a user's query be footnote-size /site/regions/america/item for example. The target node of the user's query is the *item* node. Although the (PRE, POST) pairs of the *item* are (3, 8) and (13, 18), (3, 8) is not a suitable (PRE, POST) pair of the given query. Only (13, 18) is a child node of (12, 19) of the *america* node. Its main idea is that the preorder (postorder) value of each node of a user's query is less (greater) than that of the target node of the user's query. Figure 3 shows the pruning algorithm that eliminates the unsuitable (PRE, POST) pairs of a user's query.

```
Input : a user's query
Output : suitable (PRE, POST) values of the target node of the query

BEGIN
1. for each (PRE_tn, POST_tn) value of projection node of the query
2. {   for (PRE_step, POST_step) value of each step of the query
3.        If (!(PRE_step < PRE_tn and POST_step > POST_tn))
4.           break;
5.     suitable_(PRE, POST) set := (PRE_tn, PRE_tn)
6. }
END
```

Fig. 3. The Prune-TNs Algorithm

4.1   First Phase Filtering: Rule Filter

The objective of the *Rule Filter* is to extract the necessary ACRs out of the *ACRs* database. As shown in Figure 4, namely, the PRE/POST plane of ACRs, the target node of a user query induces four partitions of the plane. Each partition has a special relation with the user query.

Let (Pr_Q, Po_Q), (Pr_{ACR}, Po_{ACR}), and $(Pr_{Q'}, Po_{Q'})$ pairs be (PRE, POST) values of a user query Q, an ACR, and a safe modified query Q', respectively.

Definition 4. [**upper-right partition: FOLLOWING ACR**] *FOLLOWING ACR* means that the preorder and postorder values of an ACR are greater than those of a user query: $Pr_Q < Pr_{ACR}, Po_Q < Po_{ACR}$.

Definition 5. [**lower-left partition: PRECEDING ACR**] *PRECEDING ACR* means that the preorder and postorder values of an ACR are less than those of a user query: $Pr_Q > Pr_{ACR}, Po_Q > Po_{ACR}$.

The *FOLLOWING* and *PRECEDING ACRs* have no connection with the query Q. Thus, we can put aside the ACRs for processing the query Q.

Definition 6. [**upper-left partition: ANCESTOR ACR**] *ANCESTOR ACR* (including *PARENT ACR*) means that the preorder (postorder) value of an ACR is less (greater) than that of a user query, respectively. In this case, the (PRE, POST) value of the target node of the modified query Q' is equal to that of the target node of the user query Q: $Pr_Q > Pr_{ACR}, Po_Q < Po_{ACR}, Pr_{Q'} = Pr_Q, Po_{Q'} = Po_Q$.

Definition 7. [**lower-right partition: DESCENDANT ACR**] *DESCEN-DANT ACR* (including *CHILD ACR*) means that the preorder (postorder) value of an ACR is greater (less) than that of a user query, respectively. In this case, the (PRE, POST) value of the target node of the modified query Q' is equal to that of the target node of the ACR: $Pr_Q < Pr_{ACR}, Po_Q > Po_{ACR}, Pr_{Q'} = Pr_{ACR}, Po_{Q'} = Pr_{ACR}$.

Definition 8. [**SELF ACR**] *SELF ACR* means that the (PRE, POST) pair of an ACR is equal to that of a user query. In this case, the (PRE, POST) value of the target node of the modified query Q' is equal to that of the target node of the user query Q (or ACR): $Pr_{Q'} = Pr_Q = Pr_{ACR}, Po_{Q'} = Po_Q = Po_{ACR}$.

Recall *Q1* in Figure 2(b). The (PRE, POST) value of the target node *phone* is (27, 24). Only *R2* is necessary for *Q1* because the target node of *R2* is an *ANCESTOR ACR* of *Q1*. R1 and R5 (*R3*, *R4*, *R6*, and *R7*) are a *PRECEDING* (*FOLLOW-ING*) *ACRs* of the query in Figure 4(a). They are identified as unnecessary ACRs for *Q1*. Figure 4(b) shows the *Rule Filter* algorithm which finds *DESCENDANT-or-SELF* (or *ANCESTOR-or-SELF*) *ACRs* that correspond to a user's query.

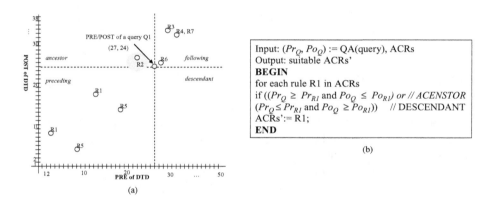

Fig. 4. (a) Semantics of PRE/POST Plane of Positive ACRs, (b) The *Rule Filter* Algorithm

Theorem 1. The Rule Filter algorithm abstracts all access control rules related to a user query.

Proof. The Rule Filter algorithm abstracts the ANCESTOR (Definition 6), DE-SCENDANT (Definition 7), and SELF ACRs (Definition 8), accordingly we see that the FOLLOWING and PRECEDING ACRs have no connection with the user query.

Let (Pr_{TN}, Po_{TN}) be the (PRE, POST) value of the target node of a user query Q. Suppose that SN is any node in sub-nodes of Q. Then the (PRE POST) value of SN is as follows:

$$Pr_{TN} < Pr_{SN} < Pr_{TN} + SIZE(TN), Po_{last-sibling-node-of-TN} < Po_{SN} < Po_{TN}$$
$$(1)$$

Suppose that FN is any node in following nodes of Q. Then the (PRE, POST) value of FN is as follows:

$$Pr_{TN} < Pr_{FN}, Po_{TN} < Po_{FN} \qquad (2)$$

Especially the (PRE, POST) value of the first following node (first_FN) of Q is as follows:

$$Pr_{first_FN} = Pr_{TN} + SIZE(TN) + 1 \qquad (3)$$

Thus, by (1) and (2), $Po_{SN} < Po_{TN} < Po_{FN}$, and by (1) and (3), we obtain (4).

$$Pr_{SN} < Pr_{TN} + SIZE(TN) < Pr_{first-FN} = Pr_{TN} + SIZE(TN) + 1 \qquad (4)$$

The inequality (4) means that the preorder value of any node (SN) in sub-nodes of Q is less than that of the first following node (first_FN) of Q. Therefore, $Pr_{SN} < Pr_{FN}$. So we can obtain $Pr_{SN} < Pr_{FN}$ and $Po_{SN} < Po_{FN}$. That is, the FOLLOWING ACRs have no connection with the user query, as was to be proved. The same is the case with PRECEDING ACRs.

4.2   Second Phase Filtering: Query Filter

The goal of the *Query Filter* is to make a safe query by extending/eliminating query tree nodes and combining a set of nodes by the operators.

The positive and negative access control rules passed by the *Rule Filter* are classified into three groups (*SELF, ANCESTOR,* and *DESCENDANT ACRs*). The process of the *Query Filter* is as follows:

1. Compares the user query with each negative access control rule and produces a modified query.
2. Combine each modified query by UNION operation.
3. Compares the user query with each positive access control rule and produces a modified query.
4. Combines each modified query by UNION operation.
5. Combines each result query of 4 and 2 by EXCEPT operation.
6. Outputs the final result query of 5.

Before describing our method in detail, we give sample queries as follows:

(*Q2*): */site/people/person/creditcard/*
(*Q3*): *//open_auction[@id<100]*

4.2.1   Assistant Functions

Before describing the process of the *Query Filter*, we introduce two functions. The *REFINE* function focuses on replacing a wild card "*" with an actual node name (element tag) and removing superfluous "//" axes. A "*" element is superfluous if the DTD shows an actual element from the element (*i.e.*, parent node) before "*" to the element (*i.e.*, child node) after "*". In addition, the "//" axis is also

superfluous if the DTD shows that there is a single path from the element before
"//" to the element after "//". If so, the "//" axis is replaced with the deterministic sequence of "/" steps. For example, the *REFINE* function gets the XPath
expression:

/site/regions/*/item.

Since the (PRE, POST) value set of the target node (*item*) of the XPath is (3,
8) and (13, 18), the *REFINE* function begins first (3, 8). In the reverse order, once
the *REFINE* function meets the "*" node, it obtains *item* before the node. The
(PRE, POST) value of *item* is (3, 8). The *REFINE* function gets the parent node
(*asia*) of the *item* as shown in Figure 1(b). Finally, the *REFINE* function gives
the output /site/regions/asia/item (Line (5) - (9) in Figure 5). In the case of (13, 8)
value, the *REFINE* function results in /site/regions/america/item.

Another example is /site/people//name. Although the (PRE, POST) value set
of the target node (*name*) of the XPath is (8, 4), (18, 14) and (25, 22), only (25,
22) is selected by the Prune_TNs algorithm as shown in Figure 3 . Once the *RE-
FINE* function meets the "//" node, it obtains *name* before the node and the next
node (*people*). As shown in Figure 1(b), each LEVEL of *name* and *people* is 3 and
1, respectively. $LEVEL_{name} - LEVEL_{people} = 2$. In this case, it is the same as

```
Input: PPS, an original XPath, and (Pr_p, Po_p) of the target node of the XPath
Output: Refinedpath //Refined XPath expression
BEGIN
1. Refinedpath := null string;
2. for reverse order of path
3. {    if node is not * and $                      // $ means "//" axis
4.            Refinedpath := concatenate( "/node", Refinedpath);
5.        else if node is *
6.        { find (Pr_before-node, Po_before-node) value set before "*" node;
7.                for each   (Pr_before-node, Po_before-node) value
8.                    if ((Pr_before-node ≤ Pr_p) and (Po_before-node ≥ Po_p))
9.                        Refinedpath := concatenate(Get_parentnode(Pr_before-node, Po_before-node,
   Refinedpath));
10.        }else if node is $                       // $ means "//" axis
11.        { while(1)
12.            { find (Pr_before-node, Po_before-node)   value set before "//" node;
13.                for each (Pr_before-node, Po_before-node) value
14.                    if ((Pr_before-node ≤ Pr_p) and (Po_before-node ≥ Po_p))
15.                    {next-node := get the next node of   "//" node
16.                        find (Pr_next-node, Po_next-node) value set of next-node;
17.                for each (Pr_next-node, Po_next-node) value
18.                    if ((Pr_next-node ≤ Pr_p) and (Po_next-node ≥ Po_p))
19.                        if( Level_before-node – Level_next-node = 1)
20.                            pass;
21.                        else if( Level_before-node – Level_next-node = 2)
22.                            Refinedpath := concatenate(Get_parentnode(Pr_before-node, Po_before-node),
                                Refinedpath));
23.                        else
24.                            { Refinedpath := concatenate(Get_parentnode (Pr_before-node, Po_before-node),
   Refinedpath));
25.                            break while;
26.                        }
27.                }
28.            }
29.    }
```

Fig. 5. The *REFINE* function

```
Input   : nodeACR, nodeQ
Output : RefinePredicate
BEGIN
1. ACR_simple_predicate = getsimplepredicate(nodeACR);   // array
2. ACR_path_predicate = getpathpredicate(nodeACR);       // array
3. Q_simple_predicate = getsimplepredicate(nodeQ);       // array
4. Q_path_predicate = getpathpredicate(nodeQ);           // array

5. if(Q_path_predicate != null && ACR_path_predicate != null)
6.       Refinedpredicates := concatenate path_predicate by Path- MERGE function;
7. else if(Q_path_predicate != null)
8.       Refinedpredicates := concatenate Q_path_predicate;
9. else if(ACR_path_predicate != null)
10.      Refinedpredicates := concatenate ACR_path_predicate;
11. if(Q_ simple _predicate != null && ACR_ simple_predicate != null)
12.      Refinedpredicates := concatenate simple _predicate by Simple-MERGE
                                                              function;
13. else if(Q_ simple _predicate != null)
14.      Refinedpredicates := concatenate Q_ simple _predicate;
15. else if(ACR_ simple _predicate != null)
16.      Refinedpredicates := concatenate ACR_ simple _predicate;
END
```

Fig. 6. The pseudo-code of PREDICATE function

people/*/name. Finally, the *REFINE* function results in */site/people/person/name*. If the difference between LEVELs of two nodes is equal to 1, the two nodes are a parent-child relation. If the difference between LEVELs of two nodes is more than 3, the two nodes are an ancestor-descendant relation (Line (17) - (26) in Figure 5).

In addition, we introduce the *PREDICATE* function. From the query rewriting point of view, it is desirable to keep the predicate's position of a user query or ACRs in the process of refining the user query. At compile time, each predicate content and position information of the ACRs is stored in the *PREDICATES* database as shown in Figure 2(b). When the *Query Filter* prompts the *REFINE* function, the latter subsequently prompts the *PREDICATE* function which adds

Predicate of a query	Predicate of a positive ACR	Predicate of a negative ACR	Optimization
[@id = "1"]	[@id = "1"]		[@id = "1"]
[@id = "1"]	[@id = "3"]		reject
[@id > "1"]	[@id > "3"]		[@id > "3"]
[@id > "1"]	[@id < "3"]		[@id > "1" and @id < "3"]
[@id = "1"]		[@id = "1"]	[@id = "1"]
[@id = "1"]		[@id = "3"]	[@id = "3"]
[@id > "1"]		[@id > "3"]	[@id > "3"]
[@id > "1"]		[@id < "3"]	[@id < "3"]

Fig. 7. Examples of Predicates Optimizations in simple-*MERGE* function

predicates of ACRs into the user query. Figure 6 shows the *PREDICATE* function whose core is the two *MERGE* functions. The Path-*MERGE* function performs to merge path predicates in the ACR and the user query. The Simple-*MERGE* function performs to merge simple predicates in the ACR and the user query. The simple-*MERGE* function also considers some optimizations in Figure 7. Furthermore, with the EXCEPT operation, a returned answer will not include the unauthorized part of an XML instance. Accordingly, we think that the optimized predicates between a query and a negative ACR are the same with predicates of the negative ACR. In the future, we will consider some other optimizations.

4.2.2 *Query Filter* Algorithm
Step 1. (Handling negative ACRs)

- **Case 1.1 (*SELF ACR*).** *SELF* means that the (PRE, POST) pair of a user's query is equal to that of an ACR. If a negative ACR is a *SELF* rule related to a user query, the output of the *Query Filter* is that the query is rejected. The (PRE, POST) pair of Q2 is (28, 25). As shown in Figure 2(b), R6 (in the negative *ACRs* database) has a value of (28, 25). In this case, the *Query Filter* rejects Q2. However, when predicates exist in negative ACRs, the output range part of the user query is disallowed access. As a result, the *Query Filter* transforms the query except the region of the negative ACR.
- **Case 1.2(*ANCESTOR ACR*).** If a negative ACR is an *ANCESTOR* rule related to a user query, it is similar to Case 1.1.
- **Case 1.3 (*DESCENDANT ACR*).** If a negative ACR is a *DESCENDANT* rule related to a user query, the *Query Filter* rewrites the query except the region of the negative ACR. For example, R7 (33, 31) is a *DESCENDANT* rule related to Q3 (30, 38) by the ACR-FINDER algorithm. Thus, the *Query Filter* prompts the *REFINE* function, and Q3 is transformed as follows:
  Q3': *Q3* EXCEPT
  (*/site/open_auactions/open_auction[@id>50]/seller[@person="chang"]*).
  Then *R4* (go to Step 2) should be taken for granted.
- **Case 1.4 (Null).** If any negative ACR does not exist against a user's query, the *Query Filter* proceeds to Step 2.

Step 2. (Handling positive ACRs)

- **Case 2.1 (SELF ACR).** If a positive ACR is a *SELF* rule related to a user query, the *Query Filter* prompts the *REFINE* function.
- **Case 2.2 (ANCESTOR ACR).** It is similar to Case 2.1.
- **Case 2.3 (DESCENDANT ACR).** If a postive ACR is a *DESCENDANT* rule related to a user query, the user query may contain the unsafe parts of an XML document. Thus, the user query should be transformed into a safe query. *R4* (33, 31) is also *ANCESTOR* rule related to *Q3* (30, 38). First, the *Query Filter* prompts the *REFINE* function whose output is
  /site/open_auctions/open_auction[quantity][@id<100]/seller.
  Second, the *Query Filter* combines the refined query of positive ACRs with

those of negative ACRs as shown in Case 1.3 of *Step1* by injecting the EX-CEPT operation between them:

(*/site/open_auctions/open_auction[quantity][@id<100]/seller*)
EXCEPT
(*/site/open_auactions/open_auction[@id>50]/seller[@person="chang"]*)

5   Experiments

We compared the performance of our work with the QFilter [18] according to syntactic data sets generated by the publicly available XMark [21]. We present two experiments[4] based on this implementation. To estimate the effectiveness and efficiency of our work, we generated 25 ACRs (7 positive and 18 negative) for each experiment. We implemented the 2PF (Two Phase Filtering), 2PF-NFA (combining 2PF with the NFA technique) and QFilter in the Java programming language using the Eclipse v.3.1.1 development tool.

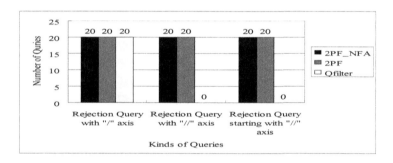

Fig. 8. The number of rejecting prohibited queries corresponding to various query types

5.1   Experiment 1: Correctness of Detecting Rejection Queries

Rejection query is a user query that is always denied. First, we made 20 intentional rejection XPath queries for each query type, and actually measured the number of filtering the rejection queries. The result is shown in Figure 8. From this, we can see that the 2PF and the 2PF-NFA completely filter the rejection queries. However, the QFilter does not. If there is more than one ACR starting with "//" axis in positive ACRs, rejection queries are never filtered by the QFilter. In particular, the QFilter's rate of filtering rejection queries starting with the "//" axis is 0%. If a user's query contains //-child and a shared NFA does not contain /-child or //-child state, the navigation of the shared NFA runs to each final state. If answer model is "answer-as-nodes", the query is rejected. However, if answer model is "answer-as-subtrees", the QFilter appends //-child to each final state so that the query is not rejected.

---

[4] The experiments were performed on a Pentium IV 2.66GHz platform, with an MS-Windows XP OS and 1 GB of main memory.

5.2   Experiment 2: Estimating the Average Processing Time

We measured the average processing time for the output (rejection, re-written query) of the 2PF, 2PF-NFA, and QFilter per 30, 50, 100, 200, 300, and 500 random XPath queries. Before estimating the average processing time, we measured the speed of each filter construction. The 2PF or the 2PF-NFA construction time means hash table generation time of a DTD as shown in Figure 1(b). QFilter construction time means two shared NFA generation time (i.e., negative and positive ACRs). Figure 9(a) shows each construction time. From this, the metadata of a DTD has minimal overhead. By the *Rule Filter* in Section 3.1, the 2PF and the 2PF-NFA use fewer ACRs than the QFilter. By the PPS as shown in Figure 1(b), the SQ-Filter and the SQ-NFA can rewrite queries with the "*" wildcard and the "//" axis faster than the QFilter. The result is shown in Figure 9(b). Each processing time includes the construction time as shown in Figure 9(a). From this, we can also see that the 2PF and the 2PF-NFA can better degrade the processing time than the QFilter can.

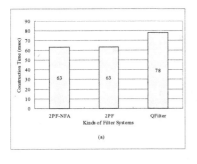
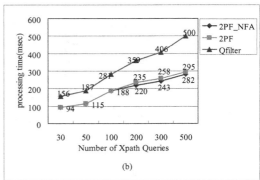

Fig. 9. (a) The Construction Time of each Filter System, (b) The Processing time of the security check on XPath queries

6   Conclusion

Our XML access control enforcement mechanism exploits the tree properties encoded in the PRE/POST plane to eliminate unnecessary access control rules for a user query, and to reject unauthorized queries ahead of rewriting. In addition, we exploits the simple hash tree of a DTD to find an actual node of a "*" node and a parent node of a node with the descendant-or-self axis ("//"), and to rewrite an unsafe query into a safe one by receiving help from operations combining the two sets of node. Our experiments demonstrate the *Rule Filter* algorithm and the *Query Filter* algorithm to be more effective and efficient and show how to modify an unsafe query into a safe one.

We note that our work is the first to explore this important area of a secure yet efficient access of XML data using only the necessary access control rules of a user in an XML document. It establishes the foundation for correct yet safe query rewriting from the access control point of view.

In the future, we are going to take into consideration the scalability of our approach and some optimizations(*i.e.*, value-based predicates optimization and nested path optimization) of a returned safe query to save query processing cost. In addition, the techniques proposed in this paper can be applied to any XML database management system. We are looking forward to applying our work to any real XML database management system. we are going to plan to progress our XML access control system combined with some access right models.

Acknowledgements

This work was supported by grant No. (R01-2006-000-10609-0) from the Basic Research Program of the Korea Science and Engineering Foundation.

References

1. T. Bray, J. Paoli, C. M. Sperberg-McQueen, E. Maler, F. Yergeau. Extensible Markup Language (XML) 1.0, World Wide Web Consortium (W3C), 2004. (http://www.w3.org/TR/REC-xml)
2. A. Berglund, S. Boag, D. Chamberlin, M. F. Fernández, M. Kay, J. Robie, and J. Siméon. XPath 2.0, World Wide Web Consortium (W3C), 2005. (http://www.w3.org/TR/xpath20/)
3. F. Rabitti, E. Bertino, W. Kim and D. Woelk, "A Model of Authorization for Next-Generation Data-base Systems", ACM Transaction on Database Systems, Vol 126, No 1. March 1991, PP. 88-131.
4. E .Damiani, S.Vimercati, S.Paraboschi, and P.Samarati, "Securing xml document", *Proc. of the 2000 International Conf. on Extending Database Technology* (EDBT2000), Konstan, Germany, March, 2000, pp.121-135.
5. E. Damiani, S. Vimercati, S. Paraboachk and P.Samarati, "XML Access Control Systems: A Compo-nent-Based Approach", *Proc. IFIP WG11.3 Working Conference on Database Security*, The Nether-lands, 2000. 8.
6. E. Damiani, S. Vimercati, S. Paraboachk and P.Samarati, "Design and Implementation of Access Control Processor for XML Documents", Computer Network, 2000.
7. E. Damiani, S. Vimercati, S. Paraboachk and P.Samarati, "A Fine-grained Access Control System for XML Documents", ACM Trans. Information and System Sec., Vol.5, No.2, May 2002.
8. E. Bertino, S. Castano, E. Ferrari, M. Mesiti, "Specifying and Enforcing Access Control Policies for XML Document Sources", WWW Journal, Baltzer Science Publishers, Vol.3, N.3, 2000.
9. E. Bertino, S. Castano, E. Ferrai, "Securing XML documents with Author-x", IEEE Internet Comput-ing, May.June, pp.21-31, 2001.
10. E. Bertino and E. Ferrari, "Secure and Selective Dissemination of XML Documents", TISSEC, 5(3), pp. 237-260, 2002.
11. E. Bertino, M. Braun, S. Castano, E. Ferrari, and M. Mesiti, "Author-X: A Java-Based System for XML Data Protection", *Proc. IFIP WG11.3 Working Conference on Database Security*, Netherlands, 2002. 8.

12. A. Gabillon and E. Bruno, "Regulating Access to XML Documents", *Proc. IFIP WG11.3 Working Conference on Database Security*, 2001.
13. A. Stoica and C. Farkas, "Secure XML Views", *Proc. IFIP WG11.3 Working Conference on Data-base and Application Security*, 2002.
14. T. Grust, "Accelerating XPath Location Steps", *Proc. of the 21st Int'l ACM SIGMOD Conf. on Management of Data*, pages 109-120, Madison, Wisconsin, USA, June 2002.
15. T. Grust, M. van Keulen, and J. Teubner, "Staircase Join: Teach a Relational DBMS to Watch its Axis Steps", *Proc. of the 29th VLDB Conference*, Berlin, Germany, September 2003.
16. M. Murata, A. Tozawa, and M. Kudo, "XML Access Control using Static Analysis", *ACM CCS*, Washington D.C., 2003.
17. Jae-Myeong Jeon, Yon Dohn Chung, Myoung Ho Kim, and Yoon Joon Lee, "Filtering XPath expres-sions for XML access control", Computers & Security, 23, pp.591-605, 2004.
18. B. Luo, D. W. Lee, W. C. Lee, P. Liu, "Qfilter: Fine-grained Run-Time XML Access Control via NFA-based Query Rewriting", *Proc. of the Thirteenth ACM Conference on Information and Knowledge Management 2004* (CIKM'04), November 8, 2004, Washington, USA.
19. S. De Capitani, S. Marrara, P. Samarati, "An Access Control Model for Querying XML Data", *Proc. of the 2005 ACM Workshop on Secure Web Services*, pages 36-42, Nov. 11, 2005, Fairfax, Virginia, USA.
20. S. Mohan, A. Sengupta, Y. Wu, J. Klinginsmith, "Access Control for XML - A Dynamic Query Rewriting Approach", *Proc. of the 31st VLDB Conference*, Trondheim, Norway, 2005.
21. A. R. Schmidt, F. Waas, M. L. Kersten, D. Florescu, I. Manolescu, M. J. Carey, and R. Busse. The XML Benchmark Project. Technical Report INS-R0103, CWI, April 2001.

Hybrid Authorizations and Conflict Resolution

Amir H. Chinaei and Huaxin Zhang

David R. Cheriton School of Computer Science, University of Waterloo,
200 University Ave. W, Waterloo, ON, N2L3G1, Canada
{ahchinaei, h7zhang}@uwaterloo.ca

Abstract. Numerous authorization models have been proposed in recent years. While some models support either positive or negative authorizations, hybrid models take advantage of both authorizations simultaneously. However, resolving authorization conflicts is quite a challenge in such models due to the existence of sophisticated hierarchies and diversity of types of resolution strategies. There are works that have addressed conflict resolution for *tree-structured* subject hierarchies. Yet, no widespread framework has been proposed for *graph-based* structures. A widespread resolution framework ought to provide several resolution strategies and to support sophisticated structures. Our attempt is to define such a framework. In particular, our framework resolves conflicts for subject hierarchies that form directed acyclic graphs. It also unites major resolution policies in a novel way by which thirty-two combined strategies are simultaneously expressed. We also provide parametric algorithms to support the strategies and to justify the framework with our analysis and experiments.

Keywords: Access Control, Conflict Resolution, Combined Strategies.

1 Introduction

With the fast growth of information systems, many enterprises require efficient and effective access control mechanisms. In such systems, it is extremely important to determine if a *user* (or any subject such as application, process, etc.) who is trying to access *data* (or any object such as programs, resources, etc.) is *authorized* or *not*. Proposed access control models deal in various ways with such a problem. Some models based on a closed (or open) world assumption support positive (or negative) authorizations only [6, 11]. Some other models, *hybrid models*, support both positive and negative authorizations [2, 7, 8].

On the other hand, access control data is potentially quite large (the product of the number of subjects and the number of objects), yet sparse. Researchers have exploited the existing hierarchy among subjects, where users belong to one or more groups and groups can contain other groups as members, to improve the required space by storing raw access controls (explicit authorizations) only, and propagating explicit authorizations recursively from groups to members to derive the rest of the authorizations. For example, the user hierarchy of UNIX can be exploited to define an explicit mode for a group to access a file, and then members of that group are implicitly authorized to access the file.

W. Jonker and M. Petkovic (Eds.): SDM 2006, LNCS 4165, pp. 131–145, 2006.

Defining a hybrid model that exploits the subject hierarchy to derive implicit authorizations from explicit ones may cause conflicts, for example if a user is in two groups, one of which is authorized to access the data and the other which has been assigned negative authorization. An *authorization conflict* is defined as either *no authorization* or *both positive and negative authorizations* for a given subject. Such models need a conflict resolution component to decide whether to grant access to such a subject. Yet, none of the existing models has proposed a resolution component that simultaneously supports a variety of policies for graph-based nesting structures. We should emphasize that the conflict resolution problem is quite a challenge in graph-based structures because a node may have multiple parents.

In this work, we propose a conflict resolution framework for hybrid authorization models in which the subject hierarchy is an arbitrary directed acyclic graph. Our framework provides a suite of conflict resolution models that are of interest in a variety of different applications, from more restricted environments such as military organizations to relaxed systems such as commercial Web-based information services. One contribution of this work is the unification of common yet distinct conflict resolution policies introduced by other researchers. Our framework builds on four practical conflict resolution policies, and consequently brings together thirty-two strategies under one umbrella. Therefore, security providers can use our framework and, by changing a few parameters, design the type of the resolution model demanded by a particular client. Thus, this work demonstrates preliminary steps of combining different strategies in a single framework; one can extend our framework to include additional conflict resolution policies too. We also provide efficient algorithms both to implement our framework and to demonstrate the similarity of selected strategies. We assume applications in which there are significantly more objects than subjects, and there are sufficiently many authorizations that they must be stored on secondary storage. Our algorithms have small footprints and are based on common data structures, thus they can be implemented and maintained cost-effectively.

This paper is organized as follows. Section 2 restates major resolving policies exploited in our framework. Section 3 defines all legitimate conflict resolution models based on the resolving policies. Section 4 provides details of algorithms applicable to our most practical model. Section 5 explains how our algorithms can be extended to cover other models, and our experiment results are shown in Section 6. Section 7 discusses related works and Section 8 summarizes with future research directions.

2   Conflict Resolution Framework

In this section, we outline the four main conflict resolution policies underlying our framework: *preferred authorization*, *locality/globalization*, *majority*, and *default authorization*. As stated in Section 1, these policies are articulated by other researchers and appear in various real world applications. Here, we restate each policy briefly and independently of other policies, as well as providing some examples of their applicability. Then, in Section 3, we explain how legitimate combinations of these policies lead us to define five conflict resolution models and thirty-two consequent strategies.

Our framework assumes that the subjects for whom authorizations are to be determined are structured as a directed acyclic graph. Individuals are represented as leaf nodes; a group of individuals is represented by a node with outgoing edges to each member of the group; a group of groups is represented by a node with outgoing edges to each subgroup member of that group In general, a group can have zero or more subgroups and zero or more individual nodes. However, we do not restrict the subject hierarchy to form a tree.

A member of a group enjoys all authorizations of that group. Recall from Section 1, propagating explicit authorizations to derive effective authorizations of the group members may cause conflicts. Here, we outline popular conflict resolution policies that we exploit in our framework.

Preferred Authorization Policy. Preferred authorization (either positive or negative) is determined by the system installer at configuration time. This policy states which authorization wins when at least one of each exist for a particular subject. Precedence of negative authorization (known as closed policy) is preferred in more restricted systems such as military; and, precedence of positive authorization may be preferred in more open applications such as public information systems.

Locality Policy. This policy states that the most specific authorization takes precedence. It applies to distributed organizations whose local branches may recognize an exception to a general rule. For instance, a department in a university may admit an outstanding applicant although the general admission requirement is not completely met. Thus, when for a given subject, both positive and negative authorizations can be derived from different ancestors, the one that is closer to the subject wins. Note that the distance between two nodes (subjects) in a directed acyclic graph is measured by computing the shortest directed path. The locality policy is not deterministic since no authorization wins when the distances are equal.

Globalization Policy. In contrast to the locality policy, globalization states that the most general authorization takes precedence. One application of this policy is in distributed organizations whose headquarters makes the final decision on a pre-approved task by a local office. For instance, a supreme court may override the appealed decision. When, for a given subject, both positive and negative authorizations can be derived from different ancestors, the one that is farther from the subject wins. Similar to the locality policy, the distance between two nodes is measured by computing the shortest path, and globalization is not deterministic since no authorization may win.

Majority Policy. This policy states that the conflict can be resolved based on votes, and the authorization that has the majority wins. The application of this policy is where several parties have different opinions of giving or not giving the authorization to a particular member; then, the decision is made by votes. For instance, GATT's current members vote to determine if a new application can get into the group. By applying this policy, the dominant authorization takes precedence. This policy is also non-deterministic since it can result in a tie.

Default Authorization Policy. This policy is applied only to root subjects for which no authorization has been defined. Closed systems, such as in the military, require negative authorization by default; however, open systems, such as public information applications, initially allow any subject to enjoy a positive authorization. This policy is deterministic, but applies to root subjects only.

3   Conflict Resolution Models

Having defined several popular conflict resolution policies, we are able to introduce five different conflict resolution models namely DLP, DLMP, DP, DMLP, and DMP, in which D, L, M, and P indicate Default, Locality/globalization, Majority, and Preferred authorization policies, respectively; see Figure 1. Recall that only the Preferred authorization policy is deterministic, we guarantee two facts: first, none of the policies are redundant, and second, there is no conflict after applying the last step. Moreover, Figure 1 illustrates that the Default and Preferred authorization policies are always the first and the last applicable policies, respectively, in our framework; the other two policies, the Locality/globalization policy and the Majority policy, are optional. Furthermore, since the Default, Locality/globalization, and Preferred authorization policies can take two modes each, in total, there are thirty-two different strategies derived from our conflict resolution models. (Paths a, b, and d generate eight instances each, and paths c and e generate four instances each.) We chose the Default authorization policy as the first step of our framework since explicit and implicit authorizations have equal priorities in our model. However, as an alternative, one may choose the Default authorization policy as the last step in order to give more priority to explicit authorizations. This will produce another yet very similar set of thirty-two strategies, which we refrain from discussing in this work due to the space limit.

Figure 2 depicts how the above models resolve different cases of conflicts. Hierarchies are directed acyclic graphs in which, for simplicity, the direction is assumed from higher nodes (parents) to lower nodes (children), and dash-dot lines between two nodes means that their distance is more than one node. In all cases, we are interested in resolving the authorization of the subject that is at the bottom of the hierarchy. Moreover, explicit authorizations are shown by regular fonts while derived authorizations are shown in bold *italics*. We have labeled nodes with special names to emphasis the role of each node in the graph; nodes with no label have no role in the conflict resolution.

In particular, Figure 2(a) illustrates the DLP model in which Locality has the highest priority. (The Default authorization policy is only applied to root subjects.) Therefore, regardless of authorizations of other nodes, the effective authorization will be the same as authorization of L that is the immediate ancestor of the node. Similarly, Figure 2(a') illustrates an instance of the DLP model in which *globalization* has the highest priority. Therefore, regardless of authorizations of intermediate nodes, the effective authorization will be the same as authorization of G that is the most global ancestor of the node. Figure 2(b) (and 2(b')) illustrates the DLMP model in which Locality (or globalization) has more priority than Majority. Therefore, we only look at the most local (global) ancestors, and whichever authorization is in majority will be assigned to the node. In Figure 2(b'), we assume that distances of three root subjects (-, +, and GM) from the leaf subject are the same. In Figure 2(c), we describe the case in which neither the locality nor the majority is important. Therefore, in case of conflict, the preferred authorization (P) will be assigned to the node; this is the DP model. Figure 2(d) (and 2(d')) illustrates the DMLP model in which Majority has more priority than Locality (or globalization). Therefore, in case of a tie on the majority of conflicting authorizations, the one that is closer to (farther from) the node will be the winner. Figure 2(e) illustrates the DMP model in which Majority has the highest priority. Therefore, regardless of the distance of other nodes, the authorization in majority will be the winner.

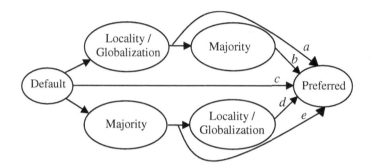

Fig. 1. Access control conflict resolution models

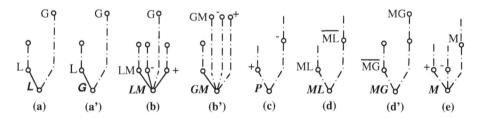

Fig. 2. Resolving conflicts by applying (a) the DLP model, (a') the DGP instance of DLP, (b) the DLMP model, (b') the DGMP instance of DLMP model, (c) the DP model, (d) the DMLP model, (d') the DMGP instance of DMLP, and (e) the DMP model

4   Algorithms for Conflict Resolution in the DLP Model

In this section, we provide algorithms for conflict resolution in the DLP model in which the most significant authorization takes precedence. The Default and Preferred authorization policies are set to positive or negative by parameters of the model. The closed DLP model, in which both Default and Preferred authorizations are negative, is the most practical resolution model demanded by real world applications. Later in Section 5, we show how to extend these algorithms for all other models.

Throughout the rest of the discussion, we assume that the subject hierarchy is stored in a table of *<parent, child>* edges, and also the authorizations are kept as *<subject, object, authorization-annotation>* tuples, denoting that *subject* has been positively (or negatively, according to *authorization-annotation*) authorized to access *object*. We assume the number of objects is overwhelming, and the explicit authorizations must be stored at secondary storage. Therefore, giving an object o and a leaf-subject (user) u, the procedure of computing compute u's accessibility to o involves loading the explicit authorizations from disk (disk IO) and resolving the conflicts from the set of explicit authorizations (CPU operation). In the following, we use "authorization" to denote "explicit authorization" if not otherwise specified. We list in Table 1 the symbols used throughout the rest of the discussion.

Table 1. Symbols

Symbol	Representation
S	All subjects
O	All objects
S_u	Subjects that are ancestors of subject u
S_o	Subjects that are authorized with object o
O_s	Objects that are authorized to subject s
$S_{u,o}$	Ancestors of u that are authorized with object o

We first show two semi-naive algorithms that compute the accessibility from user u to an object o. Both of them need to load *all* authorizations from disk having o as its object attribute, and resolve conflicts within $O(|S_u|^3)$ and $O(|S_{u,o}|^2 + |S_o|)$ time, respectively. We will then introduce the Dominance algorithm (Section 4.3), which only need to load *partial* authorizations from disk, and outperforms both semi-naive algorithms in CPU time. All three algorithms take space quadratic in the size of the subject hierarchy.

4.1 Bottom-Up Algorithm

This algorithm first loads all authorizations for S_o, then it first checking user u's authorization, and annotating u accordingly (``+''/``-'' or blank, depending if u is positively/negatively authorized with object o or no authorization is specified). After that, the annotation of the u is propagated to its parent (if the subject is blank annotated, it does not propagate to its parents). Then each parent in turn propagates its annotation to its own parents in the same manner (if that parent is not already annotated from its child, it tries to load its annotation from the explicit access controls stored on secondary storage). This process goes on until the annotations on the subject hierarchy stabilize. At this moment, if none of the ancestors is annotated, and the Default authorization policy of DLP is positive (or negative), the user may (not) access the object. If at least one of the ancestors is annotated positively (or negatively), and none of the other ancestors is annotated negatively (or positively), the user may (not) access the object. Otherwise, if the Preferred authorization policy of DLP is positive (or negative), this user may (not) access the object. The pseudo code is shown in Algorithm I. We have the following theorem on the algorithm's correctness. For readability of the proof, and without loss of generality, we assume both Default and Preferred authorizations are negative:

Theorem 1. *Bottom-Up algorithm correctly computes the semantics specified by DLP model. Particularly, this is true regardless what in order the children override their common parent's annotation at Line 9.*

PROOF (sketch): Both the policy combination and the algorithm compute well-defined access controls for each *<subject, object>* pair. Therefore, we only need to show they agree on the "negative" decisions. If the algorithm returns *negative*, either there are no authorization annotations after running the algorithm (Line 13), or there is at least one negative ancestor (Line 17). For the first situation, no explicit annotated subjects from the table of explicit authorizations must exist, since the algorithm will never decrease the number of annotations in the subject hierarchy. Similarly, if there are no explicit annotated subjects from the table of explicit authorizations, this algorithm will not generate any new annotated subjects. For the second situation when there is at least one explicit annotated subject, we observed that the user is not accessible to the object if and only if there exists at least one negative subject that has no positive descendants (NNPD for short) as the user's ancestor. We show that the algorithm generates at least one negatively annotated subject (*NA subject* for short) if and only if there exists a NNPD subject before running the algorithm. For the "only if" direction, our proof uses induction on the number of NNPD subjects and omitted here for brevity. For the "if" direction, we show that if every negative subject has positive descendant(s), the algorithm will not generate a NA subject. Assume there exist NA subject(s) after running the algorithm. We pick the NA subject that does not have any other NA children. Apparently, this NA subject gets its negative annotation from the table of explicit authorizations, and all its descendants are not positively annotated after running this algorithm. However, this NA subject should have an explicit positively annotated descendant before running this algorithm according to our assumption. This positive descendant will not lose its annotation after running this algorithm (since our algorithm will not decrease the number of annotations), hence a contradiction. ∎

The number of lookups in the explicit authorizations table in the algorithm (the IO operations) is bounded by $O(S_{u,o})$. The number of annotation propagations (the dominant CPU time in this algorithm) is bounded by $(1+d_{out}+d_{out}^2+\ldots+d_{out}^{l-1})$, where d_{out} is the maximum fan-out among the ancestors of *user*, and l is the length of the longest path in the sub-hierarchy consisting of these subjects. The above procedure can be optimized by Lines 10 and 11 to ensure that no subject appears more than once in the queue (this can be done by using a hash table on the content of the queue). This optimization is valid since a subject's previous occurrence in the queue will be overridden anyway. Thus, the number of *enqueue* operations is bounded by $(S_u.l)$, and checking if a parent exists in the queue is bounded by $(E.l)$, where E is the number of edges between all subjects in S_u. It is easy to verify that $(E.l)$ is in turn bounded by S_u^3, which is the algorithm's time complexity. The above algorithm only requires a queue, a hash table on its content, and a placeholder for the ancestors' authorizations on the object. All these data structures grow linearly in S_u. We have the following space requirement:

Proposition 1. *Bottom-Up algorithm requires $O(S_u)$ space (excluding the edge table representing the subject hierarchy). Moreover, the subject hierarchy table can be transitively reduced [1] to save space, while keeping the accuracy of the algorithm.*

With this nice property, the Bottom-Up algorithm is particularly suitable for memory-constrained computing environments where there are significantly more objects than subjects, and the explicit authorizations must be stored on secondary storage.

Algorithm I. Bottom-Up algorithm

```
BOTTOM-UP (u, o)
    ¤ To check if u has access to o
    ¤ default and preferred authorizations have been set by the DLP model
 1:     Q ← u
 2:     while Q is not empty do
 3:         s = dequeue(Q)
 4:         if s is not annotated
 5:             then if <s, o, +/-> is in raw AC table
 6:                 then annotate s accordingly
 7:         for each parent p of s do
 8:             if s is annotated
 9:                 then put s's annotation on p
10:             if Q already contains p
11:                 then remove p from Q
12:             enqueue(Q, p)
13:     if no ancestors of u is annotated
14:         then return default
15:     if no ancestor of u is annotated by authorization
16:         then return authorization
17:     return preferred
```

4.2 PairWise Algorithm

The Bottom-Up algorithm needs to check each ancestor of *user* even if that ancestor is not authorized with *object*. This causes a lot of overhead when the subject hierarchy is sparsely authorized. Moreover, it is likely that a parent subject gets enqueued/dequeued multiple times, each time being overridden with an annotation from one of its children, resulting in a huge amount of overhead. The PairWise Algorithm overcomes these disadvantages by directly overriding ancestors' annotations from its descendants. It does so by keeping in memory the ancestor-descendant relationship of the whole subject hierarchy (i.e., a materialized transitive closure of the subject hierarchy as a lookup table), which can be shared by subsequent queries. After loading authorizations on *object*, the algorithm first picks the ones that are authorized for the ancestors of the *user*. This step takes (S_o) time with the help of the ancestor-descendant table. If there is no annotated ancestor, the algorithm returns the Dfault authorization. Otherwise, the algorithm checks if at least one of the ancestors is annotated positively (or negatively) without any negative (positive) descendant, and none of the other ancestors is annotated negatively (or positively) without any positive (negative) descendant, the user may (not) access the object. Otherwise, the algorithm returns the Preferred authorization.

The correctness of the algorithm is directly derived from the definition of the DLP model and closed world assumptions. Although the PairWise algorithm loads slightly more explicit tuples than the Bottom-Up algorithm (S_u rather than $S_{u,o}$), it only needs to check Ancestor-Descendant relationship between $S_{u,o}$ subjects. Furthermore, in the closed world assumption where both Default and Preferred authorizations are negative, it may not need to check all pairs of negative and positive subjects before it returns "non-accessible"; also, one can state a similar argument for the open world assumption. These are accomplished at the cost of computing the transitive closure of the subject hierarchy beforehand and caching it in memory. We found from real applications [16] that transitive closure is moderately large for a hierarchy consisting of several thousands of subjects.

4.3 Dominance Algorithm

In this section, for the sake of readability, we assume both Default and Preferred authorizations are negative; one can easily extend the argument and algorithm to cover the other three cases too. In the closed world assumption, if a user has only one parent subject, and that parent is negatively authorized for *object*, we can conclude that the user may not access the object no matter how its ancestors are authorized. However, the PairWise algorithm will still compare its negative parent with each positive ancestor. The *dominance algorithm* overcomes this disadvantage and further improves query performances. We first introduce the concept of *dominating subjects*:

Definition 1. (Dominating Subject): Given a pair of *<user, object>*, in which *user* has two ancestors A and B that are both authorized with *object*, yet their annotations are different. Then, A *dominates* B (w.r.t. *user* and *object*) if A is on *any* path from B to *user*; or A is negative, B is positive, and B is not on *any* path from A to *user*.

Intuitively, a dominating ancestor will have a "stronger" effect on deciding accessibility for its descendant. Using such a property, we have the following result:

Lemma 1. *If there exists an annotated ancestor X that is not dominated by any other annotated ancestor w.r.t. user and object, X's annotation decides accessibility from user to object.*

Therefore, the existence of such a subject immediately tells the accessibility from *user* to *object*. However, sometimes we cannot find such a subject, e.g., where four annotated subjects dominate one another in a chain ($B^{+} \rightarrow_{dominates} A^{-} \rightarrow_{dominates} C+ \rightarrow_{dominates} D^{-} \rightarrow_{dominates} B+$). Nonetheless, we have the following special property of negative subjects:

Lemma 2. *A negative subject dominates all its successor positive subjects in (any) reverse topological ordering of the subject hierarchy. It can be dominated only by its preceding positive subjects.*

This lemma suggests that we scan the annotated subjects in a reverse topological order: for each positive subject encountered, we store it (in *P-Set*). For each negative subject encountered, we check if it is ancestor to any subjects in the *P-Set*. We stop scanning once we encounter a negative subject that is not an ancestor of (dominated by) any positive subjects in the *P-Set*. We call such negative subject a *frontier subject*. We only need to look at the subjects before the frontier subject if there exists such a frontier subject. Moreover, we only need to check the ancestor-descendant relationship between positive subjects with their successor negative subjects (This also requires keeping the transitive closure of the subject hierarchy in memory), reducing half of the ancestor descendant checks required by the PairWise algorithm. The complete procedure based on this idea is shown in Algorithm II. Its correctness follows directly from Lemma 2. Note that the *sort* operation Algorithm II is not necessary if tuples of explicit authorizations are clustered on objects and sorted in reverse topological order of the subjects inside each cluster. By this data layout, we do not even need to load all tuples of explicit authorizations on the object.

It is clear that Algorithm II can be easily parameterized to support all eight strategies of the DLP model at once. In next section, we show the similarity of DLP to other models such as DLMP, as well as to prove the efficiency of our approach by experiments.

5   Extending the Algorithms to Other Models

Algorithms for the DLP model can be exploited to define corresponding algorithms for other models illustrated in Figure 1. In particular, in this section, we provide Algorithm III to implement the Dominance algorithm for the DLMP model in which the most significant authorization (locality) takes precedence; however, if there are both positive and negative authorizations with the same locality, the one that is in majority wins. Similar to Algorithm II, we assume both Default and Preferred authorization are negative.

Algorithm II. Dominance algorithm for the closed DLP model

```
DOMINANCE1(user, obj)
      ¤ To check if user has access to obj
      ¤ default and preferred authorizations have been set to negative by the DLP model
1:   locate explicit authorizations tuples with object=obj
2:   sort them by subject's reverse-topological order
3:   P-Set ← ∅
4:   for each tuple <s, o, annotation> in sorted order with best
             locality do
5:      if s is not ancestor of user
6:         then continue
7:      if annotation="-" and none of s'∈P-Set is descendant of s
8:         then return non-accessible
9:      if annotation is "+"
10:        then P-Set ← s
11: if P-Set is not empty
12:    then return accessible
13: return non-accessible
```

Algorithm III is similar to Algorithm II except for the followings: Line 3' initializes a counter to count number of negative authorizations; Line 8' increases the number of negative authorizations; in Line 11', the algorithm returns "accessible" if majority of authorizations are positive; otherwise, it returns "non-accessible".

Algorithm III. Dominance algorithm for the closed DLMP model

```
DOMINANCE2(user, obj)
  ¤ To check if user has access to obj
  ¤ default and preferred authorizations have been set to negative by the DLP model
  1:    locate tuples of explicit authorizations with object = obj
  2:    Sort them by subject's reverse-topological order
  3:    P-Set ← ∅
  3':   negativeCnt =0
  4:    for each tuple <s, o, annotation> in sorted order with
           best locality do
  5:       if s is not ancestor of user
  6:          then continue
  7:       if annotation="-" and none of s'∈P-Set is descendant of s
  8':         then inc(negativeCnt)
  9:       if annotation is "+"
  10:         then P-Set ← s
  11':  if negativeCnt < |P-Set|
  12:      then return accessible
  13:   return non-accessible
```

Having defined algorithms for models DLP and DLMP, and recall from Figure 1 the similarity of these models to the DMP and DMLP models, respectively, interested readers can easily define corresponding algorithms for the rest of our framework. (Note that the DP model is a trivial case of other models.) Using the parameterized algorithms, security providers can define the type of the resolution model demanded by a particular client.

6   Experiments

Our experiments are conducted using JDK1.5 on a Sun workstation (sun4u, SunOS 5.8), with 512 Megabytes memory. We have compared Algorithms Bottom-Up, PairWise, and Dominance1, using the subject hierarchy of a practical system called LiveLink with random authorizations on 2000 objects. We have applied varying authorization ratio (the percentage of subjects explicitly authorized to access an object) of 0.1% (sparse), 0.7% (medium), and 5% (dense), and accessibility ratio (percentage of positive authorizations) from 10% to 90%. The explicit authorizations are stored on disk using BerkeleyDB (available at http://www.sleepycat.com). We store two copies for the explicit authorization tuples: one copy is clustered on the object attributes and secondarily sorted on subjects (according to reverse topological order of the subject hierarchy); the other copy is clustered on subjects and secondarily sorted on the objects. Each copy has an index on its clustering attribute.

We have run ten queries for each authorization ratio and accessibility ratio configuration. Each query corresponds to a random *<object, leaf-subject>* pair. Figures 3(a), 3(b), and 3(c) show the wall clock times for the ten queries using our three algorithms. The Dominance1 algorithm outperforms the other two under all authorization/accessibility ratios. The superiority of the Dominance1 algorithm is most significant when the authorization ratio is high (i.e., more authorized ancestors for each user for a given object). When the authorization ratio decreases, the gap between Dominance1 and PairWise becomes smaller. The reason is that when authorization is sparse, the number of authorized subjects per object is low, and around 30% of the users (leaf-subjects) do not have a single authorized ancestor for the object. In this case all three algorithms instantly returned *non-accessible*. For users with a few authorized ancestors, a single disk page read will load all authorized subjects for the object, therefore the I/O cost between Dominance1 and PairWise are the same. Figure 3(d) compares disk reads between Dominance1 and the two other algorithms (Bottom-Up and PairWise algorithms always load the same amount of data). The y-axis is the ratio of disk reads of Dominance1 algorithm to the ones of the PairWise algorithm (remember that the PairWise and Bottom-Up algorithms have the same amount of disk reads). We noticed that even when the I/O difference is under 3% between Dominance1 and PairWise for sparse authorization (0.1%), the Dominance1 algorithm still outperforms PairWise by around 10% from CPU time saving. The accessibility ratio does not affect the Bottom-Up algorithm, but it affects both Dominance1 and PairWise algorithms, since these two algorithms both rely on raw negatively authorized subjects to reach a *non-accessible* decision early-on. We conclude that Dominance1 algorithm is the best choice if we can sort the access control data on disk *a priori*. If the data is not sorted, PairWise algorithm is the right choice when the accessibility ratio is low. Bottom-Up algorithm suits the best when we do not have memory to hold the transitive closure of subject hierarchy.

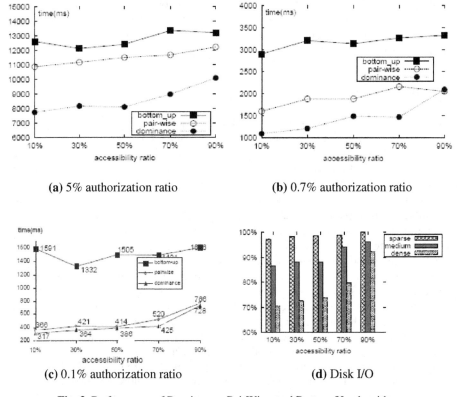

(a) 5% authorization ratio

(b) 0.7% authorization ratio

(c) 0.1% authorization ratio

(d) Disk I/O

Fig. 3. Performance of Dominance, PairWise, and Bottom-Up algorithms

7 Related Work

Bertino et al. [2] propose an authorization mechanism for relational models in which conflicts are mainly resolved based on the negative takes precedence rule, and the concept of weak and strong authorizations which is equivalent to one strategy instance of our DLP resolution by which eight different strategies are covered. Jajodia et al [8] use Datalog programs to model access controls of hybrid authorizations with a wide range of conflict prevention/resolving policies. Their modeling stores the raw authorizations and computes the effective authorizations for a *<subject, object>* pair in time linear to the size of the Datalog program (rules and ground facts). However, their ground facts include the transitive closure of the subject hierarchy (otherwise it is not linear time to infer ancestor descendant relationship between subjects, which is required for conflict resolution) plus all the raw authorizations. Taking into account the gigantic size of the ground facts, even a linear time solution is not efficient (e.g., consider searching a tuple using a sequential scan on the table). One approach to efficiently compute access control queries is by materializing (memorization of) the entire effective access control, as suggested by Jajodia et al. [8]. The accessibility check for a given *<subject, object>* pair is thus equivalent to checking the materialized effective (implicit) access control table (constant time). However, considering the formidable size of the effective access controls, which is the product of the number of objects and the number of subjects, this approach is not practical for very large systems. Moreover, the materialized effective access controls are not self-maintainable with respect to updating the explicit authorizations, and even a slight modification to the raw access controls (explicit authorizations) would possibly result in a drastic modification to the effective ones, making the maintenance task very expensive.

Some existing solutions on computing effective authorizations typically assume that the raw authorizations are propagated on tree-structured data [4, 13, 15, 16]. Propagation on a tree path makes conflict resolution trivial since there is only one path between all ancestors to a leaf. Moreover, the number of ancestors for a leaf is bounded by the depth of the tree, which is usually a small value in real world data [12]. However, when the raw access controls are propagated on a DAG subject hierarchy, a leaf subject would potentially have all subjects as its ancestors, and each ancestor may have several paths reaching to that leaf. Therefore, none of the approaches for tree-structured data are appropriate in this setting. We must emphasize that real world subject hierarchies are mostly DAG-structured rather than trees. E.g., the UNIX file system allows a user to be member of several groups at the same time; in role-based access control systems, a user can be assigned several roles while each role can be assigned to multiple parent roles [5].

Cuppens et al [3] propose a conflict resolution model for documents containing sensitive information. They solve the problem of downgrading the classification of these documents when their contents become obsolete. Their approach basically suggests a strict order of preference between rules. They do not exploit any hierarchy among subjects or objects other than the object classification. Koch et al [10] provide a systematic graph-based conflict detection and resolution based on two properties namely, *rule reduction* and *rule expansion*. Using these properties, they transform a conflicting graph into a conflict-free one. However, their approach is applicable only to the rules that are related to one another, whereas our approach addresses independent policies. Finally, our approach is also different than the combining algorithms in XACML [13], in which the resolution model relies on the data hierarchy rather than the subject hierarchy.

8 Conclusions and Future Works

In this work, we have designed a conflict resolution framework for hybrid authorizations. Our framework includes a variety of resolution models, including DLP, DLMP, DP, DMLP, and DMP, to support both closed an open systems as well as both restricted and relaxed applications. Using these models, security providers can choose, among thirty-two different instances yet extensible, the type of the resolution strategy demanded by a particular client. We have also presented a suite of algorithms for resolving access controls for subject hierarchies of form directed acyclic graph under DLP and DLMP rules. In addition to providing the correctness proof of our algorithms, we have experimented with different sets of data layouts. Our pilot experiments show the superior performance of the Dominance algorithm.

We propose several directions for continuing this research. First, our algorithms serve as the building blocks towards a flexible yet efficient hierarchical multi-user access control system. It would be interesting to extend the framework by adding more conflict resolving rules to our model. In particular, *separation of duties* and *conflict of interest* [9, 14] are among challenging properties that significantly affect the conflict resolution problem. Another possible direction to extend this framework to support more sophisticated subject hierarchies, such as graphs, as well as resolving conflicts in mixed hierarchies of subjects and objects.

Acknowledgements

We gratefully acknowledge the Natural Science and Engineering Research Council of Canada, Communications and Information Technology Ontario, Open Text Corporation, and the University of Waterloo for their financial support. We would also like to express sincere thanks to Professors Frank Wm. Tompa and Kenneth Salem for their advices.

References

1. A. V. Aho, M. R. Garey, and J. D. Ullman. The Transitive Reduction of a Directed Graph. SIAM Journal on Computing, vol. 1, pp. 131–137, 1972.
2. E. Bertino, S. Jajodia, and P. Samarati. A Flexible Authorization for Relational Data Management Systems. ACM Transactions on Information Systems, vol. 17, no. 2, pp. 101–140, April 1999.
3. F. Cuppens, L. Cholvy, C. Saurel, and J. Carrere. Merging Security Policies: Analysis of a Practical Example. In Proceedings of the 11th Computer Security Foundations Workshop, pp. 123–136, 1998.

4. E. Damiani, S. De Capitani di Vimercati, S. Paraboschi, and P. Samarati. A Fine-Grained Access Control System for XML Documents. ACM Transaction on Information and System Security, vol. 5, no. 2, pp. 169–202, May 2002.
5. D. F. Ferraiolo, and D. R. Kuhn. Role Based Access Control. In Proceeding of the 15th NIST-NCST National Computer Security Conference, pp. 554–563, October 1992.
6. M. A. Harrison, W. L. Ruzzo, and J. D. Ullman. Protection in Operating Systems. Communications of ACM, vol. 19, no. 8, pp. 461–471, August 1976.
7. J. H. Howard, M. L. Kazar, S. G. Menees, D. A. Nichols, M. Satyanarayanan, R. N. Sidebotham, and M. J. West. Scale and Performance in a Distributed File System. ACM Transactions on Computer Systems, vol. 6, no. 1, pp. 51–81, 1988.
8. S. Jajodia, P. Samarati, M. L. Sapino, and V. S. Subrahmanian. Flexible Support for Multiple Access Control Policies. ACM Transactions on Database Systems, vol. 26, no. 2, pp. 214–260, 2001.
9. J. Joshi, E. Bertino, B. Sahfiq, and A. Ghafoor. Dependencies and Separation of Duty Constraints in GTRBAC. In Proceeding of the 8th ACM Symposium on Access Control Models and Technologies, pp. 51–64, June 2003.
10. M. Koch, L. V. Mancini, F. Parisi-Presicce, Conflict Detection and Resolution in Access Control Specifications, In Proceedings of the 5th International Conference on Foundations of Software Science and Computation Structures, pp. 223–237, 2002.
11. B. W. Lampson. Protection. In Proceedings of the 5th Annual Princeton Conference on Information Sciences and Systems, pp. 437–443, March 1971.
12. L. Mignet, D. Barbosa, and P. Veltri. The XML Web: A First Study. In Proceedings of the International World Wide Web Conference, pp. 500–510, 2003.
13. T. Moses. eXtensible Access Control Markup Language Version 2.0, Technical Report, OASIS, February 2005.
14. M. Nyanchama, and S. L. Osborn. The Role Graph Model and Conflict of Interest. ACM Transaction on Information Systems Security, vol. 2, no. 1, pp. 3–33, 1999.
15. T. Yu, D. Srivastava, L. V. S. Lakshmanan, and H. V. Jagadish. Compressed Accessibility Map: Efficient Access Control for XML. In Proceeding of the 28th International Conference on Very Large Data Bases, pp. 478–489, 2002.
16. H. Zhang, N. Zhang, K. Salem, and D. Zhuo. Compact Access Control Labeling for Efficient Secure XML Query Evaluation. In Proceedings of the 2nd International Workshop on XML Schema and Data Management, April 2005.

Analysis of a Database and Index Encryption Scheme – Problems and Fixes

Ulrich Kühn

Deutsche Telekom Laboratories
Technische Universität Berlin, Germany
ukuehn@acm.org

Abstract. The database encryption scheme of Elovici et al. [3] uses encryption of individual cells in a data base table to preserve the database structure. A suitable index encryption scheme is also given for prevention of information leakage from the index. An updated and improved method for index encryption is described by the same authors in [12].

The security goals of these schemes are privacy and authenticity of the cell data at the given position in the table. Furthermore, the encrypted index data shall not have any correlation to the table column data to avoid information leakage. The index shall be protected against unauthorised modification of the index data.

In the present paper we cryptanalyse these schemes with respect to possible instantiations and give counter-examples, i.e. give instantiations of these schemes with usual components that are insecure. These counter-examples highlight that the schemes involve assumptions about cryptographic primitives that do no necessarily hold.

Furthermore, we show how to modify the schemes so that the original basic ideas of [3] and [12] lead to secure database and index encryption.

Keywords: Database Security, Applied Cryptography, Cryptanalysis.

1 Introduction

When a database holds sensitive information appropriate protection measures must be taken. Access control schemes are put in place to protect the database contents from unauthorised access. However, this still leaves the data vulnerable to a database administrator or other person with high privileges, or even a machine administrator without database privileges. Furthermore, anyone with physical access to the machine or storage system holding the actual data can copy or modify it.

Therefore, some threat scenarios require to protect the actual database contents with regard to privacy as well as authenticity. This can be achieved by a database encryption scheme. Here typical security goals are protection of data privacy and data authenticity against adversaries that have access to the database on a low enough level to bypass the access control scheme.

A scheme to achieve these goals is presented by Elovici et al. [3], which works on a granularity of individual table cells. Additionally they provide an encryption scheme for index tables that allows separation of structural data (which

W. Jonker and M. Petkovic (Eds.): SDM 2006, LNCS 4165, pp. 146–159, 2006.

is left unencrypted) from database contents. Their encryption schemes preserve the structure of the database, i.e. change only the contents of table cells. Furthermore, they are flexible with respect to which columns to protect or leave in clear. An improved version of the index encryption scheme is presented by the same authors in [12].

The security goals of these schemes are privacy and authenticity of the cell data at the given position in the table. Furthermore, the encrypted index data shall not have any correlation to the table column data to avoid information leakage. The index shall also be protected against unauthorised modification of the index data.

CONTRIBUTION. In this paper we analyse this database and index encryption schemes of [3] and [12] with respect to their security goals. We show that possible instantiations of these schemes with usual schemes like encryption in CBC mode are not secure. By giving counter-examples we show that the underlying assumptions made on the cryptographic functions are not necessarily met by standard cryptographic methods.

Based on an analysis of the requirements of the basic ideas of [3] and [12] we propose fixes to the schemes that achieve the security goals. We show that authenticated encryption with associated data leads to secure schemes where proofs of security carry over to the database and index encryption case. We examine the storage and performance overhead necessary for these renewed database encryption schemes.

2   Description of the Database and Index Encryption Scheme

In [3] two encryption schemes are presented that we will describe briefly below: One for encrypting table cell data and a second for encrypting parts of an index. The index encryption scheme allows searches with knowledge of the key only, but preserves the structure of the index. Furthermore, in [12] an updated and improved index encryption scheme is presented which we will also briefly describe in this section.

Notation. Let $x||y$ denote the concatenation of the bit strings x and y. Let $x \oplus y$ denote the bitwise exclusive-or operation of the bit strings x and y; if x and y have different lengths, the shorter string is extended by implicitly appending 0-bits.

2.1   Threat Model

The threat model of [3] and [12] assumes that the database storage is not trusted. Therefore encryption and authentication is applied. Furthermore, the server the DBMS runs on is temporarily trusted: During a secure session the encryption keys are handed over to the DBMS server, and securely removed at the end of the session. See [12] for a detailed description, including methods to implement discretionary access control. Thus the schemes assume a partially-trusted server and untrusted storage.

This way the server is in a position where it can efficiently execute queries on the database using the encrypted indexes. No data is returned that does not belong to the answer to the query and has to be sorted out by the querying client. It is helpful here that the database and index encryption schemes presented in [3] and [12] preserve the structure of the database resp. index. A rogue storage or machine administrator however cannot obtain the plaintexts of database contents, as long as they are prohibited from compromising the server software.

Remark 1. Note that handing over the key to the DBMS server might be avoided at the cost of additional running time and logarithmic many additional communication rounds between client and server. When searching in the index tree structure the node data is retrieved on the server and sent to the client. The client decrypts the index data and returns a decision (left/right in the case of a binary tree) to the server, until the leaf level of the index tree is reached. Such a scheme might be worthwhile if the index uses d-nary B^+-trees with $d \gg 2$. Instead of the client, a trusted component in the server or in an intermediate system can also do this query-support work. However, moving the cryptographic operations away from the DBMS server severely changes the threat and trust model of the schemes.

2.2 Table Cell Encryption Scheme

The encryption scheme encrypts each attribute value V in a table's cell individually, but includes a cell address in the plaintext. The cell address is a triple (t, r, c) of table id t, row r, and column c. The scheme employs a function μ to convert the cell address triple before inclusion in the plaintext. Then the encryption scheme is either

$$C = E_k(V \oplus \mu(t, r, c)), \quad \text{or} \tag{1}$$
$$C = E_k(V || \mu(t, r, c)) \tag{2}$$

where $E_k(.)$ denotes symmetric encryption under key k. Here E is a fully deterministic encryption function, i.e.

$$\forall k : (x = y) \Rightarrow (E_k(x) = E_k(y)). \tag{3}$$

As examples DES[8] and AES[9] are mentioned. The form (2) is used whenever there is not enough redundancy in the allowed type of data for the specific column, however no specific threshold is given in [3]. It is suggested that the function μ is instantiated with a cryptographic hashfunction to obtain collision resistance.

Notation. We will call the scheme (1) the *XOR-Scheme*, the scheme (2) the *Append-Scheme*.

The schemes shall achieve (among others) the following security goals (see [3, Sect. 2]:

- Protection against pattern matching,
- Prevention of substituting encrypted values by values from other cells, and
- Data and position authentication, such that unauthorised modification or relocation of data should be noticed at decryption time.

2.3   Index Encryption Scheme of [3]

The index encryption scheme proposed in [3] encrypts the indexing key, but not the structural part of the index. That way managing the structure of the index shall still be possible.

The description of the index encryption scheme starts from a table representation of a B^+-tree. The table rows contain structural elements and index keys. The structural elements are left and right child nodes for inner nodes, and the right sibling for leaf nodes. The index keys are data elements of the indexed table column.

In [3] the index keys are the only encrypted parts. This works as follows. Given a row r_I in the index containing data V held in row r of the indexed table, it is stored in encrypted form as

$$E_k(V||r_I) \quad \text{for inner nodes, resp.} \tag{4}$$
$$E_k((V, r)||r_I) \quad \text{for leaf nodes.} \tag{5}$$

The security goals of this index encryption scheme are (see [3, Sect. 4]):

- No information about the plaintext value can be learned from the index.

Furthermore, index integrity is a goal of the encryption scheme of (4), (5).

2.4   Improved Index Encryption Scheme of [12]

The scheme of [12] is an improved version of the index encryption scheme described above. To describe it we need some notation: Let V_{trc} denote the data entry in the indexed table at the cell given by address (t, r, c). Let further

- Ref_I denote internal references between index entries, e.g. for building a B^+-tree,
- Ref_T denote references to the indexed table, i.e. the table row the data entry comes from,
- Ref_S denote self-references, e.g. the address of the entry in question, like r_I for the index encryption scheme described above in Sect. 2.3.

Furthermore, different cryptographic functions are used, i.e. a nondeterministic encryption function $\tilde{E}$, another encryption function E' which is described as "ordinary", which obviously shall mean "deterministic", and a message authentication scheme MAC.

The nondeterministic encryption function $\tilde{E}$ is suggested to be implemented based on a deterministic encryption function E, with a key k, as

$$\tilde{E}_k(x) := E_k(x||a), \tag{6}$$

where a is a fixed-size random number.

Based on the assumption that a standard index entry consists of a triple $(V_{trc}, \text{Ref}_\text{I}, \text{Ref}_\text{T})$, the encrypted index entry is proposed, given key k, as

$$(\tilde{E}_k(V_{trc}), \text{Ref}_\text{I}, E'_k(\text{Ref}_\text{T}), \text{MAC}_k(V_{trc}||\text{Ref}_\text{I}||\text{Ref}_\text{T}||\text{Ref}_\text{S})). \tag{7}$$

The security goals of this scheme are

– Prevention of information leakage arising from linkage leakage, i.e. correlation between entries in the index and the indexed table.
– Protection against unauthorised modification: Replacing ciphertexts or parts of ciphertexts by generated, copied, or old values.[1]

3   Attacking the Schemes

We will show here that all schemes described above fail to achieve the security goals when instantiated with usual efficient cryptographic components. By giving concrete counter-examples we show that the schemes involve some subtle implicit assumptions about the cryptographic schemes that are not necessarily met.

INSTANTIATION OF $E_k(.)$. For illustration of the problems with the cell encryption scheme it should be noted that standard block ciphers like AES[9] operate on a fixed number of bits at one time, i.e. 128 bits or 16 octets for AES. Longer data requires multiple applications of the block cipher, a *mode of operation*. Several such modes are defined [2]. We chose AESwith the widely-used CBC mode of operation to instantiate E.[2] This mode requires an initialisation vector IV. In [3] determinism of E is explicitly assumed, see (3). Thus, to construct our counter-examples, we use a constant IV $= (0, \ldots, 0)$ for all encryptions. Note that this is not secure, see the pattern matching attack, but we argue that the description of the encryption function in [3] and [12] could easily lead to such an implementation[3](a purely deterministic mode like ECB which does not need an

---

[1] In [12] pseudo-code is given to illustrate how queries are evaluated on the encrypted index. However, this code contains two bugs: While it checks the integrity of the data in inner nodes during the tree-walk, it fails to do so on the leaf-level, both for finding the right starting place for the answer, and for generating the answer from the list of right-sibling references. Both bugs can be easily fixed.

[2] Stream ciphers and streaming modes for blockciphers like OFB or counter mode would be insecure due to the reuse of the same key-stream resulting from the assumed determinism (3). This would be easily breakable if the attribute in question contain some redundancy.

[3] Note that the encryption scheme from [4] uses a zero IV for CBC mode. This has similar consequences for the security as in the pattern matching attacks shown here.

IV would be even worse). Input data with a length not being a multiple of the block size is padded according to some padding scheme, e.g. PKCS#5 [11].

By $\mathsf{ENC}_k(x)$ we will denote the encryption of a single block x under key k, by $\mathsf{DEC}_k(y)$ the decryption, e.g. a single application of AESen- resp. decryption. We instantiate $E_k(.)$ as $E_k(x) = \mathsf{CBC}[\mathsf{ENC}_k, \mathrm{IV}](x)$: Given a padded plaintext P with blocks $P = P_1||P_2||\ldots||P_s$, its encryption $C = C_1||C_2||\ldots||C_s = E_k(P)$ is computed as

$$C_1 = \mathsf{ENC}_k(P_1 \oplus \mathrm{IV}) = \mathsf{ENC}_k(P_1) \tag{8}$$
$$C_i = \mathsf{ENC}_k(P_i \oplus C_{i-1}), 1 \leq i \leq s. \tag{9}$$

3.1   Attacks on the Cell Encryption Scheme

Here we present attacks on the cell encryption schemes. We assume here that the basic encryption function $E_k(.)$ is implemented according to the general method described above.

PATTERN MATCHING ATTACK ON THE APPEND-SCHEME. Assume that a table column contains attributes comprised of strings that are possibly much longer than the blocksize of the cipher (e.g. 16 octets for AES). Assume further that two cells at t, r, c and t, r', c store attributes V, V' that share a common prefix of –for illustration– two blocks, i.e. decomposed into blocks

$$V = M_1||M_2||M_3||\ldots||M_p \tag{10}$$
$$V' = M_1||M_2||M_3'||\ldots||M_q'. \tag{11}$$

Encrypting these values under the same key with the scheme defined above will result in

$$C = E_k(V||\mu(t, r, c)) = C_1||C_2||C_3||\ldots \tag{12}$$
$$C' = E_k(V'||\mu(t, r', c)) = C_1||C_2||C_3'||\ldots. \tag{13}$$

Thus, common prefixes in the plaintext (longer than one block) will result in common prefixes in the ciphertext, clearly violating the goal of protection against pattern matching.

ATTACK ON AUTHENTICATION OF THE APPEND-SCHEME. Assume a cell with address t, r, c that contains the encrypted attribute

$$C = C_1||\ldots||C_{s-1}||C_s||C_{s+1}||\ldots||C_{s+u}. \tag{14}$$

Let P denote the corresponding plaintext (unknown to any adversary) with

$$P = P_1||\ldots||P_{s-1}||P_s||P_{s+1}||\ldots||P_{s+u} = V||\mu(t, r, c). \tag{15}$$

where we know from public information about the output length of μ according to (2) that $\mu(t, r, c)$ is contained in the *address checksum blocks* $P_{s+1}, \ldots, P_{s+u}$, whereas $P_1, \ldots, P_s$ do not contain any bits of $\mu(t, r, c)$.

For the attack we replace C by a modified ciphertext

$$C' = C'_1 || \ldots || C'_{s-1} || C_s || C_{s+1} || \ldots || C_{s+u}, \tag{16}$$

where for at least one $1 \leq i \leq s-1$ we have $C'_i \neq C_i$. Note that in C' the blocks $s, \ldots, s+u$ are the same as in C. By decrypting C' we obtain P'

$$P' = P'_1 || \ldots || P'_{s-1} || P'_s || P_{s+1} || \ldots || P_{s+u}. \tag{17}$$

Note that the plaintext of all checksum blocks $s+1, \ldots, s+u$ is the same as for the original plaintext, because $P_j = \mathsf{DEC}_k(C_j) \oplus C_{j-1}$ for $s+1 \leq j \leq s+u$, and blocks $s, \ldots, s+u$ are the same in C and C'.[4] Therefore $\mu(t,r,c)$ is found intact in the plaintext P', so P' is accepted as valid. We have produced an existential forgery, thus breaking the authentication of data and cell address.

Furthermore, an attack using partial ciphertext substitution is possible which changes blocks $C_1, \ldots, C_{s-1}$, i.e. blocks that precede the block before the address checksum blocks, However, in this case the plaintext block following the last replaced block is destroyed during decryption, as it cannot be controlled by an adversary.

SUBSTITUTION ATTACK ON THE XOR-SCHEME. We follow the suggestion in [3, Sect. 6.2] and implement $\mu(.)$ by

$$\mu(t,r,c) = h(t||r||c)$$

with a cryptographic hash function h, if necessary shortened to the block size of the blockcipher underlying $E_k(.)$. Assume that this block size is b octets. Further assume that an attribute V consists of b characters chosen from the ASCII character set and represented as a single octet each, i.e. for each character x we have $0 \leq x \leq 127$. Here V fits into a single block.

We show here that the data can be moved to certain other cells without detection. When moving $C = E_k(V \oplus \mu(t,r,c))$ to another cell with address t', r', c', we would obtain $V' = D_k(C) \oplus \mu(t', r', c')$ after decryption. In order to be accepted as valid all octets in V' must be in the range given above. This gives a condition on the most significant bit every octet, so in total a b-bit condition.

An adversary can try to impose this condition on the result of μ, so that only certain cell addresses are possible. Here all those t', r', c' are possible where in $\mu(t,r,c) \oplus \mu(t',r',c')$ the high bits of every octet is zero. The adversary can find such cell addresses offline. After about 2^b trials such a partial-second-preimage (where only the high bits are of concern) can be expected to be found. Furthermore, partial collision attacks are possible, and yield a result with about $2 \cdot 2^{b/2}$ work on average. Such a partial collision indicates cells where the contents can be moved from one cell to the other.

To illustrate this in practice we ran an experiment with a blocksize of 16 octets (suitable for AES) and SHA1 for h (truncated to the first 128 bits).

---

[4] This is well-known error propagation of CBC-decryption, where a changed ciphertext block affects only its own and the next block's decryption.

Among 1024 trial addresses (same t and c, running r) we found 6 collisions, i.e. (truncated) hashes where for all octets the corresponding high bits were the same. Exchanging the ciphertexts of those cells yields, after decryption, an allowed output which is valid at a different position than the original one.

3.2 Attacks on the Index Encryption Scheme in [3]

Here we show that the index encryption scheme does not achieve its security goals when instantiated with the encryption function described above.

PATTERN MATCHING ATTACK. Assume again that the table column for which an index is held according to the scheme described in Sect. 2.3 contains long strings of characters, typically much longer than the block size of the employed blockcipher. Further assume that the Append-Scheme of (2) is used for the encryption of cell data.

The observation used in Sect. 3.1 for the pattern matching attack will again be used here. Let V be an attribute in the indexed column with address t, r, c that shows up as a key in the index in row r_I. Then the input to the encryption function for the cell encryption will be

$$P^\mathrm{T} = P_1^\mathrm{T}||\dots||P_p^\mathrm{T} = V||\mu(t, r, c),$$

and in the index table either

$$P^\mathrm{I} = P_1^\mathrm{I}||\dots||P_q^\mathrm{I} = \begin{cases} V||r_\mathrm{I} & \text{for an inner node, or} \\ (V, r)||r_\mathrm{I} & \text{for a leaf,} \end{cases}$$

all including suitable padding to the block size of the cipher.

In case of an inner node P^T and P^I have a common prefix that, depending on V's length, can span several blocks. Thus their encryption will contain a common prefix. Depending on the representation of P^I for a leaf this property might also extend to the leafs of the tree. As a consequence an adversary succeeds with a partial pattern matching between the index tree and the table data, allowing to derive information on ordering between table elements or classes of table elements.

ATTACKING INDEX INTEGRITY. A partial substitution of key entries in the index table might be possible along the same lines as explained in Sect. 3.1 in the attack on the data integrity of the append-scheme. If an adversary can use this successfully depends on the specific implementation and the type of data in the table. However, if an adversary can successfully mount such an attack, observation of access patterns as reaction to adaptively triggered queries can leak information on table data.

3.3 Attacking the Improved Index Encryption Scheme in [12]

Here we show that, although a non-deterministic encryption function is employed, pattern matching attacks are still possible. Further we describe potential problems with the authentication of the scheme.

PATTERN MATCHING ATTACK. This attack works similar to the one given in the last section. We assume here again that the indexed column in the table contains (possibly) long strings of data that span more than one block of the underlying blockcipher (16 octets for AES), and, without loss of generality, that the fixed-size random numbers a according to (7) fit into one block, e.g. have bitlengths $|a| < 128$. We also assume that for cell encryption the append-method (2) is used. Let $V_{t,r,c}$ be a cell entry that spans several blocks. Then the index ciphertext is computed by $E_k(V_{t,r,c}||a)$. Decomposing the plaintext input to E into blocks we get

$$P^{\mathrm{I}} = V_{t,r,c}||a = P_1^{\mathrm{I}}||\ldots||P_s^{\mathrm{I}}||\ldots||P_{s+v}^{\mathrm{I}}, \qquad (18)$$

where s is such that P_s^{I} is the last block not containing parts of a; because of the bitlength of a we have $1 \leq v \leq 2$.

On the other hand, the corresponding cell ciphertext is $E_k(V_{t,r,c}||\mu(t,r,c))$. Also decomposing the input to E into blocks we have

$$P^{\mathrm{T}} = V_{t,r,c}||\mu(t,r,c) = P_1^{\mathrm{T}}||\ldots||P_s^{\mathrm{T}}||\ldots||P_{s+u}^{\mathrm{T}}, \qquad (19)$$

where again the block P_s^{T} does not contain parts of $\mu(t,r,c)$, and u is determined by the length of μ's output.

Then we know that $P_1^{\mathrm{I}} = P_1^{\mathrm{T}}$, ..., $P_s^{\mathrm{I}} = P_s^{\mathrm{T}}$, and thus the corresponding ciphertexts resulting from $E_k(.)$ are also the same. This allows partial pattern matching attack resp. partial correlation of index and table values. In fact, appending randomness to the plaintext does not prevent this.

UNAUTHORISED MODIFICATION. We notice that in the scheme of (7) the message authentication covers the plaintext plus some additional data, so that we have a variant of the encrypt-and-MAC method in the sense of [6]. This has been shown to not be necessarily secure.

We further notice that in (7) the same key k is used for encryption as well as for the MAC algorithm. This may lead to insecure interaction of the encryption and MAC algorithms. The following example is pathological, but shows that the original specification in [12] leaves too much room form interpretation.

Given our choice for the encryption function E above (CBC mode with zero IV), instantiating the MAC with a CBC-MAC variant like OMAC [5] – that itself is secure for variable-length inputs – results in a loss of authenticity. The essential point about CBC-MAC is that it works basically the same way as CBC mode encryption (see the beginning of Sect. 3), but the intermediate ciphertexts are not made public, only the final one is used as authentication tag. The details where OMAC deviates from this rough description are irrelevant for the attack.

The attack works as follows: Let V_{trc} be the cell data in the index node, and $P = V_{trc}||a = P_1||\ldots||P_s||\ldots||P_{s+q}$ the input to $E_k(.)$ in the first component in (7). Here we assume that $P_1, \ldots, P_s$ do not contain any bits of a, and that $s > 2$. Let the corresponding ciphertext be $C = C_1||\ldots||C_s||\ldots||C_{s+q}$. In the computation of $\mathrm{MAC}_k(V_{trc}||\ldots)$ in (7) we have the same plaintext inputs $P_1, \ldots, P_s$ followed by additional blocks. Thus, during the computation of the CBC-MAC of these plaintext blocks the first s intermediate ciphertext block will again be $C_1, \ldots, C_s$ due to the same key being used.

Now replacing the ciphertext in the first component in (7) by

$$C' = C_1'|| \ldots ||C_{s-1}'||C_s|| \ldots ||C_{s+q} \tag{20}$$

results in a decryption $P' = P_1'|| \ldots ||P_{s-1}'||P_s'||P_{s+1}|| \ldots ||P_{s+q}$ (from the error propagation in CBC decryption). Note that the removal of the random bits of a takes place in block P_{s+1} which is left unchanged. Computing again a CBC-MAC (using the same key k) on these values results in the intermediate chaining values $C_1', \ldots, C_{s-1}'$, followed by C_s, so that the further computation will be the same as for the original plaintext, yielding the same authentication tag as before. Thus the scheme fails to to detect this modification of the ciphertext.

4   Fixing the Schemes

We have seen above that the successful pattern matching attacks result from determinism in the encryption process (despite appended randomness) and the way in which long plaintexts are decomposed into blocks before encryption. Furthermore, we have seen that encryption schemes do not necessarily provide authenticity to prevent substitution. The reason is that usual modes of operation provide only limited error propagation during decryption. Here strong message authentication is required.[5]

In the following we will highlight how to repair the schemes such that the original security goals are reached. Proofs of security for the employed cryptographic schemes carry over to our proposal. Furthermore we will describe the cost in terms of performance and storage overhead imposed by our proposal.

REQUIREMENTS. We notice that there is no need to explicitly store the cell address or other self-references along with the cell or index contents. However, such position information needs to be authenticated along with the cell's contents. Thus, the security goal "authentication of data and position" to prevent partial substitution or modification of data or moving data to a different place in the table requires schemes which explicitly provide authentication. This is typically *not* provided by encryption alone.

Regarding the privacy of cell data an encryption scheme needs to produce ciphertext that cannot be distinguished from random values. In fact, such a scheme automatically ensures that there is no correlation between encrypted cell or index contents that an adversary can derive information from. This requires a nondeterministic encryption scheme.

Preferably the encryption and authentication schemes come with proofs of security, i.e. results on the concrete strengths against powerful attacks.

---

[5] Thus, explicitly adding a MAC in [12] is the right move, however, we have seen that there is still room for fatal interaction between components.

Authenticated Encryption with Associated Data. To achieve the goals identified above we employ an authenticated encryption scheme with associated data (AEAD). Examples for such schemes are EAX [1], OCB · PMAC [10], or CCFB [7]; see also [7] for an overview over recent developments regarding AEAD schemes. Such encryption schemes provide confidentiality of the data, and explicitly provide authenticity of the ciphertext along with other unencrypted information – the associated data. The schemes describe all necessary details, e.g. how to chose initialisation vectors as well as keys for encryption and authentication.

Formally, an AEAD scheme is a triple (Key-Gen, AEAD-Enc, AEAD-Dec) consisting of a key generation algorithms and two algorithms for encryption and decryption

$$\text{AEAD-Enc} : \mathcal{K} \times \mathcal{N} \times \mathcal{M} \times \mathcal{H} \to \mathcal{C} \times \mathcal{T} \tag{21}$$

$$\text{AEAD-Dec} : \mathcal{K} \times \mathcal{N} \times \mathcal{C} \times \mathcal{T} \times \mathcal{H} \to \mathcal{M} \cup \{\text{invalid}\} \tag{22}$$

with a key space $\mathcal{K}$, a nonce space $\mathcal{N}$, a space $\mathcal{H}$ of associated data, the plaintext resp. ciphertext space $\mathcal{M}$ resp. $\mathcal{C}$, and an authentication tag space $\mathcal{T}$. Note that neither the nonce nor the header data is included in the ciphertext, they must be handled separately.

No plaintext will be available if invalid is returned by AEAD-Dec. In this case we know that the key is not correct, the cell address is wrong, or the nonce, ciphertext, or authentication tag have been tampered with. There is no possibility to distinguish which of these cases has occurred.

Notation. For convenience and to distinguish between keys and data, we use AEAD-Enc$_k$(.) resp. AEAD-Dec$_k$(.) to denote the encryption resp. decryption under a key $k \in \mathcal{K}$.

Formally, we require that the AEAD scheme is secure under the strongest available security notions (see [1]):

- The ciphertext shall be indistinguishable from random under adaptive chosen plaintext attacks.
- The authenticity of the associated data and the plaintext shall be protected against existential forgery under adaptive chosen message attacks, i.e. adaptive chosen plaintext / chosen ciphertext attacks[6] .

Fixing the Database Encryption Scheme. The associated data part is typically used for header data, but we place the cell address here, so there is no need to store it explicitly. Nevertheless, it's integrity is guarded by the authentication tag.

For encrypting (under a key $k \in \mathcal{K}$) a value V for a cell with address $\text{Ref}_T = (t, r, c)$, a unique nonce N is generated, and we store

$$(N, C, T) \quad \text{with} \quad (C, T) = \text{AEAD-Enc}_k(N, V, \text{Ref}_T). \tag{23}$$

---

[6] Some models make the decryption oracle only available for checking that an forgery attempt succeeds, not for regular oracle queries by the adversary. This is polynomially equivalent.

For decryption of (N, C, T) at cell address $\text{Ref}_T = (t, r, c)$ we compute

$$\text{AEAD-Dec}_k(N, C, T, \text{Ref}_T) \tag{24}$$

and raise a decryption error if invalid is returned.

FIXING THE INDEX ENCRYPTION SCHEME. The index encryption scheme, i.e. encrypting the attributes from the indexed table, can be repaired in much the same way as the cell encryption. However, some differences arise because the column is fixed in an index table, and because the reference into the indexed table needs to be encrypted and authenticated. Furthermore, some binding between the table column and its index should be provided.

We now describe how to encrypt/decrypt (under a key $k \in \mathcal{K}$) an index entry for a cell address (t, r, c) with data value V_{trc}. Let the index be implemented as a table identified by t_I, and let r_I be the row number of the entry to be encrypted. Then we use the following references:

$\text{Ref}_T = r$

$\text{Ref}_I = $ *index-internal references, e.g. left child / right child / next sibling*

$\text{Ref}_S = (t_I, t, c, r_I)$

Note that t_I, t, c are fixed for a given index, and r_I is also known. On encryption a unique nonce N is generated, and we store

$$(\text{Ref}_I, (N, C, T)) \quad \text{with} \quad (C, T) = \text{AEAD-Enc}_k(N, (V, \text{Ref}_T), (\text{Ref}_S, \text{Ref}_I)). \tag{25}$$

For accessing an encrypted index entry $(\text{Ref}_I, (N, C, T))$ we first derive Ref_S and compute

$$\text{AEAD-Dec}_k(N, C, T, (\text{Ref}_S, \text{Ref}_I)), \tag{26}$$

and raise an error if invalid is returned. Otherwise we obtain the pair (V_{trc}, Ref_T) from the decrypted plaintext.

SECURITY ANALYSIS / PROOFS. The security properties of the schemes proposed above directly relate to the security properties of the used AEAD scheme:

- The confidentiality of the encrypted data can be reduced to the privacy protection of the AEAD scheme, i.e. indistinguishability from random. This guarantees that no efficient adversary can derive any information from the ciphertexts, match patterns, correlate data and index, etc. with non-negligible probability.
- For the database encryption scheme the authentication of the data and the cell address can be reduced to the authenticity provided by the AEAD scheme. This prohibits any modification, substitution, relocation, etc.
  For the index encryption scheme the authentication of the data, its table reference, the index structure, i.e. Ref_I, and the position of the entry in the index, i.e. Ref_S, can be reduced to the authenticity provided by the AEAD scheme. Thus modification, substitution, relocation, etc. are prevented.

Some AEAD schemes come with proofs for their security properties under the assumption that the underlying blockcipher is secure. See e.g. [1], [10], or [7] for details. Based on our analysis of the requirements such proofs directly carry over to our proposals.

STORAGE OVERHEAD. The AEAD schemes require a nonce that must be stored in addition to the ciphertext itself. Furthermore, the authentication tag must also be stored. The analysis here assumes a 128-bit blockcipher like AESas the basis for the AEAD scheme. Then using nonces and tags of 128 bits each appears a good choice. For CCFB matters are slightly different, as the nonce and the tag fit into one block, e.g. using a 96-bit nonce and a 32-bit tag as suggested in [7].

The associated data, containing the cell address resp. references, is not stored explicitly. As our example schemes EAX, OCB · PMAC, as well as CCFB do not require additional padding of the plaintext data, the storage overhead thus is limited to the nonce and the tag, i.e. 256 bits or 32 octets for EAX and OCB · PMAC, per cell resp. index entry, and 128 bits or 16 octets for CCFB.

PERFORMANCE OVERHEAD. The existing AEAD schemes vary a great deal in performance: Some schemes like EAX make two passes over the to-be-encrypted data, while others like OCB · PMAC make only one; CCFB is, depending on parameters, somewhere in between. Therefore we assess the overhead in terms of blockcipher invocations, depending on the size of the attribute to be encrypted, for EAX and OCB · PMAC. Let n be the number of blocks needed to cover the plaintext P to be encrypted, and m the number of blocks to cover the associated data. With a nonce of one block EAX needs $2n + m + 1$ blockcipher invocations (plus 6 for precomputations that can be reused), while OCB · PMAC needs $n + m + 5$ blockcipher invocations.

5   Summary

In the present paper we have shown instantiations of the encryption function that result in the schemes of [3] and [12] being insecure. The most prominent reason for these counter-examples is the handling of data larger than one block of the underlying blockcipher.

We have shown that the basic ideas of [3] and [12] for encrypting cell and index data can achieve the desired security goals when implemented with suitable cryptographic methods. We have proposed to employ an authenticated encryption scheme with associated data that provides explicitly both privacy and authenticity. Proofs of security for such schemes carry over to the database and index encryption case. Furthermore, we have briefly analysed the performance and storage impact of possible choices for such schemes.

Acknowledgements

Thanks are due to Ehud Gudes and Stefan Lucks for helpful discussions.

References

[1] M. Bellare, P. Rogaway, and D. Wagner. The EAX Mode of Operation. In B. Roy and W. Meier, editors, *Proceedings of the 11th International Workshop on Fast Software Encryption*, volume 3017 of *Lecture Notes in Computer Science*, pages 389–407. Springer-Verlag, 2004.

[2] M. Dworkin. Recommendation for Block Cipher Modes of Operation – Methods and Techniques. NIST Special Publication 800-38A.

[3] Y. Elovici, R. Waisenberg, E. Shmueli, and E. Gudes. A structure preserving database encryption scheme. In W. Jonker and M. Petković, editors, *Proceedings of Secure Data Management: VLDB 2004 Workshop*, volume 3178 of *Lecture Notes in Computer Science*, pages 28–40. Springer-Verlag, 2004.

[4] T. Fanghänel. *Using Encryption for Secure Data Storage in Mobile Database Systems*. Diplomarbeit, Friedrich-Schiller-Universität Jena, 2002.

[5] T. Iwata and K. Kurosawa. OMAC: One-key CBC MAC. In T. Johansson, editor, *Proceedings of the 10th International Workshop on Fast Software Encryption*, volume 2887 of *Lecture Notes in Computer Science*, pages 129–153. Springer-Verlag, 2003.

[6] H. Krawczyk. The order of encryption and authentication for protecting communications (or: how secure is SSL?). In J. Kilian, editor, *Advances in Cryptology – CRYPTO '2001*, volume 2139 of *Lecture Notes in Computer Science*, pages 310–331. Springer-Verlag, 2001.

[7] S. Lucks. Two-pass authenticated encryption faster than generic composition. In H. Gilbert and H. Handschuh, editors, *Proceedings of the 12th International Workshop on Fast Software Encryption*, volume 3557 of *Lecture Notes in Computer Science*, pages 284–298. Springer-Verlag, 2005.

[8] National Institute of Standards and Technology (NIST). Data Encryption Standard (DES). Federal Information Processing Standards Publication (FIPS PUB) 46-3, Oct. 1999. (Withdrawn May 19, 2005).

[9] National Institute of Standards and Technology (NIST). Advanced Encryption Standard (AES). Federal Information Processing Standards Publication (FIPS PUB) 197, Nov. 2001.

[10] P. Rogaway. Authenticated-encryption with associated-data. In *Proceedings of the 9th ACM Conference on Computer and Communications Security*, pages 98–107, Washington, DC, USA, Nov. 2002. ACM Press.

[11] RSA. PKCS #5: Password-based encryption standard. Technical report, RSA Laboratories, Nov. 1993. Version 1.5.

[12] E. Shmueli, R. Waisenberg, Y. Elovici, and E. Gudes. Designing secure indexes for encrypted databases. In S. Jajodia and D. Wijesekera, editors, *Proceedings of Data and Applications Security, 19th Annual IFIP WG 11.3 Working Conference*, volume 3654 of *Lecture Notes in Computer Science*, pages 54–68. Springer-Verlag, 2005.

Information Disclosure by XPath Queries

Stefan Böttcher and Rita Steinmetz

University of Paderborn (Germany)
Computer Science
Fürstenallee 11
D-33102 Paderborn
stb@uni-paderborn.de, rst@uni-paderborn.de

Abstract. Hospitals, organizations and companies are responsible keeping data and information about their customers private even if many internal employees have access to this data or information. When accused of an unauthorized disclosure of private information, it is important for the hospital to know which employees had the opportunity to disclose concrete private information. Our approach describes secret information in form of a secret query and performs two steps to detect which employees have used 'suspicious' queries, i.e., queries the result of which allows the user to derive secret information. First, we analyze the structure of queries and of the secret query to exclude non-suspicious queries. Second, we derive a formula from user query, query result and secret query, which is satisfiable if and only if the query is non-suspicious.

1 Introduction

1.1 Motivation

Whenever a hospital or a company that has to store sensitive information of its customers is suspected that this information was disclosed to a third party by one of its employees, it may be crucial for this company to uncover and close this privacy leak. We focus on the case that multiple employees have an access right to secret information and a company wants to identify who accessed the disclosed secret information.

One scenario for such a problem is the following: A patient – Alice – has been in a hospital – HealthCo – for a few days. During her stay there, it was discovered by a bloodtest that Alice suffers from diabetes. Some weeks later, Alice gets a letter on some sweets for diabetics. Alice therefore suspects HealthCo that they have disclosed her name and the fact that she suffers from diabetes to a third party. HealthCo's security specialists know that they have a well working security system such that no intruder from the outside could have accessed the database; the privacy leak has to be within HealthCo's employees: someone who had the right to access Alice's data has disclosed her data to a third party. Now HealthCo either wants to prove Alice, that no one has accessed her data – and thus no one was able to disclose it – or to find the employee responsible for this privacy leak and to call this employee to account.

The approach presented in this paper is completely independent of any existing access control system, i.e., we assume that each database user can only access that part of the database, he is allowed to according to his access rights. In contrast to access

W. Jonker and M. Petkovic (Eds.): SDM 2006, LNCS 4165, pp. 160–174, 2006.

control systems, our approach allows the company to check ex post, which user had had sufficient database access to get knowledge of the secret information.

1.2 Paper Organization

This paper is organized as follows: The remainder of the first section summarizes the underlying assumptions and the problem definition, and it outlines the audit language. Section 2 gives an overview of the audit system architecture of our approach. The third section gives the fundamental definitions and theorems used in Section 4 to develop the algorithm checking for suspicious queries. This algorithm is then optimized by three pre-tests. Section 5 gives an overview on related work on this topic. The paper concludes with a summary and conclusions.

1.3 Audit Language

Secret information involves more than just stored values of private data: it includes that data values are in certain ranges and it includes associations of some values and their relation within the XML database. For the above-described scenario, the secret is the association of two (node,value)-pairs, i.e., "the name Alice" and "the diagnosis diabetes". Both (node,value)-pairs regarded isolated do not form a secret, i.e., neither "the name of a patient is Alice" nor "one of the patients suffers from diabetes" is a secret. Therefore, in our system, we model a secret in form of an XPath query that represents the association of the values.

Secret queries are defined in the EBNF grammar given below, where SecretQuery is the start symbol.

```
SecretQuery    ::= DuringTo 'audit' cxp
DuringTo       ::= 'during' time 'to' time
cxp            ::= locationpath | '/' locationpath
locationpath   ::= locationstep ('/' locationstep)*
locationstep   ::= x '::' Σ | x '::' Σ '[' pred ']'
pred           ::= cxp | cxp comp constant
comp           ::= '=' | '<' | '≤' | '>' | '≥' | '≠'
```

time is a timestamp, Σ is the set of elements and attributes specified by the DTD of the XML database, and constant is a constant of some standard type, such as String, Long or Integer. x is one of the following axis specifiers: 'ancestor', 'ancestor-or-self', 'child', 'descendant', 'descendant-or-self', 'following', 'following-sibling', 'parent', 'preceding', 'preceding-sibling', 'self'. Note that besides the grammar rule for pred, our supported subset of XPath expressions corresponds to Core XPath as defined in [13].

Consider the example of Alice given in Section 1.1, and assume that "diabetes" means a glucose value of 200 mg/dL or more, an audit query specified for Alice is:

```
S=during 3pm,05/05/06 to 11am,05/17/06
audit /descendant-or-self::Patient[Name="Alice"]
[./descendant-or-self::Glucose≥"200"]
```

The DuringTo-clause is used to specify a time period during which the query must have been answered in order to be considered further.

The set of XPath queries supported by our system is defined by starting with the start symbol cxp in the grammar given above.

1.4 General Assumptions and Problem Definition

We assume that some technical and some general requirements are met, because otherwise, the leak may lie outside of the system and cannot be detected by our approach.

First, we assume that the private data is only stored in an XML database with a known schema description, e.g., defined by a DTD. Second, we assume that the answer to an XPath query only returns the selected node itself, and not a complete subtree of selected elements stored in the XML database with the following exception. If the child of a selected node is a text node, this child is included in the answer as well.

Third, we assume that a security and access control system is working correctly within the company providing the following: No intruder from the outside can access the data, and the employees can only access that fragment of the XML database which they have an access right to, according to the access control system. Fourth, we assume that an employee, who communicates sensitive information e.g. by fax or phone or stores it outside of the database e.g. as printouts, is responsible to care that no unauthorized party can access the information. In other words, we search for employees who accessed the uncovered secret information from the database, as these employees will be interviewed at first to reconstruct the flow of uncovered secret information.

Whenever these assumptions are met, our approach solves the following problem: Given a user query Q, and a secret information specified by a secret query S, our approach decides whether the employee can derive the secret (i.e., the answer to the secret query S) from the pair (Q,R), where R is the answer to Q.

2 Audit System Architecture

Our system architecture consists of an XML database, combined with a query log and a backlog that are defined as follows:

Query log: The query log is a table consisting of three attributes. It stores for each query submitted to the XML database the user ID, the query itself and a timestamp of when the query was answered. Furthermore, a query is computed and stored together with a user ID and a timestamp in the query log for each write operation, where the query describes the part of the database which has been read by the write operation. Due to space limitations, we skip the details on how to compute such a query here.

Backlog: The backlog is used for a later restoration of the database state valid at a certain time and stores information about write operations in a table consisting of 4 attributes. For each write operation (i.e., delete, insert or update) the index number of the changed node, an identifier for the write operation (delete, insert, update), the new value, and the timestamp representing the time when the operation was performed are stored. If the operation is an insert operation, the new value is the subtree inserted, if the operation is a delete operation, the value is the deleted subtree. An update operation is stored as a deletion followed by an insertion of a new subtree with the same index number and a new value.

3   Basic Definitions and Concepts

3.1   Secret Information and Suspicious Queries

In order to define when a query should be called suspicious, we first have to define what secret information and what a secret query are - besides from that the information shall not be disclosed.

Definition 1 (secret information and secret query). *secret information* is information about the existence of a combination of nodes and their axis-relation within an XML database DB that can be expressed by a Boolean XPath expression S, where S(DB)=true. The XPath expression S is called *secret query*.

For the user, the concrete database state Dt at the time when his query was answered is like a black box. The user gets only that knowledge of the concrete database state that can be derived from his query and the answer to the query. The concrete database state is replaceable by another database state DB as long as the result to the user's query stays the same. This leads us to our definition of suspicious queries:

Definition 2 (Suspicious Queries). Let Q be a user query, R the result of the query Q and S be a secret query. The pair (Q,R) has uncovered the secret information if and only if for each database state DB holds:

$$Q(DB)=R \implies S(DB)=true$$

In this case, we call the pair (Q,R) *suspicious*; otherwise we call it *non-suspicious*.

The goal of our algorithm is to systematically classify as many queries as possible as being non-suspicious queries. For this purpose, we use an equivalent characterization of non-suspicious queries, which is a given in Corollary 1:

Corollary 1 (Non-suspicious Queries). Let Q be a query, Dt be the XML database at the time t when the query Q was answered, and R be the result to the query Q, Q(Dt)=R. Let S be a secret query with S(Dt)=true. A pair (Q,R) is non-suspicious if and only if there exists a database state DB2 such that

$$Q(DB2)=R \land S(DB2)=false$$

This corollary means that if at least one database state DB2 can be guessed (or constructed) with S(DB2)=false, but which leads to the same query result R of Q as the database state in which the query was answered, the query is non-suspicious.

3.2   Normalized XPath Expressions and Binary XML Trees

In order to reduce the number of different XPath axes for our algorithm, we normalize each XPath expression (user queries as well as secret queries). The normalization is similar to the rewriting of XPath axes into the primitive axes 'first-child' and 'next-sibling' and their inverse and reflexive and transitive closure as proposed in [13]. In contrast to [13], we compute the normalization nested with the elimination of inverse axes as shown in [18], so that we only get the axes 'child' and 'next-sibling' and their reflexive and transitive closure. In other words, the axes remaining after this normalization step are the 'child'-axis and its reflexive and transitive closure 'descendant-or-self', the 'next-sibling'-axis and its reflexive and transitive closure 'following-sibling', and the 'self'-axis.

For example, the user query `Q1=//Name[ancestor-or-self::Patient//Glucose≥"200"]` is normalized to an equivalent query: `Q=/descendant-or-self::Patient[/child::*/descendant-or-self::Glucose≥"200"]/descendant-or-self::Name`.

Similar to our normalization of XPath queries, we regard the XML database tree as a *binary tree XML bX*, i.e., the binary XML tree `bX` representing the XML database only contains the axes 'first-child' and 'next-sibling'. Note that we regard the binary representation of an XML document in order to simplify the presentation of our approach (especially the embedding of Definition 5), however, our approach is applicable to non-binary XML document trees as well.

3.3 Minimal Readset Fragments

Our final algorithm tries to construct a database state `DB2` for a given pair `(Q,R)`, such that `Q(DB2)=R` and the secret does not hold in `DB2`, i.e., `S(DB2)=false`. If we can construct such a database state `DB2`, we can be sure that according to Corollary 1, `(Q,R)` is non-suspicious. In order to explain how we construct such a database state `DB2`, we introduce graph patterns and embeddings to define minimal readset fragments, which are the atomic fragments read by a query (a minimal readset fragment in the XML context is similar to a tuple in the relational context).

Definition 3 (Graph Pattern [17, 9]). Let Σ be the set of element names and attributes defined by the underlying DTD. A *graph pattern* is a directed graph G, the nodes of which are labeled with symbols of Σ, with five distinguished subset of edges, and four distinguished subsets of nodes.

The five distinguished subsets of edges are the set of child edges ($\rightarrow$), the set of descendant-or-self edges ($\Rightarrow$), the set of next-sibling edges (arrow with a rhomb at the end), the set of following-sibling edges (double arrow with a rhomb at the end) and the set of self edges (single line).

The first distinguished subset of nodes contains only the root node, which corresponds to the root element of the DTD. The second distinguished subset of nodes is called the *set of element nodes*. Each element node is denoted by a circle. The third distinguished subset of nodes is called the *set of output nodes*. Each output node is denoted by a double circle. The set of output nodes is empty if a pattern represents a Boolean valued query. The fourth distinguished subset of nodes is called the *set of comparison nodes*. Each comparison node is denoted by a rectangle. The label of a comparison node is either a comparison operator (i.e., $=, <, \leq, >, \geq, \neq$) followed by a constant or it is '=*'.

Definition 4 (Tree Pattern). Let G be a graph pattern according to Definition 3. G is called a *tree pattern*, if each node of G is reachable from the root node by exactly one path.

The tree pattern `TS` for secret query `S` of section 1.3 can be seen in Fig. 1(a) and the tree pattern `TQ` for the query `Q` of section 3.2 can be seen in Fig. 1(b).

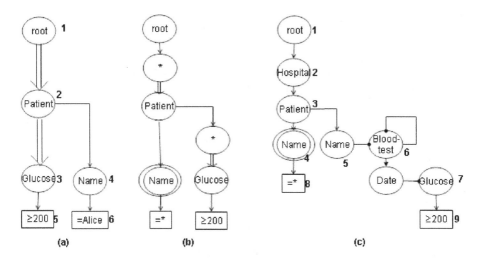

Fig. 1. (a) tree pattern for secret query S (b) tree pattern for query Q (c) graph pattern of query Q, computed using the DTD

Definition 5 (Embedding of a Tree Pattern in an XML database). An embedding of a tree pattern T of an XPath expression XP into a binary tree bX representing an XML database is defined to be a function e:Nodes(T)→Nodes(bX) with

1. e(root(T)) = root(bX)
2. ∀ x ∈ ElementNodes(T) : Label (x) = Label(e(x))
3. ∀x,y ∈ ElementNodes(T):
   a) if (x,y) is a child edge in T then (e(x),e(y)) is a first-child edge or a path of one first-child edge followed by any number of next-sibling edges in bX
   b) if (x,y) is a descendant-or-self edge in T then there exists a path of arbitrary length of first-child edges and next-sibling edges in bX
   c) if(x,y) is a next-sibling edge in T then (e(x),e(y)) is a next-sibling edge in bX
   d) if(x,y) is a following-sibling edge in T then(e(x),e(y)) is a path of arbitrary length of next-sibling edges in bX
   e) if(x,y) is a self edge in T then e(x)=e(y) in bX
4. ∀x ∈ ElementNodes(T) .∀y ∈ ComparisonNodes(T): if(x,y) is a child edge in T, then e(x) has to fulfill the condition stated in Label(y).

Definition 6 (Minimal readset fragment and Readset of an XPath query within an XML database). Let XP be an XPath expression and bX be a binary tree representation of an XML database. Let e be an embedding of the tree pattern T of XP in bX. The *minimal readset fragment* $mrf(XP,bX) = \{N, E, O\}$ *of Q within bX induced by* e is that subtree of bX that contains all nodes nT, nT ∈ e(T), all nodes x on paths from root(bX) to a node nT, nT∈e(T) and the set E of all incident edges, i.e. N := {nT ∈ bX | nT ∈ e(T)} ∪ {x ∈ bX | exists path from root(bX) to x and from x to a node `nT`, `nT ∈ e(T)}`,

`E := {(x,y) ∈ bX | x ∈ N and y ∈ N}`, and

`O := {n ∈ N | n = e(oT) and oT is an output node of T}`.

ReadSet(XP,bX) is the set of all minimal readset fragments `mrf(XP,bX)` for all possible embeddings `e` of the tree pattern `T` of `XP` in `bX`.

4 Algorithms

4.1 Replaceable Minimal Readset Fragments

In order to show that a pair `(Q,R)` with `Q(Dt)=R` is non-suspicous in a given database state `Dt`, we try to construct an XML database state `DB2` from `Dt`, such that `Q(DB2)=R`, but `S(DB2)=false`. DB2 is constructed from `Dt` by replacing each minimal readset fragment `mrf(Q,Dt)∈ReadSet(Q,Dt)` of `Q` in `Dt` by a fragment `mrf'(Q,DB2)` which is a minimal readset fragment of `Q` in `DB2`[1]. Whether or not a minimal readset fragment is replaceable, such that the replacing fragment provides an answer to the query but does not provide an answer to the secret, depends on three conditions outlined in the following definition.

Definition 7 (Replaceable). Let `Q` be a query, `S` be a secret query and `Dt` be a database state. A minimal readset fragment `mrf(Q, Dt)` is called replaceable, if a minimal readset fragment `mrf'(Q,DB)` of any (virtual) database state `DB` exists s.t.:

  a)   there exists an embedding `e` of the tree pattern `TQ` of `Q` in `mrf'(Q,DB)`
  b)   there exists no embedding of the tree pattern `TS` of `S` in `mrf'(Q,DB)`
  c)   `O(mrf(Q,Dt)) = O(mrf'(Q,DB))`.

Proposition 1. Each minimal readset fragment `mrf(Q,Dt)∈ReadSet(Q,Dt)` `\ReadSet(S,Dt)` is replaceable.

Proof Sketch: As condidtions (a), (b), and (c) of Definition 7 hold for each minimal readset fragments `mrf(Q,Dt)∈ReadSet(Q,Dt)\ReadSet(S,Dt)`, `mrf(Q,Dt)` is replaceable by itself.   ☐

If all minimal readset fragments `mrf(Q,Dt)∈ReadSet(Q,Dt)` are replaceable, the database state `DB2` that is constructed by replacing each minimal readset fragment `mrf(Q,Dt)∈ReadSet(Q,Dt)` has exactly the desired property `Q(DB2)=R` and `S(DB2)=false`. But if at least one minimal readset fragment `mrf(Q,Dt)∈ReadSet(Q,Dt)` is not replaceable, we know that for each database state `DB` with `Q(DB)=R` the secret holds, `S(DB)=true`, i.e., according to Definition 2, the pair `(Q,R)` is suspicious. This is stated in Theorem1.

Theorem 1. Let `Q` be a query and `S` be a secret query and `Dt` be the XML database at the time `t` when the query `Q` was answered and `R` be the result of the query `Q`, `Q(Dt)=R`. The pair `(Q,R)` is non-suspicious if and only if each minimal readset fragment `mrf (Q,Dt)∈ReadSet(Q,Dt)∩ReadSet(S,Dt)` is replaceable.

---

[1] Only those database states DB2 are considered that are valid according to the given DTD.

Proof sketch: (a) First, assume that the pair `(Q,R)` is non-suspicious. According to Corollary 1, there exists a database state `DB2` such that `Q(DB2)=R∧S(DB2)= false`. Choose any minimal readset fragment `mrf(Q,Dt)∈ReadSet(Q,Dt)∩Read-Set(S,Dt)`. As `Q(DB2)=R` there exists a minimal readset fragment `mrf'(Q,DB2)` with `O(mrf(Q,Dt))=O(mrf'(Q,DB2))`. As `S(DB2)=false`, there does not exist an embedding of `S` in `DB2`, and as `mrf'(Q,DB2)` is a subtree of `DB2`, there does not exist an embedding of `S` in `mrf'(Q,DB2)`. Therefore, the minimal readset fragment `mrf(Q,Dt)` is replaceable by the minimal readset fragment `mrf'(Q,DB2)`.

(b) Now, assume that each minimal readset fragment `mrf(Q,Dt)∈Read-Set(Q,Dt)∩ReadSet(S,Dt)` is replaceable. As according to Proposition 1, each minimal readset fragment `mrf(Q,Dt)∈ReadSet(Q,Dt)\ReadSet(S,Dt)` is replaceable, and as `(ReadSet(Q,Dt)\ReadSet(S,Dt))∪(ReadSet(Q,Dt)∩ReadSet(S,Dt))=ReadSet(Q,Dt)`, each minimal readset fragment `mrf(Q,Dt)∈ReadSet(Q,Dt)` is replaceable. According to Definition 7, for each minimal readset fragment `mrf(Q,Dt)∈ReadSet(Q,Dt)` there exists a minimal readset fragment `mrf'(Q,DB)` of a (virtual) database state DB such that the conditions (a), (b), and (c) of Definition 7 hold. Let `DB2` be the database state that contains only the union of all those minimal readset fragment `mrf'(Q,DB)`. Then, `Q(DB2)=R` holds because of conditions (a) and (c), and `S(DB2)=false` holds because of condition (b). According to Corollary 1, the pair `(Q,R)` is non-suspicious. □

In general, this leads us to the following algorithm to decide, whether or not a user query Q and its result R are suspicious:

1. Use the backlog to reconstruct the database state `Dt` at the time when the query was answered. This step can be performed in `O(|bl|*log(width(db))* depth(db))` time [8], where `|bl|` is the number of entries in the backlog, `width(db)` is the maximum number of children that one node of the XML database has, and `depth(db)` is the depth of the XML database.
2. Check whether each minimal readset fragment `mrf(Q,Dt)∈ReadSet(Q,Dt) ∩ReadSet(S,Dt)` is replaceable.
3. If all minimal readset fragments `mrf(Q,Dt)∈ReadSet(Q,Dt) ∩Read-Set(S,Dt)` are replaceable, return 'suspicious'; otherwise, return 'non-suspicious'.

Step 2 is performed as follows. The goal of this step is to check whether each minimal readset fragment `mrf(Q,Dt)` can be replaced by a minimal readset fragment `mrf'(Q,DB2)`, i.e., whether `mrf'(Q,DB2)` exists with `Q(mrf(Q,Dt))=Q(mrf'(Q,DB2)) ∧ S(mrf'(Q,DB2))=false`. Let eQ be an embedding of Q in `Dt` which induces `mrf(Q,Dt)`. Assume that there exists an embedding eS of S in `Dt` with `eS∩N(mrf(Q,Dt))≠∅`. To check whether `mrf'(Q,DB)` exists with `Q(mrf(Q,Dt))=Q(mrf'(Q,DB2)) ∧ S(mrf'(Q,DB2))=false` means that the following three conditions must hold:

a) Each node eQ(nQ) of Dt which is an embedded node of a node nQ, where nQ is the parent node of a comparison node cQ of TQ, can be changed only in such a way that the condition of the comparison node is not violated. We can express this as a Boolean formula `fqi=x op value`, where x is the label of nQ and `op value` is the label of the comparison node cQ.

b)   At least one node `eS(nS)` of `Dt` which is an embedded node of a node nS, where nS is the parent node of a comparison node cS of S must be changed in such a way that the condition of the comparison node does not hold any more. This can be expressed as a Boolean formula `fsj=not x op value`, where x is the label of nS and `op value` is the label of the comparison node cS.

c)   Each node `eQ(oQ)` of `Dt` which is an embedded node of an output node oQ of the tree pattern `TQ` of Q must not be changed. This can be expressed as a Boolean formula `fqi=x = value`, where x is the label of the element `eQ(oQ)` and `value` is the value of the element `eQ(oQ)` found in the XML database.

Let n be the number of comparison Nodes of the tree pattern of Q. The atomic formulas fqi, 1≤i≤n generated by the rules (a) and (c) are combined to a single formula FQ, i.e. `FQ = ( fq1 ∧ … ∧ fqn )`. Similar, we combine all formulas fsj, 1≤j≤k, where k is the number of comparison nodes of the tree pattern of S generated by the rule (b), to a single formula `FS = (fs1 ∧ … ∧ fsk)`. Then, meeting all conditions (a), (b) and (c) means that the formula (`FQ ∧ not FS`) is satisfiable. Let `Fj=(not fsj ∧ FQ)` for 1≤j≤k. Then (`FQ ∧ not FS`)=(`F1∨ … ∨ Fk`). If at least one of the formulas Fj, 1≤j≤k, is satisfiable, we can be sure, that we can construct a pattern `mrf'(Q,DB2)` to replace `mrf(Q,Dt)`, i.e., for which conditions (a), (b) and (c) of Definition 7 are met. As each formula Fj consists of n+1 atomic formulas and of at most n+1 different variables x, each formula Fj can be tested for satisfiability in `O(n²)` using the single source shortest path algorithm [10]. Thus, the total runtime of Step 2 is `O(k*n²)`.

So the overall runtime is polynomial.

```
<Hospital>
   <Patient>
      <Name>Alice</Name>
      <Bloodtest>
         <Glucose>264</Glucose>
      </Bloodtest>
   </Patient>
</Hospital>
```

Fig. 2. Example fragment of a Hospital XML database Dt

For example, consider the query Q of Section 3.2 applied to the fragment of an XML database `Dt` shown in Fig. 2. The tree pattern `TQ` of Q shown in Figure 1(b) contains an output node pQ with label 'Name' and a comparison node cQ with the label '=*' and the parent pQ. Since the result R of Q applied to `Dt` is `<Name>Alice</Name>`, e(pQ) has the value "Alice". Additionally, `TQ` contains a comparison node with label ≥200 and a parent node that has the label 'Glucose'. Therefore, the formula FQ computed for the minimal readset fragment of query Q in Dt above is `FQ=(Name="Alice" ∧ Glucose≥"200")`. Similarly, the formula

FS=(Name="Alice" ∧ Glucose≥"200") is computed for the secret S. Because FQ ∧ not(FS) is insatisfiable, the minimal readset fragment mrf(Q,Dt) is not replaceable, thus the pair (Q,R) is suspicious.

However, if we consider a second secret query

```
S2= during 3pm,05/05/06 to 11am,05/17/06
audit /descendant-or-self::Patient[Name="Alice"]
[./descendant-or-self::Glucose="264"]
```

and the same user query Q applied to the same database state Dt, the formula FS2 computed for S2 is FS2=(Name="Alice"∧Glucose="264"), i.e., FQ ∧ not(FS2) is satisfiable, and the minimal readset fragment mrf(Q,Dt) is replaceable for example by a database fragment

```
<Patient>
    <Name>Alice</Name>
    <Bloodtest>
        <Glucose>260</Glucose>
    </Bloodtest>
</Patient>
```

4.2 Identifying Proper Candidate Queries

Although checking whether (Q,R) is suspicious in a given database state Dt requires only polynomial time, it can be avoided in three situations by applying tests based on the query strings only, i.e., without access to the database. Therefore, we apply these tests to identify non-candidate queries, before testing the remaining queries for suspiciousness.

The first test is based on the during-to interval specified by the secret query and the time stamp of the user query. If the time stamp of the user query does not lie within the during-to interval, the query is not a candidate for having accessed the uncovered private information, even when it were suspicious according to our definition. Therefore, the query does not need to be examined further.

A further test, called *candidate test*, compares the tree pattern TS of the secret query S with the graph pattern GQ of the user query Q with the following idea. If TS contains subtrees and comparisons that neither occur in nor can be deduced from the structure of GQ, then TS depends on conditions not reflected by GQ. Therefore, the database can be modified in a way that violates the secret S without changing the result R of Q, i.e. (Q,R) is non-suspicious. This kind of non-suspicious queries shall be excluded by the candidate test.

In order to regard what can be deduced from the structure of GQ, we replace all recursive edges (i.e. 'descendant-or-self' and 'following-sibling') in GQ, as recursive edges GQ represent a path of several nodes. Recursive edges are replaced by a DTD graph as follows.

1. For each right-hand[2] side of a DTD rule, we build a non-deterministic finite automaton. The transitions of the NFA are 'next-sibling' edges.

---

[2] For the rule <!ELEMENT a (b,(c|d), e)*> the right-hand side is: '(b,(c|d), e*)'.

2. From each node of the NFA representing an element, we draw a 'first-child' edge to each start-node of the NFA representing the right-hand side of this element definition.

Altogether, GQ is built by replacing all 'descendant-or-self' axes within the tree pattern TQ of Q by the sub-graph of DTD graph that contains all paths from the start node to the end node of the 'descendant-or-self' edge. However, the 'following-sibling' edges of TQ are replaced by the set of 'next-sibling' paths within the DTD graph from the start node to end node of the 'following-sibling' edge.

After this step, GQ contains only the primitive edges 'child' and 'next-sibling'.

An example for a DTD and its DTD graph can be seen in Fig. 3.

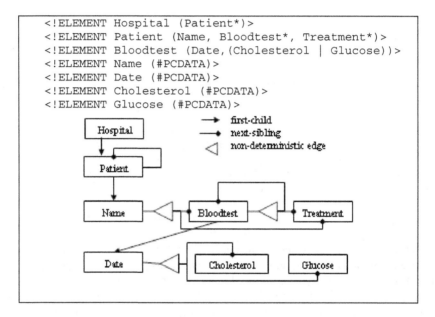

```
<!ELEMENT Hospital (Patient*)>
<!ELEMENT Patient (Name, Bloodtest*, Treatment*)>
<!ELEMENT Bloodtest (Date,(Cholesterol | Glucose))>
<!ELEMENT Name (#PCDATA)>
<!ELEMENT Date (#PCDATA)>
<!ELEMENT Cholesterol (#PCDATA)>
<!ELEMENT Glucose (#PCDATA)>
```

Fig. 3. DTD and DTD graph

This DTD graph was used to construct the graph pattern GQ of the query Q of Section 3.2, which can be seen in Fig. 1(c).

Definition 8 (Homomorphism). Let GQ be the graph pattern of the query Q, and let TS be the tree pattern of the secret query S. The homomorphism is a function h:Nodes(TS) → Nodes(GQ) such that

1. h(root(TS)) = root(GQ)
2. ∀ x ∈ ElementNodes(TS) : Label (x) = Label(h(x))
3. ∀ x ∈ ElementNodes(TS) :
   a. if (x,y) is a child edge in TS then (h(x),h(y)) is a child edge or a path of one child edge followed by any number of next-sibling edges in GQ

b. if (x,y) is a descendant-or-self edge in TS then there exists a path from h(x) to h(y) in GQ.

c. if (x,y) is a next-sibling edge in TS then $(h(x),h(y))$ is a next-sibling edge in GQ

d. if (x,y) is a following-sibling edge in TS then $(h(x),h(y))$ is a path of next-sibling edges in GQ

4. $\forall$ x $\in$ ComparisonNodes(TS): Either (a) Label(h(x)) = "=*" or (b) if cS is the comparison operator of x and cQ is the comparison operator of h(x) then the constants v(x) of x and v(h(x)) of h(x) fulfill the condition given in row cQ and column cS in Table 1.

Table 1. Conditions for a homomorphism between Comparison nodes

cQ\cS	<	≤	=	≥	>	≠
<	$v(h(x)) \le v(x)$	$v(h(x)) \le v(x)+1$	false	false	false	$v(h(x)) \le v(x)$
≤	$v(h(x)) < v(x)$	$v(h(x)) \le v(x)$	false	false	false	$v(h(x)) > v(x)$
=	$v(h(x)) < v(x)$	$v(h(x)) \le v(x)$	$v(h(x)) = v(x)$	$v(h(x)) \ge v(x)$	$v(h(x)) > v(x)$	$v(h(x)) \ne v(x)$
≥	false	false	false	$v(h(x)) \ge v(x)$	$v(h(x)) > v(x)$	$v(h(x)) > v(x)$
>	false	false	false	$v(h(x)) \ge v(x)-1$	$v(h(x)) \ge v(x)$	$v(h(x)) \ge v(x)$
≠	false	false	false	false	false	$v(h(x)) = v(x)$

The idea behind searching for a homomorphism is the following: If no homomorphism is found, there exists at least one node nS within TS that is not contained in GQ. Thus, each minimal readset fragment mrf(S,Dt)∈ReadSet(S,Dt) contains a node e(nS) that is not part of any minimal readset fragment mrf(Q,Dt)∈ReadSet(Q,Dt). Therefore, we can delete this node or change its value, such that the result R of query Q is not changed, but the secret holds no longer for the generated database state DB2.

For example, the homomorphism from the tree pattern TS of the secret query S shown in Fig. 1(a) to the graph pattern GQ of query Q shown in Fig. 1(c) is h={(1,1), (2,3), (3,7), (4,4), (5,9), (6,8)}.

In a second test, i.e., a test that is performed prior to the candidate test, we check, whether each label lS∈LS of the set LS of the labels of the tree pattern of S is contained in the set LQ of the labels of the graph pattern of Q, i.e., whether LS⊆LQ. If one label lS∈LS of a node nS of the tree pattern TS of S is not contained within LQ, there can not exist a node h(nS) in the graph pattern GQ of Q which is homomorph to nS.

5 Relation to Other Works

The hospital database as used as an example in our paper is a typical case of Hippocratic databases for which [2] lists 10 key principles. Our work mainly contributes to two of them: it provides database support, known as "compliance" [2], to identify ex post, who accessed private data (known as "Limited Disclosure" according to [2]).

An audit system for relational databases is provided in [3]. In contrast, we focus on XML trees and XPath expressions instead of on 2-dimensional tables and SQL queries. Thus, we solved a different set of problems ranging from embedding XPath queries into restored XML database content to checking for structural query similarities to more complex suspicious tests.

Note however that our approach avoids the following weakness of previous approaches. While previous approaches, e.g. [3], work correctly for select-project-join queries using only =-comparisons in selections, they do not work correctly when the secret query contains =-comparisons, but the query contains <, >, <= or >= comparisons. For example, when we submit the relational counterparts to user query Q and secret query S2 of Section 4.1 to the audit system described in [3], that audit system would call the query suspicious, although the information specified by S2 cannot be derived from the answer to the query. In comparison, our approach excludes Q from the set of suspicious queries with respect to S2.

In our algorithm, a containment test on the structure of the XPath queries is used to detect candidate queries. As our test for candidate queries uses a containment test on the structure of XPath expressions, in this paper, we propose an approach that combines and extends ideas presented in [4] and [17]. Our contribution goes significantly beyond previous approaches like e.g. [8] or [9], as we support all the axes of Core XPath (in comparison to e.g. [9] which only supported the two axes 'child' and descendant). Furthermore, the problem solved in this paper is fundamentally different from the containment problem, as we have to consider the database state given for each query, i.e., whether a query is suspicious depends on the given database state.

Although the problem of k-anonymity looks similar to the problem solved in this paper, the two problems are completely different. Contributions that aim to provide k-anonymity (as e.g., [1],[15],[16],[19],[22],[23]) change the data in published views to be more fuzzy, so that no sensitive information of concrete individuals can be derived. In our case, we are not allowed to change the data, so we cannot avoid returning query results from which a secret information can be derived, we can only detect ex post, who had access to the secret information.

The contributions [24] and [20] present approaches to prove violation of 2-anonymity from published views. However, to prove the violation of 2-anonymity for a set of published views is not sufficient to prove that the given secret information can be derived from this view set. For example, 2-anonymity can be violated for a concrete association of values (a1,b1), whereas the secret information consists of the association of values (a2,b2) for which 2-anonymity is not violated.

Our approach is fundamentally different to the field of access control techniques for XML data sources, as presented e.g. in [5], [6], [11], [12], [14] and [21], which range from policies, to user groups, to document location, to access control on fragments of XML databases are applied to the database system. We assume that our system is well protected against attacks from outside, but in contrast to access control systems, our system does not restrict the employees' access to data. Instead, each employee is allowed to access the secret information, which he needs to do his work properly, but he is not allowed to disclose the information. In contrast to the previously mentioned contributions, the goal of our paper is to detect ex post, which query accessed the secret information, i.e., which user had the possibility to expose the secret information.

6 Conclusions

Whenever a company has to handle sensitive information of its customers and whenever multiple employees of this company have to access these private information, it is crucial for the company to have a mechanism to detect privacy violations in order to prevent the abuse of the information.

In this paper, we have presented an approach on how to detect ex post, which employee had the opportunity to disclose private information. The algorithm first considers time constraints and then analyzes the structure of the user's query and the secret query to check whether the user's query has accessed all the information specified by the secret query. In the last step, the algorithm checks, whether all minimal readset fragments of the secret query are replaceable, which can be decided in $O(k*n^2)$ time by checking satisfiablity of formulas.

In order to keep our presentation as simple as possible, we have restricted it to XPath. However, as XPath forms the major part to describe data access in other query languages like XQuery and XSLT, we believe that our approach will be easily adaptable to these query languages.

References

[1] Charu C. Aggarwal: On k-Anonymity and the Curse of Dimensionality. In: Klemens Böhm, Christian S. Jensen, Laura M. Haas, Martin L. Kersten, Per-Åke Larson, Beng Chin Ooi (Eds.): Proceedings of the 31st International Conference on Very Large Data Bases. VLDB 2005, Trondheim, Norway, 2005

[2] Rakesh Agrawal, Jerry Kiernan, Ramakrishnan Srikant, Yirong Xu: Hippocratic Databases. In: Philip A. Bernstein, Yannis E. Loannidis, Raghu Ramakrishnan (Eds.): Proceedings of 28th International Conference on Very Large Data Bases. VLDB 2002, Hong Kong, 2002

[3] Rakesh Agrawal, Roberto J. Bayardo Jr., Christos Faloutsos, Jerry Kiernan, Ralf Rantzau, Ramakrishnan Srikant: Auditing Compliance with a Hippocratic Database In: Mario A. Nascimento, M. Tamer Özsu, Donald Kossmann, Renée J. Miller, José A. Blakeley, K. Bernhard Schiefer (Eds.): (e)Proceedings of the Thirtieth International Conference on Very Large Data Bases. VLDB 2004, Toronto, Canada, 2004

[4] Sihem Amer-Yahia, SungRan Cho, Laks V. S. Lakshmanan, Divesh Srivastava: Minimization of Tree Pattern Queries In: Timos Sellis (Ed.): Proceedings of the 2001 ACM SIGMOD international conference on Management of data. SIGMOD Conference 2001, Santa Barbara, California, United States, 2001

[5] Elisa Bertino, Silvana Castano , Elena Ferrari: On specifying security policies for web documents with an XML-based language In: In Proceedings of the 6th ACM Symposium on Access Control Models and Technologies. SACMAT 2001, Chantilly, Virginia, USA, 2001.

[6] Elisa Bertino, Elena Ferrari: Secure and selective dissemination of XML documents. In: ACM Transactions on Information and System Security. TISSEC, Volume 5, Number 3, pp 290–331, 2002

[8] Stefan Böttcher, Rita Steinmetz: Detecting Privacy Violations in Sensitive XML Databases In: Jonker, Willem; Petkovic, Milan (Eds.): Secure Data Management - SDM 2005, 2nd VLDB Workshop on Secure Data Management, Trondheim, Norway, 2005

[9] Stefan Böttcher, Rita Steinmetz: Finding the Leak: A Privacy Audit System for Sensitive XML Databases. Second International Workshop on Privacy Data Management (PDM), Atlanta, USA, 2006

[10] Thomas H. Cormen, Charles E. Leiserson, Ronald L. Rivest, Clifford Stein: Introduction to Algorithms. MIT-Press, Cambridge, 2nd Edition, 2001.

[11] Ernesto Damiani, Sabrina di Virmercati, Stefano Paraboschi, Pierangela Samarati: Securing XML Documents In: Carlo Zaniolo, Peter C. Lockemann, Marc H. Scholl, Torsten Grust (Eds.): Advances in Database Technology - EDBT 2000, 7th International Conference on Extending Database Technology, Konstanz, Germany, 2000

[12] Wenfei Fan, Chee Yong Chan, and Minos Garofalakis: Secure XML Querying with Security Views In: Gerhard Weikum, Arnd Christian König, Stefan Deßloch (Eds.): Proceedings of the ACM SIGMOD International Conference on Management of Data. SIGMOD Conference 2004, Paris, France, 2004

[13] Georg Gottlob, Christoph Koch, Reinhard Pichler: Efficient Algorithms for Processing XPath Queries. VLDB 2002

[14] Michiharu Kudo, Satoshi Hada: XML document security based on provisional authorization In: In Sushil Jajodia, Pierangela Samarati (Eds.): Proceedings of the 7th ACM Conference on Computer and Communications Security. CCS 2000, Athens, Greece, 2000

[15] Kristen LeFevre, David J. DeWitt, Raghu Ramakrishnan: Incognito: Efficient Full-Domain K-Anonymity. In: Jennifer Widom, Fatma Ozcan, Rada Chirkova (Eds.): Proceedings of the ACM SIGMOD International Conference on Management of Data. SIGMOD Conference 2005, Maryland, USA, 2005

[16] Adam Meyerson, Ryan Williams: On the Complexity of Optimal K-Anonymity. In: Alin Deutsch (Ed.): Proceedings of the Twenty-third ACM SIGACT-SIGMOD-SIGART Symposium on Principles of Database Systems. PODS 2004, Paris, France, 2004

[17] Gerome Miklau, Dan Suciu: Containment and Equivalence for an XPath Fragment. Journal of the ACM, Volume 51, 2004

[18] Dan Olteanu, Holger Meuss, Tim Furche, François Bry: XPath: Looking Forward. EDBT Workshops 2002

[19] Pierangela Samarati: Protecting Respondents' Identities in Microdata Release. IEEE Transactions on Knowledge and Data Engineering, Volume 13, 2001

[20] Kilian Stoffel, Thomas Studer: Provable Data Privacy. In: Kim Viborg Andersen, John Debenham, Roland Wagner (Eds.): Database and Expert Systems Applications. DEXA 2005, Copenhagen, Denmark, 2005

[21] Stonebraker, M.: Implementation of Integrity Constraints and Views by Query Modification In: W. Frank King (Ed.): Proceedings of the 1975 ACM SIGMOD International Conference on Management of Data. SIGMOD Conference 1975, San Jose, California, 1975

[22] Latanya Sweene: Achieving k-Anonymity Privacy Protection Using Generalization and Suppression. International Journal of Uncertainty, Fuzziness and Knowledge-Based Systems, Volume 10, 2002

[23] Latanya Sweene: k-Anonymity: A Model for Protecting Privacy. International Journal of Uncertainty, Fuzziness and Knowledge-Based Systems, Volume 10, 2002

[24] Chao Yao, Xiaoyang Sean Wang, Sushil Jajodia: Checking for k-Anonymity Violation by Views. In: Klemens Böhm, Christian S. Jensen, Laura M. Haas, Martin L. Kersten, Per-Åke Larson, Beng Chin Ooi (Eds.): Proceedings of the 31st International Conference on Very Large Data Bases. VLDB 2005, Trondheim, Norway, 2005

SPIDER: An Autonomic Computing Approach to Database Security Management

Hakan Hacıgümüş

IBM Almaden Research Center, USA
hakanh@acm.org

Abstract. The system management complexity is exponentially increasing for the computing systems by even threatening their viability. Researchers and practitioners are scrambling to significantly simplify the all aspects of system management complexity. One of the most notable efforts towards this direction is the autonomic computing initiative, which is inspired by how the human body works to manage itself. In this paper, we focus on the database security management. We approach the security management issues from the autonomic computing perspective. We consider situations where the database is damaged by successful malicious attacks. Our goal is to design the system in such a way that the database system should be able to isolate the damaged parts of the system and to keep the other parts of the system functioning as the damage is being repaired.

1 Introduction

The ever-increasing complexity of managing computing systems is becoming a prohibitive factor for the growth, cost-effectiveness, and adoption of those systems and new technologies. Researchers and practitioners have been venturing on significantly reducing the complexity in all aspects by introducing new approaches and solution paradigms. Arguably, autonomic computing is one of the most prominent approaches to address increasing computing systems management problems [9,14]. In essence, autonomic computing is inspired by how the human body works to manage itself without external intervention in many cases. Through various channels, the human body identifies the problems, necessary solutions, and resources to realize those solutions without requiring directions from outside and without disturbing the other parts of the body that are not related to the problem. The autonomic computing initiative aims at creating "self-managing" computing systems by following the similar model. The four main functional areas of autonomic computing are defined as: self-configuring, self-optimizing, self-healing, and self-protecting [9,14]. In this paper, we mainly focus on the self-healing and self-protecting aspects from the database systems security perspective.

The database systems are not immune to the management complexity problems we stated above as it is evident from the recent research work to make database system management simpler, more automated, and more autonomous

W. Jonker and M. Petkovic (Eds.): SDM 2006, LNCS 4165, pp. 175–183, 2006.

[6,3,16,19,15,17]. One of the biggest challenges that database systems face today is ensuring the security and privacy of the data stored in the databases [5,18,2]. The new computing models that are made viable by the Internet revolution, mounting amount of data, and more importantly the increasing value of information hidden in the data that is stored in the databases across the globe even further intensify the security and privacy issues in databases [11,10,7].

First, potential attacks to breach the database security need to be identified. This is mostly done by the Intrusion Detection Systems (IDSs). The Intrusion Detection is an active area of research [4,8,13] and we will not provide the details of IDSs as it is outside of the scope of this work. We will assume that there is an IDS available, such as [1], in the system and discuss the minimum requirements for the IDS in the following sections. IDSs aim to defend the whole computing system by using combination of detection and data analysis techniques. Most of the IDSs systems are built on two major principals, namely; anomaly detection and signature detection [4,13]. The anomaly detection tries to model the normal behavior of the system components and the users, and to identify and interpret deviations from this normal behavior. The signature detection tries to identify any behavior that is similar to previously known pattern signature of an intrusion.

Once an intrusion is detected, the system should take certain actions to stop the attack and to recover from the possible damage that is caused by the attack. If we consider this situation from a database management system perspective, an obvious and naive action is that the database system stops accepting new query requests until all of the affected transactions are rolled-back and the database is returned to a consistent state by applying re-do operations on the valid transactions. Although this solution might work, it would severely affect the systems availability even for the unrelated parts of the system. By drawing the analogy from the human defense and healing systems, the database system should be able to isolate the damaged parts of the system and to keep the other parts of the system functioning as the damage is being repaired. This is the guiding principle for our system design for the **S**elf-**P**rotect**I**ng **D**atabas**E** **R**esearch (SPIDER) project.

The remainder of the paper is organized as follows. Section 2 presents the overall system architecture and explains main architecture components. Section 3 describes the query processing protocol to achieve our design goals. We conclude the paper in Section 4.

2   System Architecture

The overall system architecture is shown in Figure 1. We explain each component of the architecture below.

Query Monitor: The user queries, which are submitted against the database, are first captured by the Query Monitor. The Query Monitor is responsible for two main tasks: 1) Formatting and annotating the queries to allow comparison with the Alert Log, which is available from the IDS and 2) Testing the queries to

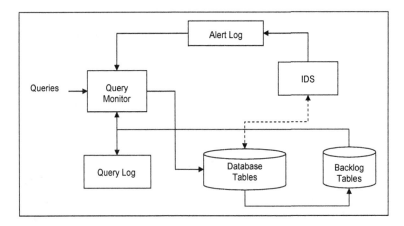

Fig. 1. SPIDER system architecture

decide whether a particular query should be granted an access to the database records.

Intrusion Detection System (IDS): We assume that an IDS is available in the system, such as [1]. The only assumption we make is that the IDS is able to provide the information items that the Query Monitor and the Alert Log need for policy enforcement. We will describe these items in Section 3 where we illustrate the query testing protocol.

We follow the attacks classification presented in [8] for the IDS. We consider the following attack types: 1) A *successful break-in*, where the attacker gains an access to the database through an unauthorized account, e.g., masquerading some other users identity, and 2) *penetration by a legitimate user*, where the attacker, who is a legitimate user in the system, tries to gain access to the parts of the system to which he/she is not entitled. These attack types are the most severe ones because in these types of attacks the malicious user may both execute read and update queries. The update queries change the state of the database, thus they may affect the outcome of the subsequent transactions. Therefore, for every new incoming query, we need to identify whether the query involves the records that have possibly been compromised by the detected attack.

Alert Log: The Alert Log keeps the list of queries that are identified by the IDS as malicious queries. The Alert Log maintains the unique query ids to identify those queries and those query ids are used by the Query Monitor.

Query Log: The Query Log keeps the log of all of the queries that change the state of the database. Select queries do not change the state of the database, however, update queries (update, insert, delete) change the state of the database.

Backlog Tables: We record all of updates in the Backlog Tables. Thus, the Backlog Tables are used to capture the state of the database at a particular point in time. Select queries do not insert any record in the backlog tables. In practice, there are far more select queries than update queries and select queries do not create any overhead for the query log and backlog tables. We will explain the schema details of the backlog tables in Section 3.2. Another observation is that even the malicious attackers avoid executing excessive number of updates against the database in order not to create a suspicious situation that can be detected by the system monitors.

3   Query Processing Protocol

In this section we present our solution to improve system availability based on the autonomic computing model. The process consists of series of tests on the submitted queries by leveraging the system components described in Section 2. Our goal is to maximize the system availability for the new incoming selection queries, while the system is recovering from the damage caused by the identified malicious queries. To achieve this goal, we try to determine what database objects are affected from the malicious transactions. After this, we try to verify whether a new user query could be executed even though the system is in recovery process. At this point, the critical question is that do the damaged database objects have any impact on answering the new query accurately? If we figured that the new query could be answered accurately, then the system could allow the execution of the query thereby improving the availability of the database system. We illustrate the process first by using examples and subsequently we will give a formal control flow that describes the query testing process.

3.1   Initial Query Testing

The most straightforward test is based on the columns names that are mentioned in the submitted query and is the malicious query from the Query Log. Let us assume that the system has been identified a *malicious query*, MQ and there is a *new user query* (or *query*, in short) Q submitted to the system. Simply, if $C_{MQ} \subseteq C_Q$, where C_{MQ} is the set of column names that are mentioned anywhere in MQ and C_Q is the set of column names that are mentioned anywhere in Q, then there is a possibility that the query results could be inaccurate due to the modifications of the malicious query on the database records. If C_Q and C_{MQ} are disjoint, then the malicious query could not have any affect on the query results, consequently the query can be executed safely. Although this test is efficient and can be quickly performed, it may create overly pessimistic results by blocking the processing of entire column (or multiple columns) because the test does not check individual records to determine whether they could impact the query results. This situation is illustrated in detail below.

Let us assume that we have a table *Customer* in the database, whose schema is given as $< ID, Name, Age >$, where ID is the unique primary key for the table. Let us consider a query $\sigma_{Age>25}(Customer)$, where σ is the relational selection operator. The initial content of the table is shown in Table 1. Let us assume that a malicious query changed the value of Age column for the $ID = 1$ from 20 to 28 as shown in Table 2. In this case, the query would select the first record, $ID = 1$, as it is qualified for the query predicate $Age > 25$. Obviously,

Table 1. Table *Customer*, the initial state

ID	Name	Age
1	John	20
2	Mary	29

Table 2. Table *Customer*, after the malicious update

ID	Name	Age
1	John	28
2	Mary	29

Table 3. Table *Customer*, the initial state

ID	Name	Age
1	John	20
2	Mary	29

Table 4. Table *Customer*, after the malicious update

ID	Name	Age
1	John	24
2	Mary	29

this is an inaccurate result because the original value, 20, which would not have been qualified, has been altered by the malicious query and now the record is a qualified record for the query. If the malicious query is detected by the IDS, it is recorded in the Alert Log. The Query Monitor combines the Alert Log information, which provides Query IDs for the malicious queries, with the Query Log, and performs the test to check whether the query and the malicious query share a common column mane(s). In this case as the *Age* column is mentioned in both of the queries the new user query is blocked until the changes that have been made by the malicious query are rolled-back. As a result, the test successfully prevents inaccuracy in the query results.

However, consider another case that is illustrated in Table 4. Let us consider that the malicious query changed the value of *Age* column for the $ID = 1$ from 20 to 24. In this case, neither the original value, 20, nor the (maliciously) changed value, 24, is qualified for the query predicate $Age > 25$. Therefore, although the system is still recovering the damage caused by the malicious query, the new query could safely be executed as the query results would not be affected. However, the first level test does not allow us to continue with the query processing causing an unnecessary blockage. We devise further levels of testing to overcome this issue and to allow for greater query processing flexibility by exploiting the backlog table structure.

3.2   Backlog Table Structure

For each table T in the database, we create a backlog table BT. BT has the schema that has the same set of columns of the schema of T and three additional columns; $timestamp, TS, Operation, OP,$ and $QueryID, QID$. This structure is somewhat akin to the approach presented in [12]. Note that the unique key of the table T is not a unique key for BT. A new record is inserted in a BT only if there is an update operation executed against the table T. Update operations are identified by one of the *Insert, Update, Delete* statements, hence *Operation* column stores one of these values depending on the update operation. After an *Insert* operation, a new record in BT is created with the identical column

Table 5. Table *Customer_Backlog*, after the malicious update

ID	Name	Age	Op	TS	QID
1	John	20	Insert	10:23:32	12
2	Mary	29	Insert	10:24:30	13
1	John	24	Update	11:30:45	35

values in T. After an $Update$ operation, a new record in BT is created with the updated values of the record in T and we retain the previous records for the corresponding record. After a $Delete$ operation, a new record in BT is created with the values of the record that exist before the delete in T and we retain the previous records for the corresponding record. TS is the timestamp of the update operation, and QID is the identifier for the update query. A sample backlog table table for $Customer$ is shown in Table 5 based on the database status for the previous case. The first two records show the initial insert operations for $John$ and $Mary$. The third record is the update by the malicious query, altering the Age value from 20 to 24 for $John$.

3.3 Advanced Query Testing

We can now describe the second level testing that exploits the backlog tables. If the first level test gives a positive answer, – i.e, the query and the malicious query have common column names– then we first look at whether the malicious query has actually changed the values for the common columns. In our example that is Age. This test is useful because even though Age column is mentioned in the malicious query, the column value might not have been altered by the malicious query at all. We can conduct this test by comparing the column value with the previous column value that is created by a non-malicious query in the backlog table. Formally, to obtain the column value, $malV$, that is updated by the malicious query $\pi_{C,TS}\sigma_{QID=mid}(BT)$, where C is the common column name between the query and the malicious query, mid is the query ID of the malicious query, and π is relational projection operator. Once the value of C is retrieved we can check the previous value, pV, that is updated by a non-malicious query by $\pi_C\sigma_{QID\neq mid \wedge TS<ts}(BT)$, where ts is the timestamp value for the malicious query. If the column value for Age has not been changed, – i.e., $malV = pV$ – then the system may allow the query execution. Otherwise, we need to check if pV is qualified for the query predicate. If pV is qualified, then the system blocks the query. Because, at this point, we know that the malicious query has been altered the column value and the original valid value was a qualified value. Therefore, the new query request needs to wait until the affects of the malicious query are rolled-back.

To continue the process, if pV is not qualified then we need to check the altered value, $malV$ against the query predicate. The new Age value is 24, which does not qualify the query predicate. Therefore, even the malicious query changed the column value the system may allow the query execution instead of blocking the execution thereby introducing greater execution flexibility.

Table 6. Table *Customer_Backlog*, after the malicious update

ID	Name	Age	Op	TS	QID
1	John	20	Insert	10:23:32	12
2	Mary	29	Insert	10:24:30	13
1	John	24	Update	11:30:45	35
1	John	26	Update	11:30:45	50

To illustrate the last level of testing consider the following case, which is also shown in Table 6. This can be thought of the continuation of the previous case from the database state perspective. After the execution of – malicious but then legitimate query – $QID = 35$, there was another legitimate query $QID = 50$ in the system. Let us assume that the IDS could not detect the malicious query, $QID = 35$, before the execution of $QID = 50$, accordingly the system allows the execution of the query $QID = 50$. Let us assume that the query $QID = 50$ selects the record where $Name =$ "*John*" and updates his age by adding 2, thereby making the $Age = 26$. Let us assume that the IDS detects the malicious query after this point and triggers the roll-back process for all of the affected transactions including $QID = 50$. In this case, the record is qualified for the new querys predicate $Age > 25$ and the system would allow the query execution based on the tests described earlier. Because the tests explained above do not check the records that have a later timestamp than that of the malicious query. Obviously, allowing the execution of the new query will create inaccurate results. Note that, had the IDS detected the malicious query before the execution of $QID = 50$, the Age value would have been 22, which is actually is not qualified for the new query, instead of 26. Therefore, the system needs to conduct additional testing for the queries that updated the columns that are included in a new query and executed after the malicious queries.

We can conduct this test by comparing the column value with the next column value that is created by a non-malicious query in the backlog table after the malicious query. Formally, to obtain the column value, $malV$, that is updated by the malicious query $\pi_{C,TS}\sigma_{QID=mid}(BT)$, where C is the common column name between the query and the malicious query and mid is the query ID of the malicious query. Once the value of C is retrieved we can check the next value, nV, that is updated by a non-malicious query by $\pi_C\sigma_{QID\neq mid \wedge TS>ts}(BT)$, where ts is the timestamp value for the malicious query. If the column value for Age has not been changed, i.e., $nV = malV$, the system may allow the query execution. Otherwise, the system blocks the execution of the new query until the affected transactions are first rolled-back and legitimate transactions are re-done.

The steps and the control flow for the testing process are shown in Figure 2. In the examples and in the process flow we assumed there is a single query for previous, next, and malicious queries. However, the techniques we describe can be extended to the cases where there are multiple instances of those queries in a straightforward manner. We follow the same notation we used in the examples where, $malQ$ is malicious query, $malV$ is the column value after the execution of the malicious query, pQ is the previous query that is executed immediately before the malicious query, pV is the column value after the execution of the

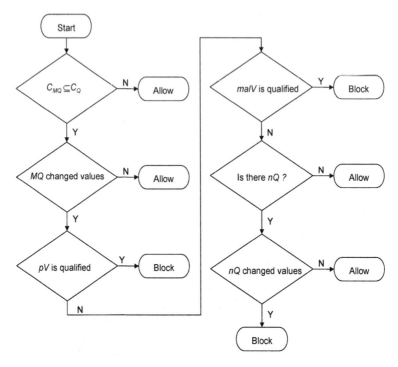

Fig. 2. Control flow for the query testing protocol

previous query, nQ is the next query that is executed immediately after the malicious query, nV is the column value after the execution of the next query.

4   Conclusions

We have presented our design approach to database security management from the autonomic computing perspective. The guiding principle for the approach is to enable a database system to isolate the damaged parts of the system and to keep the other parts of the system functioning as the damage is being repaired, if there is a successful break-in that have damaged parts of the system. We have presented the system architecture to reach this goal and illustrated query processing protocols to isolate the damaged parts of the system from the intact parts thereby keeping the undamaged parts of the system functioning. This work is based on our design experiences from a continuing project in the subject area.

References

1. IBM Tivoli Risk Manager. *Info Available at*
   http://www-306.ibm.com/software/tivoli/products/risk-mgr/.
2. R. Agrawal, J. Kiernan, R. Srikant, and Y. Xu. Hippocratic databases. In *Proc. of VLDB*, 2002.

3. S. Agrawal, S. Chaudri, and V. R. Narasayya. Automated Selection of Materialized Views and Indexes for SQL Databases. In *Proc. of VLDB*, 2000.
4. S. Axelsson. Intrusion Detection Systems: A Taxomomy and Survey. Technical report, Dept. of Computer Engineering, Chalmers University of Technology, Sweden, 2000.
5. S. Castano, M. Fugini, G. Martella, and P. Samarati. *Database Security*. Addison-Wesley Publishing Company, 1995.
6. S. Chaudhuri, E. Christensen, G. Graefe, V. R. Narasayya, and M. J. Zwilling. Self-tuning technology in microsoft sql server. *Data Engineering Bulletin*, 22(2):20–26, 1999.
7. E. Damiani, S. D. C. di Vimercati, S. Jajodia, S. Paraboschi, and P. Samarati. Balancing confidentiality and efficiency in untrusted Relational DBMSs. In *Proc. of 10th ACM Conf. On Computer and Communications Security*, 2003.
8. D. Denning. An Intrusion-Detection Model. *IEEE Transactions on Software Engineering*, 13(2), 1987.
9. A. G. Ganek and T. A. Corbi. The Dawning of the Autonomic Computing Era. *IBM Systems Journal*, 42(1):5–18, 2003.
10. H. Hacıgümüş, B. Iyer, C. Li, and S. Mehrotra. Executing SQL over Encrypted Data in Database Service Provider Model. In *Proc. of ACM SIGMOD*, 2002.
11. H. Hacıgümüş, B. Iyer, and S. Mehrotra. Providing Database as a Service. In *Proc. of ICDE*, 2002.
12. C. S. Jensen, L. Mark, and N. Roussopoulos. Incremental Implementation Model for Relational Databases with Transaction Time. *IEEE Transactions on Knowledge and Data Engineering*, 3(4):461–473, 1991.
13. R. A. Kemmerer and G. Vigna. Intrusion detection: a brief history and overview. *IEEE Computer*, 35(4), 2002.
14. J. O. Kephart and D. M. Chess. The Vision of Autonomic Computing. *IEEE Computer*, 36(1):41–50, 2003.
15. E. Kwan, S. Lightstone, A. Storm, and L. Wu. Automatic Configuration for IBM DB2 Universal Database. *Available at http://www.redbooks.ibm.com/redpapers/pdfs/redp0441.pdf*.
16. G. Lohman and S. Lightstone. SMART: Making DB2 (More) Autonomic. In *Proc. of VLDB*, 2002.
17. G. Lohman, G. Valentin, D. Zilio, M. Zuliani, and A. Skelly. DB2 Advisor: An optimizer Smart Enough to Recommend Its Own Indexes. In *Proc. of ICDE*, 2000.
18. T. Lunt and E. B. Fernandez. Database Security. *ACM SIGMOD Record*, 19(4), 1990.
19. J. Rao, C. Zhang, G. Lohman, and G. Megiddo. Automating Physical Database Design in a Parallel Database System. In *Proc. of ACM SIGMOD*, 2002.

Author Index

Lecture Notes in Computer Science

For information about Vols. 1–4062

please contact your bookseller or Springer

Vol. 4113: D.-S. Huang, K. Li, G.W. Irwin (Eds.), Intelligent Computing, Part I. XXVII, 1331 pages. 2006.

Vol. 4112: D.Z. Chen, D. T. Lee (Eds.), Computing and Combinatorics. XIV, 528 pages. 2006.

Vol. 4111: F.S. de Boer, M.M. Bonsangue, S. Graf, W.-P. de Roever (Eds.), Formal Methods for Components and Objects. VIII, 447 pages. 2006.

Vol. 4110: J. Díaz, K. Jansen, J.D.P. Rolim, U. Zwick (Eds.), Approximation, Randomization, and Combinatorial Optimization. XII, 522 pages. 2006.

Vol. 4109: D.-Y. Yeung, J.T. Kwok, A. Fred, F. Roli, D. de Ridder (Eds.), Structural, Syntactic, and Statistical Pattern Recognition. XXI, 939 pages. 2006.

Vol. 4108: J.M. Borwein, W.M. Farmer (Eds.), Mathematical Knowledge Management. VIII, 295 pages. 2006. (Sublibrary LNAI).

Vol. 4106: T.R. Roth-Berghofer, M.H. Göker, H. A. Güvenir (Eds.), Advances in Case-Based Reasoning. XIV, 566 pages. 2006. (Sublibrary LNAI).

Vol. 4104: T. Kunz, S.S. Ravi (Eds.), Ad-Hoc, Mobile, and Wireless Networks. XII, 474 pages. 2006.

Vol. 4099: Q. Yang, G. Webb (Eds.), PRICAI 2006: Trends in Artificial Intelligence. XXVIII, 1263 pages. 2006. (Sublibrary LNAI).

Vol. 4098: F. Pfenning (Ed.), Term Rewriting and Applications. XIII, 415 pages. 2006.

Vol. 4097: X. Zhou, O. Sokolsky, L. Yan, E.-S. Jung, Z. Shao, Y. Mu, D.C. Lee, D. Kim, Y.-S. Jeong, C.-Z. Xu (Eds.), Emerging Directions in Embedded and Ubiquitous Computing. XXVII, 1034 pages. 2006.

Vol. 4096: E. Sha, S.-K. Han, C.-Z. Xu, M.H. Kim, L.T. Yang, B. Xiao (Eds.), Embedded and Ubiquitous Computing. XXIV, 1170 pages. 2006.

Vol. 4095: S. Nolfi, G. Baldassare, R. Calabretta, D. Marocco, D. Parisi, J.C. T. Hallam, O. Miglino, J.-A. Meyer (Eds.), From Animals to Animats 9. XV, 869 pages. 2006. (Sublibrary LNAI).

Vol. 4094: O. H. Ibarra, H.-C. Yen (Eds.), Implementation and Application of Automata. XIII, 291 pages. 2006.

Vol. 4093: X. Li, O.R. Zaïane, Z. Li (Eds.), Advanced Data Mining and Applications. XXI, 1110 pages. 2006. (Sublibrary LNAI).

Vol. 4092: J. Lang, F. Lin, J. Wang (Eds.), Knowledge Science, Engineering and Management. XV, 664 pages. 2006. (Sublibrary LNAI).

Vol. 4091: G.-Z. Yang, T. Jiang, D. Shen, L. Gu, J. Yang (Eds.), Medical Imaging and Augmented Reality. XIII, 399 pages. 2006.

Vol. 4090: S. Spaccapietra, K. Aberer, P. Cudré-Mauroux (Eds.), Journal on Data Semantics VI. XI, 211 pages. 2006.

Vol. 4089: W. Löwe, M. Südholt (Eds.), Software Composition. X, 339 pages. 2006.

Vol. 4088: Z.-Z. Shi, R. Sadananda (Eds.), Agent Computing and Multi-Agent Systems. XVII, 827 pages. 2006. (Sublibrary LNAI).

Vol. 4087: F. Schwenker, S. Marinai (Eds.), Artificial Neural Networks in Pattern Recognition. IX, 299 pages. 2006. (Sublibrary LNAI).

Vol. 4085: J. Misra, T. Nipkow, E. Sekerinski (Eds.), FM 2006: Formal Methods. XV, 620 pages. 2006.

Vol. 4084: M.A. Wimmer, H.J. Scholl, Å. Grönlund, K.V. Andersen (Eds.), Electronic Government. XV, 353 pages. 2006.

Vol. 4083: S. Fischer-Hübner, S. Furnell, C. Lambrinoudakis (Eds.), Trust and Privacy in Digital Business. XIII, 243 pages. 2006.

Vol. 4082: K. Bauknecht, B. Pröll, H. Werthner (Eds.), E-Commerce and Web Technologies. XIII, 243 pages. 2006.

Vol. 4081: A. M. Tjoa, J. Trujillo (Eds.), Data Warehousing and Knowledge Discovery. XVII, 578 pages. 2006.

Vol. 4080: S. Bressan, J. Küng, R. Wagner (Eds.), Database and Expert Systems Applications. XXI, 959 pages. 2006.

Vol. 4079: S. Etalle, M. Truszczyński (Eds.), Logic Programming. XIV, 474 pages. 2006.

Vol. 4077: M.-S. Kim, K. Shimada (Eds.), Geometric Modeling and Processing - GMP 2006. XVI, 696 pages. 2006.

Vol. 4076: F. Hess, S. Pauli, M. Pohst (Eds.), Algorithmic Number Theory. X, 599 pages. 2006.

Vol. 4075: U. Leser, F. Naumann, B. Eckman (Eds.), Data Integration in the Life Sciences. XI, 298 pages. 2006. (Sublibrary LNBI).

Vol. 4074: M. Burmester, A. Yasinsac (Eds.), Secure Mobile Ad-hoc Networks and Sensors. X, 193 pages. 2006.

Vol. 4073: A. Butz, B. Fisher, A. Krüger, P. Olivier (Eds.), Smart Graphics. XI, 263 pages. 2006.

Vol. 4072: M. Harders, G. Székely (Eds.), Biomedical Simulation. XI, 216 pages. 2006.

Vol. 4071: H. Sundaram, M. Naphade, J.R. Smith, Y. Rui (Eds.), Image and Video Retrieval. XII, 547 pages. 2006.

Vol. 4070: C. Priami, X. Hu, Y. Pan, T.Y. Lin (Eds.), Transactions on Computational Systems Biology V. IX, 129 pages. 2006. (Sublibrary LNBI).

Vol. 4069: F.J. Perales, R.B. Fisher (Eds.), Articulated Motion and Deformable Objects. XV, 526 pages. 2006.

Vol. 4068: H. Schärfe, P. Hitzler, P. Øhrstrøm (Eds.), Conceptual Structures: Inspiration and Application. XI, 455 pages. 2006. (Sublibrary LNAI).

Vol. 4067: D. Thomas (Ed.), ECOOP 2006 – Object-Oriented Programming. XIV, 527 pages. 2006.

Vol. 4066: A. Rensink, J. Warmer (Eds.), Model Driven Architecture – Foundations and Applications. XII, 392 pages. 2006.

Vol. 4065: P. Perner (Ed.), Advances in Data Mining. XI, 592 pages. 2006. (Sublibrary LNAI).

Vol. 4064: R. Büschkes, P. Laskov (Eds.), Detection of Intrusions and Malware & Vulnerability Assessment. X, 195 pages. 2006.

Vol. 4063: I. Gorton, G.T. Heineman, I. Crnkovic, H.W. Schmidt, J.A. Stafford, C.A. Szyperski, K. Wallnau (Eds.), Component-Based Software Engineering. XI, 394 pages. 2006.